seattle city walks

seattle city walks

Exploring Seattle Neighborhoods on Foot

Laura Karlinsey

WITH RESEARCH ASSISTANCE
BY SHERRI SCHULTZ

SASQUATCH BOOKS
SEATTLE

Printed in the United States of America
Distributed in Canada by Raincoast Books, Ltd.
03 02 01   5 4 3 2

All maps and interior photographs copyright ©1999 by the author.

Cover design: Karen Schober
Cover photograph: Rick Dahms
Interior design and composition: Patrick David Barber
Research assistance and copy editing: Sherri Schultz

Library of Congress Cataloging-in-Publication Data
Karlinsey, Laura.
    Seattle city walks : exploring Seattle neighborhoods on foot / by Laura Karlinsey.
        p.   cm.
    Includes index.
    ISBN 1-57061-145-9
    1. Seattle (Wash.)—Tours. 2. Walking—Washington (State)—Seattle—Guidebooks.
I. Title.
    F899.S43K37 199
    917.97'7720443—dc21   98-48380

SASQUATCH BOOKS
615 Second Avenue
Seattle, Washington 98104
(206) 467-4300
www.SasquatchBooks.com
books@SasquatchBooks.com

Sasquatch Books publishes high-quality adult nonfiction and children's books related to the Northwest (Alaska to San Francisco). For more information about Sasquatch Books titles, contact us at the address above, or view our site on the World Wide Web.

contents

introduction

IF YOU ARE READING THIS book, it is probably because Seattle intrigues you. Seattle displays the peculiar combination of history, culture, and contemporary fashion that makes urban landscapes fascinating. In Seattle's streets the common dramas of our time exist amid half-forgotten stories of the past. The slant of a tree or the set of a stone may hint at the story of one person's good fortune or another's shattered dream.

Many city guidebooks provide practical information on urban navigation and dry lists of historical facts, but make no attempt to tell the city's stories. This book takes a different approach. It describes Seattle's diverse neighborhoods, providing background on each neighborhood's history, notable personalities, and character. Each chapter recommends a walking tour through the featured neighborhood, and includes maps, photographs, and useful information about the area. *Seattle City Walks* is for those who want to experience this unique city—not just see it.

Seattle was once known as an unsophisticated and somewhat sleepy northwestern city, but in past decades it has become the focus of much national attention. It is the birthplace of many recent economic forces and popular movements: Microsoft, grunge rock, the gourmet coffee and the microbrewery fads. Seattle frequently shows up near the top of the list in surveys of best places to live in the United States.

The reasons for Seattle's popularity are clear: its scenery is unsurpassed; its populace has a reputation for being well-read, physically fit, and extraordinarily polite; and its weather, while a little gray, is usually temperate. Seattle has bustling markets, eclectic architecture, hilltop views, lovely tree-lined streets, waterfront property on two sides, and mountains in every direction. Its picturesque urban landscape complements the natural splendor, and the surrounding landscape puts the city in perspective.

getting around

WASHINGTON STATE FERRY SERVICE: Washington State Ferries crisscross Puget Sound at various points from Tacoma north to Anacortes, connecting cities on the east side of the Sound to islands and towns on the west. In Seattle there are regular crossings between the downtown terminal at Pier 52 and Winslow, on Bainbridge Island, and Bremerton, on the Kitsap Peninsula.

If you take a vehicle on a ferry, you may be subject to a long wait during peak times (rush hour or holiday weekends); but you never have to wait if you walk on the ferry or take a bicycle (though there is an extra charge for bicycles). Most ferry routes charge for passengers in only one direction (for example, you pay to go from Seattle to Bainbridge, but can travel from Bainbridge to Seattle for free). However, vehicles have to pay both ways. Information on ferry schedules and fares can be obtained by calling (206) 464-6400 or (888) 808-7977. Automated schedule information is available at (800) 843-3779. You can also access the Washington State Ferry Service web site at http://www.wsdot. wa.gov/ferries/schedules/current.

METRO BUSES: All bus rides within downtown Seattle are free until 7:00 p.m. This is a convenience for downtown travel, but it makes traveling in or out of the downtown confusing. During the day, if you board a bus that is leaving downtown, you pay your fare when you get off; if you board a bus that is heading downtown, you pay when you board.

At most bus stops, you'll find a list of the route (bus) numbers that service that stop: often route schedules (and sometimes route maps) are also posted. From these, you can get a rough idea where the buses that service the stop go, and when to expect the next bus.

All Metro buses are equipped with bike racks on the front. You don't have to pay extra to bring along your bike, but in the ride-free (downtown) area, you will be able to load or unload a bike only at limited stops.

Many bus routes that pass through downtown stop in the bus tunnel, a subway for buses that travels along Third Avenue between Pine Street and South Jackson Street. Each of the five bus tunnel stations is decorated with a different theme. They feature murals, decorative tile, and animated light displays. All bus tunnel stops are within the ride-free zone.

Following is a list of bus routes serving the various neighborhoods mentioned in this book. For some neighborhoods only a few of the many available routes are listed. To get more complete route information, contact the Metro 24-hour rider information line at (206) 553-3000, or access their web site at http://transit.metrokc.gov.

NEIGHBORHOOD	BUS ROUTES	
alki	37	FROM DOWNTOWN
belltown	1	FROM QUEEN ANNE OR THE INTERNATIONAL DISTRICT
	2	FROM MADRONA OR QUEEN ANNE
	13	FROM DOWNTOWN OR QUEEN ANNE
capitol hill/volunteer park	10	FROM DOWNTOWN
capitol hill/broadway	7	FROM RAINIER BEACH, DOWNTOWN, OR THE UNIVERSITY DISTRICT
	9	FROM RAINIER BEACH OR THE UNIVERSITY DISTRICT
	60	FROM BEACON HILL OR FIRST HILL
downtown	5	FROM DOWNTOWN, GREENLAKE, OR SHORELINE
	6	FROM BITTERLAKE OR FREMONT
	7	FROM RAINIER BEACH OR THE UNIVERSITY DISTRICT
	13	FROM THE INTERNATIONAL DISTRICT OR QUEEN ANNE
	14	FROM CAPITOL HILL, THE INTERNATIONAL DISTRICT, OR MOUNT BAKER
	28	FROM BROADVIEW OR FREMONT
	39	FROM SOUTHCENTER, RAINIER BEACH, OR BEACON HILL
	255	FROM KINGSGATE OR KIRKLAND

NEIGHBORHOOD	BUS ROUTES
fremont	**28** FROM BROADVIEW OR DOWNTOWN
	5 FROM DOWNTOWN, GREENLAKE, OR SHORELINE
green lake	**48** FROM RAINIER BEACH OR LOYAL HEIGHTS
	16 FROM NORTHGATE OR DOWNTOWN
international district	**1** FROM QUEEN ANNE
	7 FROM RAINIER BEACH, DOWNTOWN, BROADWAY, OR THE UNIVERSITY DISTRICT
	14 FROM MOUNT BAKER OR CAPITOL HILL
	36 FROM RAINIER BEACH OR DOWNTOWN
	39 FROM SOUTHCENTER, RAINIER BEACH, DOWNTOWN, OR BEACON HILL
	42 FROM RAINIER BEACH OR DOWNTOWN
	136 FROM WHITE CENTER, SODO, OR DOWNTOWN
kirkland	**230** FROM REDMOND OR JUANITA
	251 FROM DOWNTOWN OR WOODINVILLE
	255 FROM DOWNTOWN OR KINGSGATE
	275 FROM THE UNIVERSITY OF WASHINGTON OR KINGSGATE
	234 FROM BELLEVUE OR KENMORE
	254 FROM DOWNTOWN OR REDMOND
	931 FROM WOODINVILLE
lake union	**26** FROM GREEN LAKE OR DOWNTOWN
	28 FROM BROADVIEW OR DOWNTOWN

NEIGHBORHOOD	BUS ROUTES	
leschi	**27**	FROM COLMAN PARK OR DOWNTOWN
madison park	**11**	FROM DOWNTOWN
madrona	**2**	FROM QUEEN ANNE OR DOWNTOWN
magnolia	**19 or 24**	FROM DOWNTOWN
montlake	**43**	FROM THE UNIVERSITY DISTRICT OR DOWNTOWN
	48	FROM RAINIER BEACH OR LOYAL HEIGHTS
	25	FROM DOWNTOWN OR LAURELHURST
mount baker	**14**	FROM CAPITOL HILL OR DOWNTOWN
	27	FROM DOWNTOWN OR LESCHI
pike place market	**5**	FROM DOWNTOWN, GREENLAKE, OR SHORELINE
	10	FROM CAPITOL HILL
	28	FROM BROADVIEW OR FREMONT
	39	FROM SOUTHCENTER, RAINIER BEACH, OR BEACON HILL
pioneer square	**6**	FROM BITTERLAKE OR FREMONT
	7	FROM RAINIER BEACH OR THE UNIVERSITY DISTRICT
	10	FROM CAPITOL HILL
	14	FROM CAPITOL HILL, THE INTERNATIONAL DISTRICT, OR MOUNT BAKER
	28	FROM BROADVIEW OR FREMONT
	39	FROM SOUTHCENTER, RAINIER BEACH, OR BEACON HILL
	255	FROM KINGSGATE OR KIRKLAND

NEIGHBORHOOD	BUS ROUTES
queen anne	**2** FROM MADRONA OR DOWNTOWN **13** FROM THE INTERNATIONAL DISTRICT OR DOWNTOWN
ravenna	**48** FROM RAINIER BEACH OR LOYAL HEIGHTS **74** FROM SANDPOINT OR THE UNIVERSITY DISTRICT
seattle center	**1** FROM QUEEN ANNE OR THE INTERNATIONAL DISTRICT **2** FROM MADRONA OR QUEEN ANNE **3 or 4** FROM MADRONA OR QUEEN ANNE **6** FROM BITTERLAKE OR GREEN LAKE **8** FROM CAPITOL HILL **13** FROM THE INTERNATIONAL DISTRICT, DOWNTOWN, OR QUEEN ANNE **16** FROM NORTHGATE OR DOWNTOWN **19 or 24** FROM MAGNOLIA OR DOWNTOWN **33** FROM MAGNOLIA OR DOWNTOWN
university of washington	**25** FROM DOWNTOWN, MONTLAKE, OR LAURELHURST **48** FROM RAINIER BEACH OR LOYAL HEIGHTS **372** FROM WOODINVILLE

Key

 Route Starting Point

Described route

Route extension

Footpath or stairway

Streetcar/Monorail track and station

Street

Paved road closed to vehicular traffic

Park

Stream

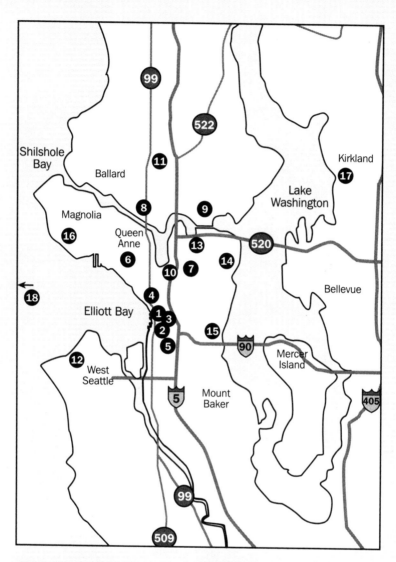

1 Pike Place Market
2 Pioneer Square
3 Downtown
4 Belltown
5 International District
6 Queen Anne
7 Capitol Hill
8 Fremont
9 University of Washington
10 Lake Union
11 Green Lake
12 Alki
13 Montlake
14 Madison Park
15 Leschi
16 Magnolia
17 Kirkland
18 Bainbridge Island

TO MARKET, TO MARKET:

AND THE WATERFRONT

Distance: 1 mile **Approximate time:** 3 hours

PEOPLE WHO COME TO DOWN-
town Seattle with no specific destination in mind usually end up at
Pike Place Market. Its mixture of
locally grown produce, fresh
seafood, handmade crafts, antique
stores, street musicians, and sidewalk vendors attracts residents and
visitors alike, providing enough
diversions to entertain all but the
most jaded. The oldest continu-
ously operated public market in
the United States, Seattle's beloved
Market is a warren of intriguing
sights and smells. If you like to
shop, you'll love it. Even if you
don't like to shop, you'll find
plenty to interest you. The atmosphere is always lively, and the
views of Elliott Bay are some of
the best in town.

The first part of this walk provides a list of buildings and attractions in Pike Place Market, but
does not suggest a specific route.
Half the fun of exploring this area
is happening upon apparently
undiscovered nooks and crannies
in the many blocks, passageways,
and levels of the Market. Also,
several of the buildings mentioned
are joined together, so it can be
unclear where one begins and
another ends.

Fruits and vegetables in the Main Arcade

When you leave the Market
(if you can pry yourself away), this
walk leads you to some of Seattle's
waterfront sites, including the
Seattle Aquarium, a carousel, and
a waterfront streetcar. You'll then

walk up a stairway park to the Seattle Art Museum on your way back to the Market.

Start this walk on the corner of First Avenue and Pike Street. This is the main entrance to **Pike Place Market**, founded in 1907. When it opened, it was on the northern edge of the young city. It had no permanent buildings, just produce wagons; buildings came later, in fits and starts, resulting in the maze of mysterious passageways found in the Market today.

Entrance to the Pike Place Market

By the late 1930s more than 600 farmers were selling at the Market, but the internment of the Japanese during World War II cut that number in half. During the war the Market declined, becoming shabby and largely unused. In the 1960s it was threatened with redevelopment: An association of downtown businesses proposed replacing the old Market buildings with a parking garage, apartments, and office towers. Fortunately, even in its neglected state, the

pike place market and the waterfront

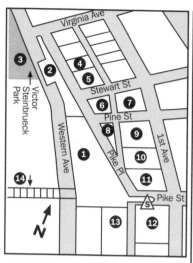

1. **Main Arcade and Down Under Shops**
2. **North Arcade**
3. **Victor Steinbrueck Park**
4. **Soames-Dunn Building**
5. **Stewart House**
6. **Seattle Garden Center Building**
7. **Inn at the Market**
8. **Triangle Market**
9. **Post Alley Market**

Pub in Upper Post Alley

10. **Sanitary Market**
11. **Corner Market**
12. **Economy Market**
13. **La Salle Hotel**
14. **Pike Place Hillclimb**
15. **Seattle Aquarium**
16. **Waterfront Park**
17. **Ye Olde Curiosity Shop**
18. **Harbor Steps**
19. **Seattle Art Museum**

View from Steinbrueck Park

Market had loyal friends. A group of citizens led by architect Victor Steinbrueck spearheaded a successful ballot initiative in 1971 to save the Market, resulting in the area's designation as a historic district.

Today the Market is an urban preservation success story, attracting locals as well as tourists from all over the world and serving as a model for public markets in other cities. No one would even think of uttering the word "redevelopment" in conjunction with Pike Place Market today.

Roam through structures ❶ through ⓭, described below, as

you please. If you like, you can pick up a list of Market merchants and eateries at the **tourist information booth** on the corner of First and Pike. (This tiny green kiosk is also an outlet for Ticket/Ticket, which sells half-price day-of-show theater tickets.)

❶ **Main Arcade and Down Under Shops.** This is a combination of two buildings, the Leland Hotel (1900) and the Fairley Building (1907–14). Above the Main Arcade is the famous Public Market Center sign and the neon clock; beneath the clock is Rachel, the enormous bronze piggy bank installed in 1986. Every year Rachel collects about $8,000 in donations for the Market Foundation, which helps support the Market's food bank, health clinic, and other social services.

Near Rachel are the fishmongers of Pike Place Fish, famous for tossing fish back and forth across the counter as a crowd gathers to watch. Also in the Main Arcade are restaurants, flower and produce stalls, and gift shops. Down the stairs are three more levels of stores, collectively called Down Under, selling everything from magic tricks to ethnic clothing. One level is largely devoted to antique shops.

❷ **North Arcade** (1911). Along this long, covered arcade are stalls selling fresh produce (much of it local), flowers, and the works of local artists and craftspeople.

❸ **Victor Steinbrueck Park** (1978). Named for the local architect who led the effort to save Pike Place Market from redevelopment in the 1960s and early '70s, this park sits atop a bluff overlooking Elliott Bay. On a sunny day, it's a fine place to enjoy the croissant or farm-fresh fruit you couldn't resist buying at the Market.

4 Soames-Dunn Building (1918). Formed when the Soames Building and the Dunn Building were joined together in 1976, this structure is home to a multitude of shops and restaurants—everything from an art gallery (upstairs) to a small grocery selling foods of India. A charming courtyard in back connects with Post Alley via a stairway. The building also houses the original Starbucks Coffee outlet: The now-ubiquitous nationwide chain opened its first store in Pike Place Market on this very site in 1971, as a plaque in the store's window proudly proclaims.

5 Stewart House (1902–11). Here you can spend $600 on eyeglasses or have your hair cut for just 10 bucks. As in several other Market buildings, low-income apartments are located upstairs, part of the Market's commitment to social services.

6 Seattle Garden Center Building (1908). Set on a small triangular block, this building is home to two stores selling a vast array of gardening supplies and kitchenware, respectively.

7 Inn at the Market (1985). You can walk through this elegant hotel's fountain courtyard, which contains a fine restaurant and some of the more upscale shops in the Market.

8 Triangle Market. This curiously shaped structure is actually two buildings: the Triangle Building (1908) and the Silver Oakum Building (1910). Above the ground-floor shops are apartments and a restaurant with an outdoor terrace overlooking Elliott Bay.

9 Post Alley Market (1983). As its name suggests, this building faces Post Alley, a quaint cobblestone street that winds its way through the Market. Post Alley Market contains an array of eateries and shops as well as an expansive coffee bar on Pine Street that, along with the tables and chairs set out in Post Alley, is a prime spot for people-watching.

10 Sanitary Market (1910). Called "sanitary" because it was the first Market building to prohibit horses inside, this structure is home to the Market's oldest business, the Three Girls Bakery, opened in 1912. The maze of passageways here always yields unexpected rewards. Bargain hunters may want to head right for the little-known rummage-sale corner, which features a different seller each day.

11 Corner Market (1912). This was the first building in the Market to be rehabilitated after the Market was declared a historic district. Enjoy the eateries and produce stalls on the ground floor, climb the stairs to the restaurants and bars on two levels above, or check out the jazz club tucked in the basement.

12 Economy Market (1900). Originally a horse stable, the Economy Market Building was later transformed into Market space where discount day-old

victor steinbrueck: father of our landmarks

SEATTLE'S THREE MOST RECOG- nizable landmarks are the Space Needle, Pike Place Market, and Pioneer Square. Victor Steinbrueck had a hand in designing or preserving all three. He was one of the principal architects of the Space Needle, and both Pioneer Square and Pike Place Market were saved from redevelopment by efforts he helped organize.

This savior of landmarks was raised in a working-class neighborhood in Seattle. The city fascinated Steinbrueck from an early age. As a child he wandered through the streets, poking into every corner and back alley. As a youth, Steinbrueck often came to Pioneer Square with his father. They would have supper at a local cafe after working late and watch the neighborhood's human spectacle of workers, street people, and soapbox orators.

Steinbrueck received his degree in architecture from the University of Washington in 1935 and entered private practice in 1938. During World War II he volunteered for the Army and spent his tour of duty designing airport runways in Newfoundland. The only conflict he saw during the war was with his superior officers. Asked if he liked the Army, he replied that if he had, he wouldn't have seen any point in going to war to fight fascism.

Back in Seattle, he opened an architectural practice and started teaching part-time at the UW. He eventually made teaching his vocation, feeling that he could have a greater effect on the field of architecture by influencing students than by designing buildings.

Steinbrueck began his activist career in the 1960s, when the Seattle City Council was considering razing the buildings in Pioneer Square to make room for high-rises and parking lots. Around the same time, Pike Place Market was also facing redevelopment. Steinbrueck was determined to save his beloved childhood haunts. He gathered support from like-minded Seattleites, and the long struggles with City Hall began. Eventually he and his compatriots prevailed: Pioneer Square was designated a historic district in 1970, and Pike Place Market was granted similar status through a 1971 initiative.

Steinbrueck spent much of his time trying to convert his colleagues to the cause of civic restoration, but he was often unsuccessful. He grew dissatisfied with what he believed was mainstream architects' lack of social conscience. For a time he even left the American Institute of Architects, frustrated by what he felt was the futility of getting Seattle's practicing architects involved in civic planning issues.

Steinbrueck passed away in 1985, but he is unlikely to be forgotten. Many of the city's landmarks are his memorials.

produce was sold. Today it holds specialty food shops and restaurants, a newsstand featuring periodicals from all over the world, and retailers selling such things as wind-up toys and herbal medicines.

⓭ LaSalle Hotel (1908). The services offered here by Nellie Curtis, who purchased the building in 1942, were very popular with the Navy boys stationed across Puget Sound at Bremerton. Nellie and her girls were known to have as many as 1,000 sailors lined up at their door. You can find a couple of upscale restaurants in parts of Nellie's old haunts today; the rest of the building is now apartments.

Leave the Market via the Main Arcade stairway near Rachel, to the right of Pike Place Fish, below the "Welcome Down Under" sign. Descend the many short flights of stairs to Western Avenue. Just before Western, on the left, you pass the playground of the Pike Market Child Care Center, another of the Market's social programs.

⓮ Cross Western Avenue and descend the stairway to the parking area below. The wide stairway, bordered by shops and restaurants, is the **Pike Place Hillclimb**. This area was once home to Seattle's only royalty: Princess Angeline, the daughter of Chief Seattle. She lived in a tiny shack below the present-day site of the Market until her death in 1896. (See "Her Majesty Kicki-somlo-Cud" on page 13.**)**

The Seattle Aquarium's back door

Walk straight ahead through the parking area, under the elevated freeway; cross Alaskan Way to the waterfront. Waterfront attractions stretch before you to the left and right. A few blocks to the right is **Pier 66**, a relatively new development you may want to explore on your own. It offers several seafood restaurants ranging from casual to upscale, a fish-shaped wading pool popular with kids, and a short-stay marina as well as a viewing plaza located on the roof of the Bell Harbor Conference

Center. The glass elevator just before the pier, on Alaskan Way at Lenora Street, connects the waterfront with the business district above.

To the left, between Pike and Marion Streets, is a stretch of **waterfront** that survives almost entirely on tourism. It has an abundance of restaurants and souvenir shops, ticket booths for boat cruises and parasailing adventures, and historical markers. The area used to be considerably more working-class, however: In his 1951 book *Skid Road,* Murray Morgan describes Seattle's waterfront as "a good, honest, working waterfront." Unfortunately, today it looks more like an amusement park, but it does have some features of interest.

🚯 The first attraction you encounter on the waterfront is the **Seattle Aquarium**. In addition to the usual collection of multicolored sea creatures from tropical climes, this aquarium places special emphasis on local aquatic fauna. They have a lively community of sea otters, river otters, and harbor seals, as well as an underwater dome where you can stand surrounded by 400,000 gallons of water and watch salmon and other fish. If you time your visit right, you can watch divers feed the fish. For a hands-on experience, visit the Discovery Lab, where you can touch starfish, anemones, and other tidepool residents.

The aquarium's site is significant in Duwamish mythology. In this spot was a legendary subterranean waterway called Sh-chapu, a mythical link between Lake Union and Puget Sound that allowed whales to travel back and forth.

Dining on the waterfront

mark tobey:
a northwestern point of view

MARK TOBEY IS PERHAPS THE best-known member of the Northwest School, an artistic movement characterized by the use of a subdued color scheme, a penchant for the mystical, and an Asian influence. The Northwest School included Kenneth Callahan, Morris Graves, and Guy Anderson. Although Tobey wasn't a Northwest native, he loved Seattle—especially Pike Place Market—and spent countless hours wandering through the Market, sketchbook in hand.

The young Tobey began his artistic career as a fashion illustrator in Greenwich Village, but in the early 1920s he grew increasingly discontented with the social demands of New York. At the age of 32, he followed a friend to Seattle, where Cornish College of the Arts hired him on commission: He kept 80 cents of the $2 tuition students paid for his art classes. A natural in the classroom, he taught at various institutions for the next three decades, finding teaching the most agreeable way to finance his art.

The Northwest's gray skies were the perfect backdrop for the muted colors and introspective, spiritual qualities of Tobey's paintings, which led critics to call him "the Northwest mystic" and "the sage of Seattle." He received his greatest acclaim when he was in his 60s, but even then he was more lauded in Europe than in his own country. In 1958 he received the international prize for painting at the Venice Biennale, an honor no American had received since James McNeill Whistler in 1895.

In 1960 this great Northwest artist left the Northwest permanently and moved to Switzerland, dismayed by the impact of growth on Seattle. In its post–World War II expansion, Tobey felt, the city had destroyed much of its beauty and erected an offensive sprawl in its place. Although he maintained contact with his Seattle friends and always intended to return, he never did: He died in his home in Switzerland on April 24, 1976, at 85 years of age. Today his paintings can be seen at the Seattle Art Museum, just a few blocks from the Market he loved so well.

SEAGULL LOVERS
ARE WELCOME TO FEED
SEAGULLS IN NEED.
(PLEASE DO NOT FEED PIDGEONS)

Seagull panhandling at Ivar's

⑯ Turn left and stroll along Alaskan Way to Pier 52. Just past the aquarium, at Pier 57, are **Waterfront Park**, which offers wonderful panoramas from several viewing platforms, and Bay Pavilion, a pier building that now contains shops and an antique carousel. At Pier 55/56, private companies offer sightseeing cruises of Elliott Bay, the Ballard Locks, and elsewhere.

Alaskan Way has two completely different faces. The waterfront side is multicolored and tourist-oriented, while the opposite side sits underneath the elevated freeway looking stark and menacing. This freeway, called the **Alaskan Way Viaduct**, has a long parking lot underneath it that, together with the freeway itself, creates an unfortunate division between downtown and the waterfront.

Yet although the Viaduct is an ugly scar through the heart of the city, it somehow still manages to be intriguing. Driving north along this elevated freeway provides one of the most unusual views of the city, but even the Viaduct's underbelly has a certain charm. A few restaurants and an abundance of antique shops peer out from unadorned old brick buildings. The businesses here operate out of what was clearly intended to be the buildings' posterior. These are not the polished faces commerce usually presents to the world.

The Alaskan Way Viaduct's design is very similar to that of the Nimitz Freeway in Oakland, which collapsed during the 1989 earthquake in the Bay Area. Seattle is also due for another earthquake, experts say. (Just a little something to think about if you choose to loiter here.)

⑰ Farther along Alaskan Way, at Pier 54, is **Ye Olde Curiosity Shop**. This shop is curious all right: It's a free museum-cum-store that lures customers in with amazing grotesque oddities and then sells them cheap mementos. "Highlights" of the collection include several shrunken heads, two mummified bodies, fleas in dresses, a three-tusk walrus skull, and more. Joe Standley opened the store in 1899, and it's still run by his descendants.

Pier 54 is also a terminal for the summertime Elliott Bay water taxi, which zips between the downtown waterfront and Seacrest Park in West Seattle.

Next to Ye Olde Curiosity Shop is **Ivar's Acres of Clams**, a local institution. Look for the statue of its namesake feeding the seagulls, just beyond the take-out window, near where children can usually be found throwing french fries to the birds. Ivar Haglund was a natural showman who became famous in Seattle for his seafood restaurants, his publicity stunts, and his bad puns. He was a media phenomenon too, sponsoring community events, appearing on TV, and always urging the public to "Keep Clam."

In 1938 Haglund displayed his knack for getting free publicity with his very first entrepreneurial attempt, a tiny aquarium operating out of a 1,000-square-foot space on the northern end of Pier 54. On a local weekly radio show, he sang familiar folk songs with humorously rewritten lyrics, many of them—not so coincidentally— about creatures in his aquarium. He took a seal to visit Santa at Christmas, and he drove around town in a truck with a drum attached, loudly proclaiming the attractions of the aquarium.

Haglund opened this restaurant in the 1940s and gradually expanded his empire to include more than a dozen Seattle-area eateries.

Because of his wide-ranging radio ads, he became a household name from British Columbia to Oregon. When he died in 1985, his estate was worth $12 million, most of which he willed to the University of Washington.

Beyond Ivar's are a waterfront fire station and the **Washington State Ferry Terminal**, which offers numerous sailings to and from Bainbridge Island and Bremerton every day. Even if you don't need to go anywhere, a ferry ride is a pleasant, inexpensive way to see Puget Sound. (Chapter 18 provides a walking tour of downtown Winslow, the town at which the Bainbridge Island ferry docks.)

Retrace your steps, strolling back along Alaskan Way for several blocks to University Street. You can also choose to ride a **waterfront streetcar** to University; catch it at the station opposite Ivar's, nicknamed "Clam Central Station" in his honor. (Since you would be taking the streetcar only to its next stop, though, you may wish to save this for a time when you can take a longer ride.) Featuring Tasmanian mahogany and white ash woodwork, the waterfront streetcars are 1927 Australian coaches that were brought from Melbourne to began service here in 1982. They run between Myrtle Edwards Park to the north and the International District to the south, and provide a pleasant tour of Seattle's waterfront. The streetcars run every 20 minutes throughout the day (and well into the evening in summer), seven days a week.

⑱ Turn right onto University Street; follow it across Western Avenue and up the grand stairway to First Avenue. The stairway promenade is called the **Harbor Steps**. Its stair-stepped fountains and attractive plantings have made it a popular spot with office workers eating lunch and tourists taking a break from sightseeing. In the summer you may even happen upon one of downtown Seattle's free noontime concerts here. The steps were created by a local development firm in conjunction with its adjacent project involving apartment towers, retail shops, a restaurant, and an inn. This sizable development has helped revitalize what was once a marginal area.

⑲ At the top of the Harbor Steps, on the northeast corner of First and University, is the **Seattle Art Museum** (SAM), housed in a Postmodern building designed by Pulitzer Prize–winning architect Robert Venturi and erected in 1991. The animated, 48-foot-tall *Hammering Man* outside, by artist Jonathan Borofsky, is a controversial addition that has been criticized as ugly and unoriginal (it has several dozen identical siblings scattered across the United States and Europe) but is nonetheless becoming a Seattle icon.

SAM has one of the world's top collections of Northwest Coast Native American art as well as an extensive African art collection. The museum has an authentic bamboo-and-cedar teahouse in the Japanese Gallery, where a Japanese master performs tea ceremonies several times a month, and is home to works by Mark Tobey, Morris Graves, and other artists of the Northwest School, who practiced an understated painting style influenced by mysticism and Asian art. SAM is open daily except Mondays. There is an admission fee except on the first Thursday of each month, when it's free.

Turn left onto First Avenue and follow it to Pike Street, where you started this walk.

her majesty kickisomlo-cud

PRINCESS ANGELINE WAS GIVEN her English name by Seattle pioneer Catherine Maynard. Named Kakiisimla at birth, the daughter of Chief Seattle was later known as Kickisomlo-Cud ("widow of Cud" in the Duwamish language). Thinking the widow "far too handsome a woman to carry a name like that," Maynard bestowed upon her the name Angeline. A much-beloved figure in early Seattle, Angeline lived in a shack near the waterfront and was often seen hobbling along the streets selling handmade baskets, wearing a bright calico scarf tied beneath her chin.

Angeline's deeply lined, solemn face was photographer Edward Curtis' inspiration. Curtis had been making a living in Seattle taking portraits of society matrons, but he changed his focus after he met the chief's daughter. He saw her digging clams in Seattle's tideflats and offered her a dollar for every picture she allowed him to shoot. Angeline was happy to comply, saying she preferred having her picture taken to digging for clams.

When Curtis found that his Indian prints sold well, he expanded his portfolio, taking thousands of photos of Native Americans across the western United States. He compiled his work into the 20-volume set *The North American Indian*, published between 1907 and 1930. (A collection of Curtis' photographs can be seen at the Flury & Co. gallery in Pioneer Square, at 322 First Avenue South.)

After Curtis' photos made Angeline's image familiar, souvenir trinkets showing her face were produced and sold up and down the Pacific coast. When she died in 1896, most of the city's prominent citizens turned out for her funeral; crowds of mourners lined the route between the church and Lake View Cemetery on Capitol Hill, where she was buried.

Today Angeline's grave bears a rough stone slab with a metal plaque upon it, installed by the Seattle Historical Society in 1958. The gravestone makes no mention of her Duwamish name.

NEW YORK BY AND BY:
pioneer square

A walk back in time to old Seattle

Distance: 1 mile **Approximate time:** 2 hours

THE FOUNDERS OF SEATTLE

originally settled on Alki Point, in West Seattle, in 1851. However, one winter in that unprotected spot was enough to convince many to look elsewhere. The following year most of them moved across Elliott Bay to the hillsides where downtown Seattle is located today. Gradually a community coalesced around the neighborhood you're about to explore, bolstered largely by Henry Yesler's decision to locate his sawmill at the foot of what is now Yesler Way. Thus, while the oldest house in Seattle is on Alki Point, the oldest neighborhood in Seattle is Pioneer Square.

One of the first names ever given to Seattle, when the city was no more than those few families camped out on a beach, was New York-Alki. "Alki" was an Indian trade-jargon word meaning "by and by." The place may have been a tiny outpost in the middle of the wilderness, but Seattle's founders were convinced it would be just like New York City—by and by.

This vision, combined with dogged persistence and a lot of luck, eventually did help Seattle grow into the Queen City of the

Bust of Chief Seattle

Northwest, as it was called in the early 1900s. The city has long since stopped trying to be New York, and most residents are glad. Unlike New York, Seattle retains an almost small-town friendliness

getting there

parking Metered parking is usually available under the Alaskan Way Viaduct, an elevated freeway near the waterfront, although it's limited to two hours. There are also several commercial lots in the neighborhood. If there's a major event at either of the sports stadiums, don't even try to park near Pioneer Square.

bus connections Many Seattle buses pass through downtown within a few blocks of Pioneer Square; get off near Cherry Street or Yesler Way and walk downhill to First Avenue. (For more information on bus routes serving this area, see the "Getting Around" section in the introduction to this book.)

and never seems all that far from the natural world. Who wouldn't choose the Emerald City over the Asphalt Jungle?

This walk explores Seattle's oldest neighborhood, historic Pioneer Square, a former skid row now full of restored historic buildings housing art galleries, shops, restaurants, and nightclubs. Along the way you'll encounter some unlikely urban features, including a waterfall, a national park, and more than two dozen walruses. The walk also visits several older buildings in the southern part of the central downtown before returning you to the heart of Pioneer Square.

One of Pioneer Square's biggest attractions is the underground tour (see "The Seattle Underground" on page 30), but did you know you can see the underground on your own? Parts of buried Seattle are still open for business, and you will visit these sites along this walk. They lack a little of the underground tour's musty allure, but they provide an interesting glimpse into Seattle's past. You can visit parts of the underground at sites ❶, ❷, and ❸ in this chapter.

❶ Start this walk at Pioneer Place, on First Avenue between Cherry Street and Yesler Way.

Pioneer Place marks the northern end of the Pioneer Square neighborhood. This cobblestone square is today shaded by large trees and encircled by elegant Romanesque Revival buildings, but in the early days of Seattle it was the site of the city's first industry: Henry Yesler's sawmill. Yesler's cookhouse, a rough log structure that served as Seattle's first public meeting place, was located across First, on what is now the site of the Mutual Life Building (1890–91). Before Yesler established his cookhouse, a Duwamish Indian winter village was located just south of this building.

In Pioneer Place today, people feed the pigeons, dine at sidewalk eateries, gather for the famous underground tour, and sometimes take shelter under the glass and iron **pergola** to escape Seattle's frequent rain showers. This ornate structure on the corner of First and Yesler was built in the early 1900s to mark the entrance to a fabulous underground restroom. Closed permanently several decades later due to plumbing problems at high tide, in its prime it must have been a remarkable sight. The stalls were

16

pioneer square

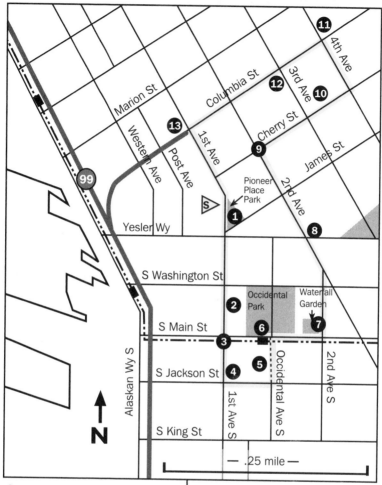

1. **Pioneer Place Park:** pergola, Pioneer Building, Pioneer Square Antique Mall, bust of Chief Seattle, totem pole
2. **Grand Central Arcade**
3. **Globe Hotel Building/Elliott Bay Book Co. and Matilda Winehill Block/Bread of Life Mission**
4. **Jackson Building**
5. **Foster/White Gallery**
6. **Klondike Gold Rush National Historical Park**
7. **Waterfall Garden**
8. **Smith Tower**
9. **Broderick, Alaska, Hoge, and Dexter Horton Buildings**
10. **Arctic Building**
11. **Rainier Club**
12. **Old Chamber of Commerce Building**
13. **Colman Building**

The Pioneer Building

solid Alaskan marble, and there was a lounge area with benches and a concession stand. The restroom is still there, underneath layers of grime, but its entrance has been cemented over and the pergola is all that remains of its former glory.

Dominating Pioneer Place is the elegant **Pioneer Building** (1892), a fine example of the Romanesque Revival architectural style, which was popular from the 1880s until about 1900. Its characteristics include bays and arches, recessed entryways, round towers, rock-faced walls, and a massive

appearance. The American Institute of Architects called this "the finest building west of Chicago" soon after it was completed. Peek inside at the marvelous interior, with its elegant atrium and refurbished elevator cage. To the right of the building's entrance, a flight of stairs leads down to the pleasantly musty **Pioneer Square Antique Mall**, one of the several parts of Seattle's underground that are accessible to the public for free. This store is full of trinkets and memorabilia. A glass display cabinet tucked away on the northwest side of the shop stands in front of a window that was once above street level. A moldy passageway is all that's visible in the dark on the other side of the glass, but if you squint, and stand there long enough, you will eventually see clientele of the underground tour file past.

In front of the Pioneer Building are a tall totem pole and a fountain featuring a **bust of Chief Seattle** (the city's namesake, a chief of the Duwamish tribe). Although totem poles are often associated with Northwest Native Americans, the tribes living in the Puget Sound area typically did not carve them. The original version of this **totem pole** was from southeastern Alaska. It arrived in Seattle illegally in 1899 after some leading Seattle citizens stole it from a Tlingit Indian village while touring the Inside Passage. The village was vacant because its residents were in their summer fishing camp.

Whether or how the Tlingit community ever received restitu-

chief seattle

THE CITY OF SEATTLE WAS named for a chief of the Duwamish tribe. Chief Seattle (also translated "Sealth") was born on Blake Island (about four miles off West Seattle) in the late 18th century. Although an old man by the time the settlers met him, he was still regal: about six feet tall, with long unbraided hair that fell to his broad shoulders.

The office of chief wasn't a hereditary post among the Duwamish. Seattle was chief because he was intelligent, diplomatic, and a good strategist. Puget Sound tribes typically granted little authority to their chiefs, but Seattle had unusual influence; he managed to unite six competing tribes under his leadership. He excelled in war as well; the Haida Indians of Vancouver Island, who often raided Puget Sound villages, reportedly avoided coming within 10 miles of him.

Seattle had many friends in the white community, although he knew enough to be wary of the settlers. He saw that members of his tribe were hung for killing whites, but every white accused of killing an Indian was acquitted, even one simple-minded enough to admit his guilt. But he realized that the tide of white settlers was an unstoppable force. He knew his tribe would fare better by cooperating than by opposing the inevitable. He helped the settlers, but he never compromised his Duwamish identity. He refused to wear the settlers' clothing or speak English, and could usually be seen in a breechcloth and a faded blue blanket.

In 1854, Governor Isaac Stevens decided that all Indians in the Washington Territory should be moved to reservations. At a gathering of the northern Puget Sound tribes, Stevens asked them to set a date for a treaty convention, telling them the great chief in Washington, D.C., loved them and would see to their every need if they would sign his treaty. Seattle agreed to the treaty convention but was unimpressed with Stevens' oratory. He responded with his own, now-famous speech, excerpts of which appear on page 20.

In Stevens' Point Elliott Treaty, signed on January 22, 1855, approximately two million acres of Indian lands were traded for $150,000—about .075 cents per acre—to be paid in "useful articles" in installments over the next 20 years. At the same time, the territorial government was selling the same land for $1.25 per acre.

The Duwamish were sent to a reservation, but the tribe was never happy there. In the summer of 1856 all but four or five Duwamish families fled the reservation at Port Madison, where they were barely subsisting. They subsequently moved to several locations on Puget Sound and Lake Washington. Today, the Duwamish who remain on reservations live on either Suquamish or Muckleshoot land. The federal Bureau of Indian Affairs doesn't recognize the Duwamish tribe, although tribal members struggle to maintain their cultural identity.

excerpts of chief seattle's speech to governor isaac stevens

DR. HENRY SMITH, A SEATTLE physician, recorded Chief Seattle's 1854 speech to Governor Isaac Stevens. Smith translated Seattle's speech into eloquent English, but he claimed that his translation, excerpts of which appear below, "lacks all the charm lent by the grace and earnestness of the able old orator and the occasion."

. . . *There was a time when our people covered the whole land, as the waves of a wind-ruffled sea cover its shell-paved floor. But that time has long since passed away.* . . .

Your God loves your people and hates mine; he folds his strong arms lovingly around the white man . . . but he has forsaken his red children. . . .

. . . *we are two distinct races and must ever remain so. There is little in common between us. The ashes of our ancestors are sacred and their final resting place is hallowed ground, while you wander away from the tombs of your fathers seemingly without regret.* . . .

Your dead cease to love you and the homes of their nativity as soon as they pass the portals of the tomb. They wander far off beyond the stars, are soon forgotten, and never return. Our dead never forget the beautiful world that gave them being. . . .

Even the white man, whose God walked and talked with him, as friend to friend, is not exempt from the common destiny. We may be brothers after all. We shall see. . . .

And when the last red man shall have perished from the earth and his memory among white men shall have become a myth, these shores shall swarm with the invisible dead of my tribe, and when your children's children shall think themselves alone . . . they will not be alone. . . . At night, when the streets of your cities and villages shall be silent, and you think them deserted, they will throng with the returning hosts that once filled and still love this beautiful land. . . ."

tion for the stolen totem is debated. When an arsonist set the totem aflame in 1938, the city shipped the scarred remains back to the village from which the pole had been plundered, along with payment for a reproduction that the local artists were to carve. Instead, according to one story, the Tlingits thanked city officials for finally paying for the stolen pole and said that if they wanted a second one, they'd have to cough up another $5,000. The city complied, and the tribe carved the replica you see today.

From the pergola, cross Yesler Way and follow First Avenue South to South Washington Street. South of Yesler, the streets in Pioneer Square take a sharp turn (First Avenue actually takes its turn half a block north). This confusing arrangement is due largely to a personality clash between two Seattle founders who each owned land here: Arthur Denny, the city's stoic, puritanical patriarch, and David Maynard, a generous, free-spirited epicurean. Denny thought the streets should follow the waterfront, which on his property ran roughly northwest to southeast, while Maynard wanted streets that ran north to south. Each man platted his streets his own way, and downtown Seattle's confusing street pattern is a permanent reminder of their dispute.

❷ After about a block and a half, step into the **Grand Central Arcade** (214 First Avenue South) on the left. Erected in 1889, this building was a hotel during the Klondike gold rush of the late 1890s, but it later became a flophouse. Today it has been restored and houses restaurants, shops, and a glass-enclosed arcade that connects with the plaza called Occidental Park. When the fireplace inside is lit, the arcade is an especially cozy place to have a bite to eat (from the adjacent bakery) or read the paper. Down the stairs at the far end of the arcade is a collection of shops and offices—a mysterious yet tidy underground passageway that is another accessible part of the underground, with

Historic cafe at First and Yesler

the good doctor

DR. DAVID "DOC" MAYNARD was an enthusiastic Seattle booster, and in the early days of Seattle, the town needed all the promotion it could get. Maynard had great energy, ingenuity, and personal influence, and he used all these qualities on Seattle's behalf. He sold much of his land cheaply, or even gave it away, because he believed that doing so would promote Seattle's growth. He was at times overly generous, and never as prudent or restrained as Seattle founder Arthur Denny thought he should be. He had a tendency to drink too much and talk too much. These qualities made Doc Maynard one of the most colorful and amiable of Seattle's founders.

Maynard was well into middle age when he decided to head toward the California gold fields. Along the way he met Catherine Broshears, who had been widowed on her journey west. Maynard was a married man—his estranged wife was back in Ohio—but that didn't prevent him from falling for Broshears. He never made it to California, instead accompanying his new love to Tumwater, Washington, where she was to stay with her brother-in-law, who encouraged the married Maynard to move on.

Doc eventually moved to Seattle and opened a general store on what is today the site of the Bread of Life Mission. The village's oldest resident, he soon held a prominent position in the new settlement, but he still found time to commute to Tumwater via canoe to see Broshears.

Eventually he decided he wanted to marry her, so he traveled to Olympia and asked the territorial legislature to grant him a divorce. It was an awkward request—his wife didn't know she was being divorced!—but Maynard was a masterful schmoozer. After some flattery and a few drinks, the legislators agreed to his request. Elated, he headed back to Seattle, stopping in Tumwater on the way to ask for Broshears' hand in marriage.

Catherine joined Doc in Seattle, and the happy couple settled into domestic bliss. Maynard returned to his store and was also appointed a justice of the peace; his store was named the county seat. He also became an Indian agent, established a hospital, and opened a law practice. But trouble was just ahead.

When Maynard arrived in Seattle, he had made a claim for the land allowed by law for a husband and wife. When he remarried, he tried to transfer his claim from the name of his first wife to the name of his new one. That got the attention of someone in the land claims office, who informed his Ohio wife, Lydia. She decided to come west and investigate the situation.

On the day Lydia was to arrive in Seattle, Maynard had his whiskers trimmed, put on his best suit, and declared, "I'm going to give the people here a sight they never had before and may never have again. I'm going to show them a man walking down the street with a wife on each arm." Doc and Catherine met the steamer and escorted Lydia home. The three of them lived together for some time, apparently without strife.

Lydia didn't withdraw her land claim, though, and a legal battle over Maynard's estate ensued. His health

Bread of Life Mission

declined as more and more he took to drink. Ironically, one of his last acts was to donate a parcel of land to St. John's Lodge of the Masons, which was raising funds for a cemetery. A few months later, when he died, he became the second person to be buried there, in Lake View Cemetery on Capitol Hill.

After Maynard's death, the courts decided that neither Lydia nor Catherine was entitled to his land claim. Instead, half of it would have to be returned to the territory of Washington. Because Maynard had already sold or given away most of his land, this meant that his widows were left with almost nothing. He had owned a portion of the Seattle waterfront that is today worth hundreds of millions of dollars, but he died a pauper.

historical photos of Seattle on the walls.

❸ Continue on First Avenue to South Jackson Street. On the corner of First Avenue and Main is the **Globe Hotel Building** (1890), a Romanesque Revival building that is now the home of the **Elliott Bay Book Company**. Prior to the recent introduction of large chain bookstores to Seattle, Elliott Bay was the city's largest bookseller. The store first opened its doors in 1973 in the space that currently houses the children's section. Since then it has expanded upward, downward, and outward, filling multiple rooms—and a bargain-books mezzanine—with books tucked into every nook and cranny.

Elliott Bay hosts readings almost every evening in the room off its downstairs cafe (another part of the underground). Best-selling authors often appear, as do the relatively obscure. The bookstore takes pride in helping lesser-known writers go on to wider acclaim.

Across the street, on the right, is the **Bread of Life Mission** in the **Matilda Winehill Block** (1890). The mission is located on the site of Seattle's first general store, opened in 1852 by David Maynard. While parts of Pioneer Square look relatively clean and upscale today, the area has been a skid row throughout much of its history, and numerous transients still wander through Pioneer Place and Occidental Park. The mission is one of the few relatively low-cost or free housing options in

First Avenue scene

the area that have survived gentrification.

④ On the corner of First and Jackson stands the building that marked the beginning of efforts to revitalize the Pioneer Square area after it had fallen into disrepair and disrepute. In the early 1960s, architect Ralph Anderson purchased and renovated the **Jackson Building** (322 First Avenue South), a three-story Italian Renaissance structure. It was the first Pioneer Square building to be rehabilitated. Anderson subsequently restored many other area structures, including the Pioneer Building and the

Grand Central Arcade, and was instrumental in the fight to save Pioneer Square.

⑤ Turn left onto South Jackson Street, follow it for a block, and turn left onto Occidental Avenue South. This is Occidental Mall, actually a tree-lined pedestrian street. Shops face the mall on both sides, with art galleries a dominant theme. This area is the epicenter of Gallery Walk, held on the first Thursday of each month, when galleries stay open into the evening and preview their new shows. On the left is the **Foster/White Gallery** (at press time, however, Foster/White was planning to move to 123 South Jackson Street). Foster/White regularly displays work by preeminent Seattle glass artist Dale Chihuly, whose brilliantly colored creations have brought international attention to Seattle's art scene. Much of Chihuly's work is in a room that is often kept locked, but the staff will let you in if you ask.

⑥ Walk through the block-long Occidental Mall, turn left onto South Main Street, and walk half a block, to just before an alley. Located in a storefront, the **Klondike Gold Rush National Historical Park** (117 South Main Street), open daily, is more of a free museum than a park. The exhibits, films, and books tell the story of the Klondike gold rush and its dramatic effect on Seattle.

The statistics of the rush are sobering. Beginning in 1897, about 100,000 people from all over the world headed for the Klondike, the majority traveling to Alaska through Seattle. Of that number, only 40,000 reached the gold fields at Dawson City; 20,000 stayed to search for gold; a mere 4,000 found any gold at all; and 300 found enough to be considered rich. Of those 300, only 50 held on to their wealth.

But the prospectors' tragedy was Seattle's good fortune. The city's new railroad terminus, together with some skillful public relations, made Seattle the natural starting point for the journey to Alaska. Because the Klondike was so desolate, the Canadian government required everyone headed for the gold fields to bring a year's supply of food and clothing. This allowed Seattle merchants to strike gold in the prospector market without even leaving home. The gold rush helped triple Seattle's population, from 80,671 in 1900 to 237,194 in 1910.

Across the street is **Occidental Park**, a former parking lot that was transformed into a park in 1972. The park now features a treed plaza, a pergola, and totem poles, several of which were donated to the city by Richard White (of the Foster/White Gallery). The most unusual one, the standing figure with arms outstretched, represents the Native American version of the bogeyman, a mythical forest dweller who tries to lure children to her house and then eats them.

❼ Retrace your steps along South Main Street and follow it to Second Avenue South. On the left at Second and Main is **Waterfall Garden**, an enclosed park built to commemorate the site where the United Parcel Service was founded in 1907. It has the feel of a private garden: A 22-foot-high waterfall cascades over granite boulders into a pool beside shade trees and flowers. You can sit at one of the small tables and watch the 5,000 gallons of falling water that stream down the rock wall every minute. It's so secluded that you may forget you're in the center of a large city.

Waterfall Garden

Smith Tower from Occidental Park

❽ Turn left onto Second Avenue South and follow for several blocks, continuing as it angles to the left, to Yesler Way. On the right at Second and Yesler is **Smith Tower** (1914). At the time it was erected, Smith Tower was the fourth-tallest building in the world, and the tallest building in the United States west of the Mississippi. (Today, of course, it's dwarfed by the city's other edifices.)

Typewriter magnate L. C. Smith, who financed the tower, had never lived in Seattle and visited the city only once, but he realized that erecting such a tall building would win his company a lot of valuable publicity. A plaque on its corner proudly announces its height: 42 stories. Sadly, Smith never got to see it; he died during its construction.

The tower is worth a peek inside. It still has its beautiful woodwork and marble floors (timeworn though they may be) and—a blast from the past—elevator operators, one of whom may pop out to greet you. For a small fee, you can ride in one of the West Coast's few remaining manually operated elevators to the observation deck on the 35th floor. (Check ahead, however, to make sure the observation deck is open. At press time, the Smith Tower was undergoing major renovation, resulting in temporary closure of the deck.) On the same floor is the Chinese Room, which boasts a hand-carved teak ceiling and a collection of Chinese art.

As you leave Smith Tower, notice the steep grade of **Yesler Way**. In early Seattle, this street (then Mill Street) was informally referred to as Skid Road because logs were regularly "skidded" down it to Henry Yesler's sawmill from the wooded lands on First Hill above. Yesler Way also was a sort of dividing line between "good" and "evil": Respectable society never ventured south of Yesler, where the undesirable element lurked in a vast tideflat littered with bars, brothels, and flophouses. Thus Yesler Way provided a graphic illustration of both logs and lost souls skidding down the slippery slope to their demise, and the nickname "Skid Road" eventually evolved into the term "skid row."

❾ Continue on Second Avenue for several blocks to Cherry Street. The buildings on the four corners of this intersection provide a small example of what downtown Seattle looked like before the high-rise boom in the 1970s and 1980s permanently changed its appearance.

Just before you reach Cherry, on the left is the **Broderick Building** (1889–91). Begun shortly after the 1889 fire that leveled much of Seattle, it's faced entirely in stone. Originally the Bailey Building, it was renamed the Broderick Building after pioneering real estate developer William Broderick, who had offices here for several decades. On the right is the terra-cotta-clad **Alaska Building** (1903–04), Seattle's first steel-framed skyscraper.

Across Cherry, on the left is the Beaux Arts **Hoge Building** (1911), which stands on the site of the first structure erected on Elliott Bay: Carson Boren's cabin, built in 1852. (According to one story, construction of the cabin was begun not by Carson Boren but by his sister, Louisa.) On the right is the massive **Dexter Horton Building** (1921–24), one of the many terra-cotta-clad buildings erected in Seattle in the late 1800s and early 1900s. Boasting an elegant arching entryway on Second

The Arctic Building

Avenue, the building was designed in an unusual E shape to maximize natural light.

Dexter Horton, Seattle's first banker, happened upon that position when he installed a safe in his store. Since it was the only strongbox in town, everyone stored their valuables with him. (Horton's safe, however, wasn't all that safe; he'd bought it at a discount because its back was missing!) The Dexter Horton Bank eventually became Seattle First National Bank, a longtime local institution commonly known as Seafirst.

Colman Building

🔟 **Follow Cherry Street uphill to Third Avenue.** Before you, on the corner of Third and Cherry, is the **Arctic Building** (1913–17). Built for the Arctic Club, an exclusive businessmen's fraternity, the building features fanciful terra-cotta ornamentation that includes 25 walrus heads. They once had real ivory tusks, but when an earthquake in the 1940s brought several of their tusks to the ground, the remainder were replaced with epoxy tusks, which were thought to be less likely to come loose and skewer pedestrians passing beneath them. The Arctic Building currently houses government offices. Its ornate Cherry Street entrance, which you pass as you continue the walk, is far grander than its unassuming Third Avenue one.

⓫ **Continue on Cherry Street to Fourth Avenue; turn left onto Fourth and follow it to Columbia Street.** On the corner of Fourth and Columbia is the venerable Seattle institution known as the **Rainier Club** (1904). Although unmarked, the building is easily identifiable: The ivy-covered brick clubhouse exudes exclusivity, along with a posh pastoral elegance that seems a bit out of place amid skyscrapers. The club began as a prestigious businessmen's fraternity; it now admits women too.

⓬ **Turn left onto Columbia Street and follow it for several blocks to First Avenue.** Just past Third, on the left, is the **old Chamber of Commerce Building** (1924), with its unusual church-inspired

facade. Its impressive main entry features sculptural friezes carved in stone on either side. The one on the right depicts early Seattle's industry, while the one on the left portrays Native American culture.

⑬ The grand **Colman Building** (1889), occupying an entire block at First and Columbia, was built by early Seattle entrepreneur James Colman. He acquired this property through squatter's rights, by beaching a ship at the site long enough to establish ownership. He purchased the hull of the wrecked clipper ship *Windward* and had it towed here around 1872. The wrecked *Windward* served as Colman's home for quite a while. Eventually the tideflats that surrounded his ship were filled in and the ship was buried, which is why this site is now three blocks from the waterfront.

Sculptural relief on the old Chamber of Commerce Building

Construction began on the Colman Building (over the partially buried ship's hull) in 1889 but was not completed until 1904, having been interrupted by the 1893 depression; additional flourishes were added in 1930. Thus the building's design includes elements of a number of different architectural styles—Romanesque Revival, Chicago School, Art Deco—each of which enjoyed popularity at some point during the several decades of its construction.

Turn left onto First Avenue and follow it to Pioneer Place, where you started this walk.

the seattle underground: through fire and high water

LOCATED BENEATH THE PIONEER Square neighborhood, Seattle's underground is an eerie realm of deserted basements and subterranean sidewalks that were once at ground level—until ground level was raised one floor in the 1890s. The underground tour offered by a private Seattle company is one of King County's top tourist attractions. Every year about 150,000 people follow quick-witted guides on a pun-filled romp through early Seattle's history, wandering through musty underground passageways and decaying 1890s-era basements—all of which are devoid of any notable art or architecture.

The story of Seattle's underground *is* interesting, however, even if the actual underground is not. Seattle has an underground because it was built on land that wasn't well suited to urban occupation. There was scarcely a flat spot along the waterfront on which to build, except for a tiny island in a tideflat, on what is now Pioneer Square, which had a very robust odor at low tide.

First Avenue (called Front Street at the time) ran along the top of a bluff that was cut with ravines so deep that the road was impassable for any significant distance. In the late 19th century a 10-year-old boy drowned in a pothole at Third and Jackson—a "pothole" that was actually more of a pond. It was a permanent feature of that intersection, and pedestrians used to row across it.

The land in Seattle that wasn't too steep was too shallow. Most of early Seattle's retail core was below sea level at high tide, which became more of a problem when modern plumbing was introduced. Rising tides traveled up Seattle's sewage system almost as regularly as sewage traveled down it. Toilets tended to become gurgling fountains at high tide.

On the afternoon of June 6, 1889, Seattle had a brush with fate that would end up solving many of its elevation problems. In a woodworking shop on the corner of Front and Madison, a pot of glue being heated by an apprentice boiled over and ignited some wood chips on the ground. Within 20 minutes, an entire block of Front Street was in flames. By the time the fire was vanquished, 120 acres in the heart of the city had been leveled.

It didn't take the city's leaders long to realize that the fire had given them an opportunity to do for the city what nature had not: lift the central core out of the reach of high tide. City engineers proposed a project to raise the streets in Pioneer Square, but with buildings going up, the city couldn't regrade by sluicing down the hills. Instead, engineers regraded only the streets, then built retaining walls along the streets and filled them with dirt. Buildings were erected with the full knowledge that what started out as the first or second floor would eventually be the basement.

When the regraded streets were finally in place, they stood as high as 10 feet above their former level. The construction of sidewalks at street level was delayed due to budget constraints. This meant that there was a deep trench between buildings and the street. To cross the street from one building to the next involved climbing a ladder to street level, crossing the street, and then climbing another ladder down the other side. These hazardous trenches cost the lives of more than a dozen men (the great fire had killed not even one!), most of whom had been returning home after stopping for a few drinks when they stepped onto the "sidewalk" and took a nasty fall.

About 5,000 men lost jobs because of the Seattle fire, but they quickly found work constructing the 3,500 buildings that went up in the two years following the fire. Seattle's population grew from an estimated 31,000 at the time of the fire in 1889 to almost 43,000 in the 1890 census. What had been a ramshackle frontier town became a respectable modern city.

Seattle's underground remained in use for many years after the streets were raised. In the early 20th century much of the underground was condemned, but some enterprising citizens still found uses for it. During Prohibition, it was the perfect hiding place for illicit activities, and in the 1940s and 1950s homeless camps were located there.

Now that Pioneer Square has been gentrified, the underground is a tourist attraction, most of it accessible only to those taking a guided tour. You can get a free peek at Seattle's underground at several of the sites in this chapter.

Interior of the Grand Central Arcade

SKYSCRAPERS AND THE SPACE NEEDLE:

AND SEATTLE CENTER

Distance: 1.5 miles (one way)   **Approximate time:** 3 hours

THIS WALK RANGES THROUGH downtown Seattle, looking at some notable architecture from many periods of Seattle's past and present. It takes you past opulent hotels and historic theaters as well as more recently built shopping centers and skyscrapers, and leads you to some little-known downtown parks and quasi-public spaces. If you like, you can then board the Monorail and ride to Seattle Center, a recreational complex that includes facilities for sporting events, theaters, museums, an amusement park, and, most famously, the Space Needle.

❶ Start this walk on the corner of Fourth Avenue and Madison Street, with Elliott Bay to your left. On the left side of Fourth stands Seattle's first modern high-rise, the black-glass tower now known as the **1001 Fourth Avenue Building**. Built a few years after the Space Needle, the skyscraper was often referred to as "the box the Space Needle came in." It's hard to imagine now, but when this building was completed in the late 1960s, Seattle's skyline boasted only three other towers: the 600-foot Space Needle (1962),

the 42-story Smith Tower (1914), and the 27-story Seattle Tower (1928), which you'll visit on this walk.

In front of the 1001 Fourth Avenue Building is *Vertebrae*, a large abstract bronze sculpture by Henry Moore, set amid a reflecting pond. On sunny days it's surrounded by office workers, who perch on the edge of the pond while enjoying their lunch break. In the 1980s a public outcry followed the news that the artwork had been sold and was moving to Japan; eventually the owners were persuaded to buy back the sculpture and keep it in Seattle.

Across Fourth Avenue, on the right, is the **Seattle Public Library**, one of Seattle's first large International-style buildings. Its design was considered progressive when the library was built in 1960, but now it looks old and tired. Plans are under way to replace this outdated structure with a new, larger library in the same location.

Follow Fourth Avenue to University Street. You pass Seneca Street, the southern boundary of the **University of Washington's Metropolitan Tract**. The land from Seneca to Union Streets, roughly between Fourth and Sixth Avenues, was the original site of the university before it moved to its current location on Lake Washington in 1895. The university still holds the title to this land, which brings in millions of dollars of revenue each year.

❷ Turn left onto University Street and follow it to Third Avenue. At this intersection are

Henry Moore's Vertebrae

several notable buildings. On the left, before you cross Third, is the **Seattle Tower** (originally the Northern Life Tower), an elegant 1928 Art Deco skyscraper. The building's design, inspired by the mountains of the Northwest, uses brickwork that graduates from darker at the bottom to lighter at the top, to emphasize the building's height. The permanence of a mountain was a desirable bit of

downtown and seattle center

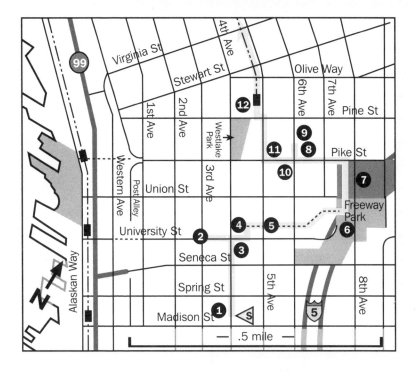

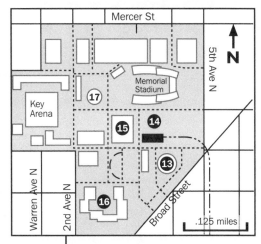

1. 1001 Fourth Avenue Building
2. Seattle Tower
3. Four Seasons Olympic Hotel
4. Rainier Square
5. 5th Avenue Theater
6. Freeway Park
7. Washington State Convention & Trade Center
8. GameWorks
9. Planet Hollywood
10. FAO Schwarz
11. Coliseum
12. Westlake Center

13. Space Needle
14. Fun Forest
15. Center House
16. Pacific Science Center
17. International Fountain

Washington Mutual Tower

Look for the tiny mouse running up the street clock outside on Third, an allusion to the nursery rhyme.

If you like, take a slight detour to visit the Washington Mutual Tower's elegant atrium and outdoor plaza on Second: Enter through the building's main entrance on Third Avenue, walk through the wood-paneled bank of elevators, and follow the low silver and marble walls to the staircase leading to the atrium below.

On the right, across Third, is **Benaroya Hall** (1998), the $118 million home of the Seattle Symphony. From the expansive, glass-enclosed lobby of the main performance hall, patrons can enjoy a view of the Seattle Art Museum and Elliott Bay beyond. Even if you're not attending a performance, you can stroll through the block-long foyer, which fronts Third Avenue and features a cafe, a coffee bar, and artfully scattered tables. Gracing the ends of the gallery are two dazzling 20-foot-long blown-glass chandeliers called *Crystal Cascade*, created especially for this space by internationally known Seattle artist Dale Chihuly.

symbolism for the building's original owner, the Northern Life Insurance Company. The polished lobby boasts intricate detailing and an 18-karat gold relief map on the far wall boldly proclaiming, "Westward the Course of Empire Takes Its Way"; enter on Third to see it.

On the left, across Third, is a building whose design is a 1980s interpretation of Art Deco: the **Washington Mutual Tower**, one of the last structures built during Seattle's high-rise boom of the 1980s. The tower's silvery accents and blue-glass windows make it a striking feature of Seattle's skyline.

❸ **Retrace your steps on University Street and follow it half a block past Fourth Avenue.** On the right, occupying an entire block, is the majestic **Four Seasons Olympic Hotel** (1924–29). The hotel was originally constructed around the Metropolitan Theater, which was demolished in 1954 so the "motor entrance" before you could be added. Step

36

dale chihuly: glass master

SEATTLEITE DALE CHIHULY, widely regarded as the world's premier glass artist, is the first person to have been named a National Living Treasure by the president of the United States. His works—often brilliantly colored and extravagantly shaped—can be found in more than 100 museums worldwide and are much in demand, with prices ranging from a few thousand dollars to hundreds of thousands. Chihuly is an institution in the art world, having secured new respect for glass as an art form. He cofounded the Pilchuck Glass School in Stanwood, north of Seattle, which has been training glass artists since 1971.

Chihuly cuts an eccentric figure: a pudgy man with wildly curly brown hair and a patch over his left eye (the result of a London car crash in the 1970s). He lives and works at a sizable studio he calls the Boathouse, located in a former boat factory on Lake Union. It's a constant swarm of activity, as Chihuly surveys his staff's work and plays host to a continuous stream of visiting artists from around the world.

Interestingly, Chihuly doesn't actually blow the glass that bears his name. Because he lost his depth perception along with his left eye, he instead uses the team approach to glassblowing that he learned while studying in a factory near Venice in the late 1960s. He designs the pieces, then presides over a team of gaffers (master glassblowers) who actually fabricate the creations; some works take up to six gaffers to complete.

Chihuly's glass artworks are in the collections of the Seattle Art Museum and the Tacoma Art Museum. You can view them for free at Benaroya Hall, the U.S. Bank Centre, the Stouffer Madison and Sheraton Seattle hotels, and the Washington State Convention & Trade Center (all in downtown Seattle) as well as at the Union Station courthouse in Tacoma.

Chihuly's Crystal Cascade *at Benaroya Hall*

inside, ascend the escalators to the ornate lobby, and admire its hushed elegance. The Four Seasons has a number of fine restaurants; the lush Garden Court, with its tall windows overlooking the motor entrance, is just off the lobby. Boutiques and salons are located on the lower level. Retrace your steps to University Street when you're done exploring.

❹ Across University Street from the Four Seasons is **Rainier Square**, a shopping area attached to **Rainier Tower** (1979). This office tower has a particularly eye-catching design; it looks as if it's teetering on a giant golf tee.

Enter Rainier Square. Rainier Square is the home of the **Seattle Architectural Foundation**; if you like, you can visit its offices to learn more about Seattle architecture from the interesting exhibit there. (You can also pick up a brochure on the foundation's popular Viewpoints tours of Seattle.) To find the exhibit, walk straight ahead to an atrium with shops surrounding it on several levels; the foundation's offices are on the top level. Retrace your steps to the Rainier Square lobby, near US Bank, when you're done.

Ascend the escalator opposite the lobby, exit the building through the door to the left, and follow the stairs all the way up. At the top is **Rainier Square Park**, actually the roof of a building that has been strewn with benches and large flowerpots. From here you can enjoy a third-story perspective on the Four Seasons Olympic Hotel, the Seattle Tower, and the Washington Mutual Tower.

You can also see the historic **Cobb Building** (1909–10) to the west, with its striking Indian-head reliefs on a terra-cotta facade. The reliefs reflect the attitudes of the era; urban residents were looking back with romantic nostalgia toward the not-so-distant past when the land was unspoiled and inhabited only by Native tribes. Famed photographer and Seattleite Edward S. Curtis was working on his 20-volume photographic archive of American Indian tribes, and Indian images commonly appeared in advertising and on souvenir trinkets. The Indian on the Cobb Building doesn't memorialize a Northwestern past, though; his feathered headdress is more typical of Plains Indians.

❺ **Leaving Rainier Square Park, cross the street to the far side of Fifth Avenue.** The **5th Avenue Theater** (1926) is a glorious reminder of early-20th-century Seattle, when grand theaters abounded downtown and the city was the headquarters of several vaudeville circuits. The 5th Avenue's extravagant interior is painted with designs inspired by those in Beijing's Forbidden City, and the ceiling, with its fantastic coiled dragon, is a nearly exact replica of the dome from the throne room of the Imperial Palace there. Call in advance to schedule a free tour, (206) 625-1418.

Descend the short staircase near the theater entrance, leading to the building's lower level. Pass several eateries, then turn right and follow the underground corridor until you reach an escalator. The corridor's walls are lined with photographs of Seattle's past, tracing the development of the city from the late 1880s to the present day.

❻ Take the escalator and follow the signs toward the Two Union Square lobby until you reach a stairway. Ascend the stairs, walk through the lobby, and exit at the opposite end. You have entered the uniquely situated **Freeway Park**, an expansive green space located atop a freeway underpass. The park was constructed in 1976 to reconnect downtown and First Hill, which were divided by I-5. Wandering here may make you feel like a kid searching for secret passageways in your grandmother's attic; there are pathways heading in mysterious directions, intimate plazas, and hidden corners. And everywhere there is water—fountains, waterfalls, and gurgling streams running through concrete channels— adding to the ambience and masking the noise of the freeway. To explore the park, take the stairway to the right, and turn right at the top. Retrace your steps when you're done.

❼ Leave Freeway Park through the large green-glass building abutting the park. This is the **Washington State Convention**

Rainier Tower

& Trade Center, which offers shops, eateries, art exhibits, and a visitors center on the main floor.

❽ Descend the escalators and exit straight ahead, onto Pike Street. Turn left and follow Pike Street to Fifth Avenue. You're now entering an epicenter of commerce and recreation. On the right, on the corner of Seventh and Pike, is a 16-screen cinema and **GameWorks,** a huge arcade featuring 250 different variations on the video game, from Pac-Man to assorted high-tech virtual-reality experiences. GameWorks has its own eateries as well as a brewpub and a coffee bar. You can walk through for free, but the games cost money. A block farther, on the right at Sixth and Pike, is **Niketown**. Don't let its futuristic decor and autographed sports memorabilia fool you: At its heart, it's still a shoe store.

9 Just beyond Niketown on Sixth is the glitzy **Planet Holly-wood**, packed with movie memorabilia, where you can take home souvenirs along with your leftovers.

10 On the left, catycorner from Niketown, is a giant bronze teddy bear beckoning you into the toy superstore **FAO Schwarz**, one of

Freeway Park

the many upscale City Centre Shops in the **U.S. Bank Centre** tower. The building owns a substantial collection of glass art, including *Puget Sound Persian*, an astoundingly large installation of brilliantly colored glass forms by renowned artist Dale Chihuly. The Chihuly installation is located on the second floor near the toy store, and most of the other glass artworks are scattered throughout this floor as well.

11 A block farther, on the right at Fifth and Pike, is another of Seattle's elegant old theaters, now an elegant Banana Republic store. Built in 1916, the **Coliseum** had more than 1,700 seats and was one of the first theaters in the world designed expressly for the display of motion pictures. Like many of its counterparts, the Coliseum suffered neglect throughout the years, and it closed in the late 1980s. Banana Republic completed a multimillion-dollar rehabilitation and remodel in 1995.

Turn right onto Fifth Avenue and follow it to Pine Street. On the right, across Pine Street, is the gleamingly restored 1918 building housing the flagship store of the **Nordstrom** empire, which began as a humble shoestore in downtown Seattle in 1901. The Seattle Walk of Fame on the sidewalk outside lets you compare your feet to those of some influential Seattle personalities, from Bill Gates to Jimi Hendrix. If Nordstrom only whets your appetite, take a short detour to the polished grandeur of **Pacific Place**, just up the street at

Sixth and Pine, where the tenants include Tiffany & Co., Cartier, and J. Peterman as well as an assortment of fashionable eateries and an 11-screen movie complex.

⑫ Turn left onto Pine Street and follow it to Fourth Avenue. On the right is **Westlake Center**, a block-size shopping mall. It faces Westlake Park, a plaza on either side of Pine Street where young people gather, protesters congregate, street musicians play, and a carousel appears every holiday season.

On the left, in Westlake Park, is Robert Maki's cleverly designed "water wall," which gives those intrepid enough to pass through it the sensation of walking through a waterfall without getting (too) wet.

Enter Westlake Center, ascend the escalators to the top floor, and enter the Monorail station, just to the left. The **Monorail**

The Coliseum Theater turned Banana Republic

makes its 90-second run between Westlake Center and Seattle Center every 15 minutes all day and into the evening. The Monorail was built for the Seattle World's Fair in 1962; afterward, opinion was divided about whether it should continue to stand. The pro-Monorail forces prevailed, and it's been chugging away ever since.

Take the Monorail to its first (and only) stop, Seattle Center. Seattle Center was also built for the World's Fair. Previously a baseball park and a civic center, today this ground sees a lot more action: Over 5,000 events are held here each year. The facilities include sports arenas, several theaters, an opera house, a science center, a children's theater and a children's museum, an amusement park, and the crowning glory of it all, the Space Needle. You can choose among the attractions outlined below and chart your own path with the help of the accompanying map. A schedule of upcoming events and performances at the center's various venues is available at the information booth in the Center House.

⓭ Space Needle. The Space Needle is the first image that comes to mind when most people think of Seattle. Visiting the city without riding the elevator to the top of the Needle is a bit like visiting Paris and missing the Eiffel Tower. This strangely shaped spire has become so much a part of Seattle's landscape that it almost seems like a natural formation. (There's a fee for the elevator ride unless you're also dining atop the Needle.)

The International Fountain

Near the Space Needle is the construction site of a $60 million museum honoring Northwest popular music. Scheduled for completion around the year 2000, it will house a vast collection of artifacts and interactive exhibits, as well as a library and a concert hall—all in a 140,000-square-foot building resembling a smashed guitar. The museum, which will be called the **Experience Music Project,** is the brainchild of local billionaire Paul Allen, a Microsoft cofounder.

⓮ Fun Forest. This modest kid-oriented amusement park offers carnival rides and an arcade.

⓯ Center House. Here you'll find restaurants, an information booth, and an informal performance space/dance floor. You'll probably end up stopping here if you need to eat, use the restroom, ask directions, or pick up an event

the space needle: pointing toward the 21st century

THE SPACE NEEDLE HAS BEEN the most recognizable symbol of Seattle ever since it was built in 1962. When the Seattle World's Fair was being planned, the United States had recently entered the space race, cars had tail fins, orbiting planets had become a common decorative theme, and science fiction was enjoying new popularity. Fair organizers decided to capitalize on the trend, calling their event the Century 21 Exposition and giving it a forward-looking theme centered around space and science.

The exposition featured exhibits from 400 companies and 40 foreign countries, but the number-one attraction was the Space Needle. During the six months of the fair, more than two and a half million people paid $1 each to ride to the Needle's observation deck, and the revolving restaurant at the top was usually filled to capacity. The Seattle World's Fair was an astounding success, one of the few world's fairs to make a profit.

Building this profitable observation tower/restaurant platform involved first digging a big hole in the ground. The Space Needle is a tall, spindly-looking spire built in earthquake country, so in order to ensure that this apparently top-heavy structure wouldn't topple over at the slightest tremor, it had to be given a low center of gravity. To accomplish this, a huge pit was filled with 5,850 tons of concrete and rebar to support the base of the Needle, which was affixed to the ground with 96 massive anchor bolts, many of them four inches in diameter and 32 feet long. If you walk around the Needle's base, you can see the huge nuts that attach the Needle to its substructure.

When the 600-foot Space Needle was completed, it was the tallest structure in the United States west of the Mississippi River. It's still one of Seattle's top attractions, and it's hard to imagine the city without it. Perhaps it does resemble a flying saucer on stilts, but that only makes it more endearing.

Chief Seattle hails the Space Needle from Tillicum Place

schedule anytime during your visit. The Center House was formerly an armory building where sock hops were held in the 1950s.

Also located in the Center House is the **Children's Museum**, which features exhibits on wilderness, culture, and technology, all designed to provide children with an interactive learning experience. (There's a modest admission fee.)

16 **Pacific Science Center.** This learning center features hands-on scientific displays where children (and adults) can meet robotic dinosaurs, experience virtual-reality hang-gliding, or ride a bicycle on a track 30 feet in the air. The center has a mega-screen IMAX theater too. (There's an admission fee and a separate charge for films.)

17 **International Fountain.** On a sunny day, the International Fountain is the social hub of Seattle Center. Children of all ages play in the water, while everyone else takes in the scenery. The fountain also dances: From midday into the evening it performs, producing a fine spray that looks like steam and then sending jets of water 50 feet into the air, all accompanied by music.

In Seattle's early days, the lawn to the north of the fountain was the flower garden of Seattle founders David and Louisa Denny, the first white couple to be married in the city of Seattle. In a house located where the Opera House is today, they raised eight children, who undoubtedly frolicked around the site of the fountain much as children do today.

When you've finished exploring Seattle Center, you can return to downtown (where you parked your car) via the Monorail or bus routes noted at the beginning of this chapter.

A REMODELED PROMISED LAND:

belltown

Urban funk and a long-vanished hill

Distance: 1.25 miles **Approximate time:** 1 hour

THE AREA BETWEEN DOWN-
town Seattle and the Space Needle
has always had a bit of an identity
crisis. It even has two names: Belltown and the Denny Regrade.
The name "Belltown" came from
the William Bell family, who originally claimed this land, while
"Denny Regrade" describes what
used to be Denny Hill. The very
steep hill that originally occupied
this part of Seattle was regraded—
washed into Puget Sound—in the
early 1900s, flattening the area in
an effort to make development
more feasible.

Belltown never became part of
the central business district as city
officials had hoped it would;
instead it became home to light
industry and other enterprises that
didn't need a prestigious address in
the downtown core. The neighborhood was also popular with
artists because of its cheap rents,
but during the past decade expensive condominiums began to
replace inexpensive studios.

Today, designer boutiques and
swanky clubs have taken up space
beside thrift stores and divey
nightspots. "Campy" may be the
best way to describe Belltown's
style. You can experience it while

Fourth Avenue and Blanchard Street

sipping a mai tai under an erupting
black-light volcano at the Lava
Lounge or dancing under papier-
mâché snakes at the Crocodile
Cafe. It's another stage in the
neighborhood's evolution; what

getting there

Belltown will be tomorrow, no one knows.

❶ Start this walk at Sit & Spin, on Fourth Avenue between Blanchard and Bell Streets. Sit & Spin (2219 Fourth Avenue) is the quintessential Belltown establishment: Not just a laundromat, it's also a cafe, a bar, and, on some nights, a live-music club. Step inside to fully appreciate its unconventional decor. Patrons can order sandwiches or juice concoctions at the counter, and then do laundry or play a board game from the cafe's ample collection while they wait for their meals.

The Crocodile Cafe

❷ Exiting Sit & Spin, turn right onto Fourth Avenue and follow it to Blanchard Street. On the corner of Fourth and Blanchard is the high-rise officially known as the **Sedgwick James Building**. It seems to be made almost entirely of black glass, and its roof comes to a sharp point that jabs the sky, which helps explain its nickname: the Darth Vader building.

This corner was once the highest point on Denny Hill. Had the hill not been washed into Puget Sound, you would now be enjoying an excellent view (although the walk here would have been

belltown

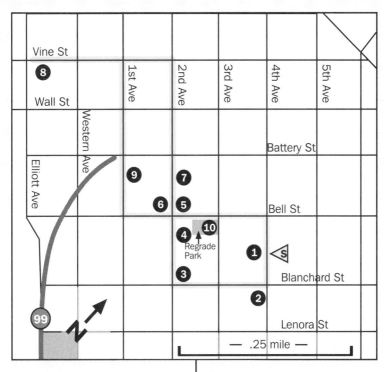

Blanchard Street

1. **Sit & Spin**
2. **Sedgwick James Building**
3. **Crocodile Cafe**
4. **Lava Lounge**
5. **Seattle Building Salvage**
6. **Street Life Gallery**
7. **William Tell Apartments**
8. **Belltown P-Patch**
9. **Austin A. Bell Building**
10. **Regrade Park**

A thrift shop on Second Avenue

considerably more strenuous). To see what the view from the top of Denny Hill might have looked like, take the elevator to the eighth floor of the Sedgwick James Building—the top of Denny Hill was as high as this floor—and gaze through the row of windows behind a work area. (Avoid disturbing the employees, of course.)

An early-20th-century civil engineer named Virgil Bogue had great dreams for this intersection. Hired by Seattle's new planning commission in 1910 to draft a plan for the growing city, he produced a two-volume document that included an extensive rapid transit system, thousands of additional acres of parkland, and, as its centerpiece, a civic center complex of impressive Beaux Arts government buildings radiating outward from a central plaza at Fourth and Blanchard, modeled after the Piazza San Marco in Venice. Sadly for this rather nondescript corner, Seattle voters rejected his vision in 1912.

❸ **Exiting the Sedgwick James Building, turn left onto Blanchard Street and follow it to Second Avenue.** On the corner of Second and Blanchard is the **Crocodile Cafe**, one of Seattle's most popular music clubs. It was opened in 1991 by local lawyer Stephanie Dorgan, who's married to Peter Buck of R.E.M. The Croc plays host to everyone from folk singers to Elvis impersonators, but the emphasis is on alternative rock. The internationally known, Seattle-born grunge-rock band Nirvana even performed here in the fall of 1992, as they were nearing the height of their fame, less

the great regrade

THE AREA CALLED THE DENNY Regrade is a flatland where a huge hill, covering about 60 blocks, once stood. Six million cubic yards of dirt were sluiced from the slopes of Denny Hill to create the Denny Regrade, and twenty millions gallons of water were pumped from Lake Union every day to wash the hill down into Puget Sound.

Today one might question whether the regrading was such a good idea. If the Regrade were still a hill, it would be a swanky address with an outstanding view. As a flatland, the Regrade has long been a neglected area that has only recently started to undergo gentrification.

The transformation of Denny Hill into Denny Regrade began in the late 1890s and proceeded in fits and starts for more than three decades. The ambitious project was the vision of one man: city engineer Reginald H. Thomson, who saw the hill as "an offense to the public" and a barrier to Seattle's progress; its sides were too steep for horse-drawn carriages to traverse.

Not everyone shared Thomson's vision. James A. Moore—owner of the luxurious Washington Hotel, which graced the hill's crest—bitterly protested the plan that would condemn his hostelry. Prominent Seattleite Thomas Burke commented that it would be better to build a tunnel underneath Denny Hill than to destroy the structure that was called "the scenic hotel of the world." The *Seattle Times* ran several editorials accusing Thomson of tyranny and fraud.

For his part, Thomson never understood his critics' objections, writing later in his memoirs, "Some people seemed to think that because there were hills in Seattle originally, some of them ought to be left there. . . ." By 1912 the entire western half of the hill had been leveled, and land values there underwent the predicted boom. Even the reluctant Moore resigned himself to the regrading.

The city regraded only the streets and other property it owned; private property owners had to either live on land that now stood many feet above street level, sell their land to the city, or pay for private regrading, which usually entailed the destruction of all buildings on their property. Thus the area looked like a strip mine for several years, with pillars of earth topped with homes towering above barren plains. Some of these pillars remained for many years, becoming known as "spite mounds" because their owners were refusing to sell or regrade in an attempt to spite a city policy they disagreed with.

Leveling was mostly complete by 1931, but the Great Depression kept the newly flat land from being developed for many years. Even today, the Regrade is somewhat of a poor relation to downtown Seattle; perhaps it still mourns the loss of its spectacular views.

kurt cobain and the irony of youth

KURT COBAIN, LEAD SINGER OF the phenomenally successful band Nirvana, was considered immortal by many of his young fans. But on April 8, 1994, his body was discovered in his home on Lake Washington Boulevard, a shotgun pointing at his chin; he had committed suicide three days earlier. Thousands of fans attended a vigil at Seattle Center to mourn the 27-year-old's passing, vowing that his music would live forever. He was suddenly one step closer to immortality.

Cobain was not only the lead singer but the creative force of Nirvana, which pioneered the sound the world came to know as grunge. Perhaps the band's music was so popular because it expressed the ironies of youth so perfectly. Some of Cobain's lyrics were sensitive and poetic, but the music that accompanied them was often loud and aggressive. Nirvana championed causes like feminism, gay rights, and racial equality, yet a large portion of its audience was attracted by the anger and edginess in the music, not by any social concerns.

Cobain grew up in Aberdeen, a small, conservative logging community near Washington's Pacific coast that was no haven for the artistically inclined. After he quit high school, he took odd jobs and spent some time homeless. A few years later he formed the first of several versions of Nirvana, and in 1989 the group's first album, *Bleach*—produced for a mere $606.17—was released by Seattle's Sub Pop Records, then a little-known independent label. Nirvana signed with a major label for its second album, *Nevermind,* and was catapulted to stardom when the record sold 10 million copies worldwide.

Many of Cobain's lyrics were downbeat. He originally wanted to title Nirvana's fourth album *I Hate Myself and I Want to Die*, after one of the songs it was to include (the song was ultimately cut from the album, *In Utero*). But although his music was often morose and intensely critical of American culture, its discontent obviously spoke to his contemporaries with unusual power.

than two years before lead singer Kurt Cobain tragically took his own life.

❹ Turn right onto Second Avenue and follow it to Bell Street. On the right, the block between Blanchard and Bell is lined with retro and avant-garde businesses, including the **Lava Lounge** and **Mama's Mexican Kitchen**, home of mediocre food and world-class kitsch (check out the Elvis Room, abundantly decorated with memorabilia).

Just before Mama's, look up; above the street-level businesses you'll see a dilapidated former boardinghouse covered with tar-paper siding. It has a peculiar historical significance: When Denny

Second Avenue street scene

Hill was regraded, this wooden structure was one of the very few buildings kept in place and lowered along with the hill.

❺ On the corner of Second and Bell is **Seattle Building Salvage**, a treasure trove of antique doors, windows, and other architectural fixtures salvaged from buildings that have reached the end of their natural lives. Just beyond this home remodeler's dreamland is the **Speakeasy**, Seattle's foremost Internet cafe. In the Belltown tradition, it also offers art, music, experimental films, and more.

❻ On the left is the **Street Life Gallery**, an art studio and exhibition space for homeless artists. Cofounded by an artist who had himself been homeless, it's run by the Catholic archdiocese and funded solely by donations. Artists

Seattle Building Salvage

must volunteer time to help run the gallery, but they receive 100 percent of the proceeds from the sale of their work.

➐ Continue on Second Avenue for several blocks to Vine Street. Beginning in the late 1920s, the next few blocks, from Bell to Wall, were known as **film row**, and all the major motion-picture studios had offices in the area. The building now housing the **William Tell Apartments** (2327 Second Avenue), with its striking classical and Mediterranean-influenced design, was an exclusive hotel frequented by film-industry types; the building just beyond it was MGM's office, as is noted on the silver "Welcome" mat embedded on the sidewalk in front of it (part of a Second

Avenue public art project). Film row served as a distribution point for almost 500 theaters—in Washington, Idaho, Montana, and Alaska—and handled as many as 15 million film shipments per year. The row also housed several small movie studios and a theatrical supply company.

The heart of the row was the Seattle Film Exchange Building, a huge plaster and brick edifice with terra-cotta ornamentation, which filled the entire west side of Second between Battery and Wall. It housed screening rooms, projectionist booths, and editing facilities. Sadly, by the 1960s the popularity of television and changes in the film industry's methods of distribution had combined to help bring about an end to this part of Belltown's history. The building was demolished in the early 1990s to make way for the **Belltown Court condominiums** after preservation efforts failed.

❽ Turn left onto Vine Street and follow it for several blocks to Elliott Avenue. On the corner of Elliott and Vine is the **Belltown P-Patch**, one of about three dozen such community gardens throughout Seattle. The city's highly popular P-Patch program provides urban dwellers with a small plot of land in return for a modest annual fee and an agreement to practice only organic gardening.

Belltown's P-Patch is a monument to the community's spirit. Both an artistic and a botanical wonder, it was once a parking lot where drug dealers loitered. Neighborhood activists convinced the city to purchase the property in 1992, and more than 5,000 hours of volunteer labor later, the former parking lot features an inviting entrance stairway accented with tile mosaics, a solar-powered fountain, a wrought-iron fence with a vegetable motif, and an ornamental entrance gate that incorporates gardening implements into its design. If the gate is open, stroll through the P-Patch, following the winding pathway past flower and vegetable beds and observing the many artistic touches added to the plots by these creative gardeners.

Behind the P-Patch sits a collection of small **cottages** that seem out of place in this urban area. Built in the early 1900s as company housing for the seafood canneries that once thrived on Seattle's waterfront, they serve as storage sheds today.

Retrace your steps up the hill to First Avenue. On the corner of First Avenue and Vine Street is the **New Pacific Apartments** (1904). This structure originally housed the New Pacific Hospital; hence its bay windows, which maximized the sunlight streaming into the sickrooms. When fire raged through Belltown in 1910, casualties were treated here. Eventually the hospital relocated to First Hill,

Belltown P-Patch

directly above downtown, which has so many medical facilities that locals call it Pill Hill.

⑨ Turn right onto First Avenue and follow it for several blocks to Bell Street. Midblock between Battery and Bell Streets, on the left, is the stately, recently remodeled red-brick **Austin A. Bell Building** (2324 First Avenue). When neighborhood founder William Bell died, his son Austin inherited this Belltown property and began planning this building, hoping that new construction would help establish Belltown as a commercial center. He never saw the finished building, though; he took his own life in 1889. It was his wife, Eva, who ensured that the building was completed and named it after her late husband.

Prosperity continued to elude Belltown, though. The Bell Building, designed as a luxury apartment building and commercial block, instead saw use as a low-rent apartment hotel; later, parts of it sat vacant for decades. Only now is this historic building coming back to life, courtesy of the current demand for upscale downtown condominiums. It has been renovated—a "renovation" that involved tearing down everything

but the brick facade, a designated Seattle landmark—to create what its builders first intended, luxury housing.

The red-brick **Barnes Building** next door (2320 First Avenue), which has retained more of its historic integrity, was constructed around the same time as the Bell Building. Intended for use as a lodge hall, it eventually became a sleeping bag factory, as the fading mural on the right side of the building still attests. Now it's home to a comfortable pub, with offices above.

⑩ Turn left onto Bell Street and follow it to Third Avenue. At Third and Bell is **Regrade Park**, a small urban park with a basketball court, some playground equipment, and a huge (9 feet by 16 feet) cement sculpture called *Gyro Jack*, which represents the simultaneous whirling and tilting of a gyroscope. The artist hoped it would invite viewers to climb to the top and survey the park from the viewing seat there, in a memorial to Denny Hill.

Continue on Bell Street to Fourth Avenue, turn right, and walk half a block to Sit & Spin, where you started this walk.

A WORLD APART: THE
International district

The exotic within the familiar

Distance: 1.5 miles (one way)   **Approximate time:** 1.5 hours

STEPPING FROM PIONEER

Square into the International District is a bit like stepping back in time. The Asian enclave has the disheveled look that Pioneer Square had before it was restored in the 1970s. Yet while the buildings tend to be rundown, the neighborhood is bustling and vibrant, providing an all-too-rare look at nongentrified Seattle.

The International District was so named because it has long been home to many different Asian communities. The Chinese were the first to settle here, in the 1860s; then came a large Japanese community. Over the years Filipinos, Vietnamese, and others have followed.

Visiting the International District is like traveling to a foreign country without leaving Seattle. Intriguing sights and smells emerge from every doorway. Exotic merchandise and figures of unfamiliar gods line the shelves. Live turtles swim in tanks at butcher shops, and unusual fruits and vegetables spill onto the sidewalks.

Several major projects are currently planned for areas near the International District. In the coming years, a million square feet of

View from the Danny Woo Garden

office space will be built around Union Station, King Street Station will become a transit center for a new regional commuter railway, and the Kingdome will be razed

starting point

South Jackson Street and Fourth Avenue South

finish point

South Jackson Street and 12th Avenue South. The text describes a one-way walk of 1.5 miles, ending at 12th and Jackson. However, you can return to the starting point by following the loop route outlined on the map. The loop route is 2 miles.

parking

Metered parking is hard to come by and limited to two hours. It's easiest to park in a commercial lot. If there's a major event at either of the sports stadiums, don't even try to park near the International District.

bus connections

Many Seattle buses pass through downtown within a few blocks of the International District; get off near South Jackson Street and Fourth Avenue South. (For more information on bus routes serving this area, see the "Getting Around" section in the introduction to this book.)

To return to the starting point or downtown via bus: Catch Route 1 (Kinnear), 7 (Broadway or University District), or 14 (Summit) on South Jackson Street near 12th Avenue South; get off near Jackson and Fourth Avenue South. The bus shelter there is decorated with tiles illustrating the history of the International District.

and new baseball and football stadiums completed. You may need to act fairly quickly to experience the International District described in this walk.

❶ Start this walk at South Jackson Street and Fourth Avenue South. In front of you is **Union Station**, a massive brick and stone building with an ornate metal awning out front. Inside is a huge hall with an elegant barrel-vaulted ceiling. Constructed in 1911, Union Station has seen no train traffic since 1971, but a project currently under way will make it the center of a nine-acre complex of office buildings and plazas.
❷ To the right is **King Street Station**, now an Amtrak depot but originally built for the Great Northern Railway in 1906. Its clock tower—a nearly exact reproduction of the campanile in Venice's Piazza San Marco—made the station the tallest building in town until 1914, when the 42-story Smith Tower eclipsed it.

King Street Station sits at the end of a railway tunnel that was

the world's longest, early wags joked, since it stretched all the way from Virginia to Washington (Streets). Though it doesn't quite span the continent, the tunnel is indeed quite long—more than 5,000 feet. It was built because the city refused to grant the Great Northern permission to run tracks along the downtown waterfront, forcing the railway to go underground. The tunnel emerges into daylight near South Washington Street and Fourth Avenue South.

King Street Station today is but a shadow of its original self. Its elaborate ceiling and wall reliefs were covered over with drywall in an insensitive renovation, and most of the building's interior is closed to the public. An effort is under way to restore some of the station's former grandeur, however, bolstered by plans to make the building a transit center for a new commuter rail system.

❸ With Union Station to your right, follow South Jackson Street for a couple blocks, turn right onto Sixth Avenue South,

international district

- **1** Union Station
- **2** King Street Station
- **3** Uwajimaya
- **4** Hing Hay Park
- **5** Chong Wa Benevolent Association building
- **6** Yick Fung Company
- **7** Milwaukee Hotel
- **8** Wing Luke Asian Museum
- **9** Danny Woo International District Community Garden
- **10** Nippon Kan Theatre
- **11** Higo Variety Store
- **12** Viet-Wah Supermarket

Higo Variety Store

Hing Hay Park

④ Turn left onto South King Street and follow it to Maynard Avenue South. On the corner of King and Maynard is **Hing Hay Park**, which features an ornate pavilion that was a gift from the city of Taipei in 1975. The park is a gathering place for community events, including the Seafair International District Summer Festival, held every year in July.

On the back wall of the **Bush Hotel**, which abuts Hing Hay Park, is a large mural of a Chinese dragon. In 1915, when the hotel was built to provide lodging for rail passengers, it offered the finest accommodations in the International District. Now it serves as low-income housing and offices for social service agencies.

and follow it to South King Street. On the corner of Sixth and King is the largest and most upscale business in the International District: the vast Japanese supermarket called **Uwajimaya**. Not just a grocery store, it's also a restaurant, a Japanese bookstore, a cooking school, and a place to buy gifts and sundries. Fujimatsu Moriguchi opened the original Uwajimaya in Tacoma in 1928, naming the market after his hometown in Japan. Uwajimaya is still a family business; six of Moriguchi's seven children work there.

Turn right onto Maynard Avenue South, then turn left onto South Weller Street and follow it to Seventh Avenue South. Weller Street was once the locus of Seattle's **Filipino community**. When the United States claimed the Philippines as a territory after the Spanish-American War, Filipinos became free to immigrate to the United States. A small community formed in the International District in the 1920s and 1930s. Although they had little in common culturally with the area's Chinese and Japanese residents, widespread prejudice against Asians elsewhere in the city made the district the most attractive place for them to live.

In 1935 the federal government curtailed Filipino immigration sharply, allowing only 50 immigrants per year. Because young men had made up most of the first wave of immigrants, and the quota made it difficult for women to join them, many Filipino men were forced to continue to live as bachelors. Not only that, most Filipinos were limited to working as menial laborers, since white employers were unwilling to hire even highly educated Asians for anything else, and labor unions wouldn't admit nonwhites. Seattle's Filipino community helped fight this discrimination, forming a Filipino cannery worker and farm laborers' union in the early 1930s.

Turn left onto Seventh Avenue South and stroll toward South King Street. In the early 1900s about 90 percent of Seattle's Chinese population was male, partly because laws restricting Chinese immigration made it difficult for immigrants to bring their wives and children into the country. Most immigrants saw the United

States as a place to accumulate riches to bring back to their native land; consequently, their ties with China were often stronger than their ties to the local area. The Chinese community established a multitude of organizations— benevolent associations, family associations, and tongs—to help immigrants adjust to life in America. Examples of all three are located nearby.

❺ First on the right is the striking 1929 **Chong Wa Benevolent Association building**, one of the only buildings in the International District with an Asian rather than a Western design. In the early part of the 20th century, Chinese immigrants were reluctant to trust government agencies, so they formed their own associations to provide aid to newcomers and oversee community functions. Chong Wa was one of these; it

China Gate Restaurant

japanese internment and the international district

ON THE EVE OF WORLD WAR II, Japanese immigrants were the largest and the most successful Asians in Seattle, with a prosperous business center and a strong community. In 1940 the Japanese made up only 2 percent of Seattle's population, but they operated 63 percent of its apartment and hotel buildings, 45 percent of its restaurants, and 17 percent of its groceries. The Japanese were also successful farmers, even though laws made it difficult for them to buy or even lease land.

On December 7, 1941, when Japan bombed Pearl Harbor, everything began to change. In Seattle, 1,300 Japanese crowded into a Buddhist temple to pledge allegiance to the U.S. government, but in the other Washington, the FBI investigated allegations of Japanese disloyalty. In the spring of 1942, President Franklin Roosevelt signed Executive Order 9066, authorizing the relocation of all West Coast Japanese Americans to inland internment camps. Seattle's Japanese were given a week to pack up their households and sell their businesses. Merchandise worth hundreds of millions of dollars was lost or sold well below cost. Detainees were loaded onto trains and taken to Camp Minidoka, on the high desert in Idaho.

Across the country, more than 110,000 Japanese—two-thirds of them American citizens—were taken to internment camps. There was only one way to leave: The young men could volunteer for the armed services. Many did, eager to prove their loyalty to the United States. The unit they formed, the 442 All Nisei Combat Unit, went on to become the most decorated unit of its size in American military history. ("Nisei" is a Japanese word that means second-generation Japanese American.) American general Charles Willoughby said the nisei soldiers "saved a million lives and shortened the war by two years."

Those who remained in the camps spent more than two years there before the Supreme Court declared internment unconstitutional in December 1944. When the Japanese returned to their home communities, they faced harassment and discrimination that made it difficult to find jobs and apartments. Seattle's Japanese also found that the city had demolished much of their former neighborhood and built a housing project in its place. The difficult circumstances forced uneasy solutions: 27 families ended up moving into a building on Weller Street that had formerly housed a Japanese language school, for instance. They hung blankets from the ceiling as room dividers and lived in conditions not much different from those in the internment camps.

While World War II dealt a crippling blow to Seattle's Japanese community, it opened up opportunities for other Asians. Chinese and Filipino people were able to find work with the

Boeing aircraft company and in the shipyards, jobs that had never before been available to Asians. In 1943 the federal government granted first-generation Chinese immigrants the right to become naturalized citizens.

Housing restrictions were eventually liberalized as well. In Seattle, as in other cities, real estate agents had observed a strict code of "honor" under which they pledged not to show properties in white neighborhoods to nonwhite buyers. The only central Seattle neighborhoods where a nonwhite could purchase a home were the Central District, Beacon Hill, and the International District. Until the late 1940s it was the policy of the federal government to finance or insure housing only in racially homogenous neighborhoods. When that policy finally changed, it became easier for Asians to move elsewhere in the city.

As postwar prosperity dulled the country's memory of the conflict, the Japanese also found their social position improving. In 1952 first-generation Japanese immigrants were given naturalization rights, and in 1965 immigration quotas were liberalized. Today Japanese residents are scattered throughout the metropolitan area, but Nihonmachi is only a memory.

was recognized by the Chinese government as the official supervisory organization for Seattle's Chinese population. Today it hosts cultural activities and offers U.S. citizenship and Chinese-language classes.

On the left is the **Gee How Oak Tin Family Association**. It's located in a plain, windowless storefront (519 Seventh Avenue South), but look for the ceremonial recessed balcony on the third floor. Early Chinatown had several family associations, clubs whose members shared common surnames. This one is the state's largest.

Next to the Chong Wa Benevolent Association is the **China Gate restaurant**, in a building constructed in 1924 as a Chinese opera house. Later, as the Chinese Gardens, it became a popular jazz venue and nightclub— one of the many that thrived along Jackson Street between the 1920s and the 1950s. Today's China Gate serves a popular Sunday buffet and has a bar that offers late-night dim sum, a popular Chinese meal consisting of an assortment of dumplings and other bite-size treats.

Just beyond the China Gate is a building housing the **Luck Ngi Musical Club**, which began in 1938 as a way to raise money for war victims in China and other community causes. The club provides a vital cultural link: Members meet regularly to sing selections from Chinese opera, accompanied by traditional instruments.

❻ Turn right onto South King Street and walk half a block.

On the right, just past the corner, is the oldest business in the International District, the **Yick Fung Company** (705 South King Street). A tiny shop selling a few vegetables and dry goods, it was once also a hotel and travel agency of sorts. The store was opened in 1913 by Mar Fook Hing, an agent for the popular Blue Funnel steamship line, which provided relatively affordable transportation between Seattle and China. The

Yick Fung Company

store's loft was once filled with cots where passengers could lodge while waiting for their ship's departure. Now run by Mar Fook Hing's sons, the shop no longer sells steamship tickets, but the gold lettering on its window still advertises the Blue Funnel line.

The Yick Fung Company is a remnant of an age when the neighborhood's Chinese businesses served many purposes. They were lodging places, labor contractors, post offices, and banks, and the merchants were respected community spokesmen and arbiters— somewhat of an irony, since the merchant class was looked down upon in China.

On the left, in a somewhat grimy brick building with a recessed red and green balcony on the fourth floor, is the headquarters for a tong called the **Bing Kung Association**. Tongs were originally secret societies formed as business organizations, but nowadays they're primarily gathering places for older Chinese Americans. The International District's tongs have a particularly infamous past: In the first half of the 20th century, they competed among themselves for control of gambling and prostitution in the district.

❼ Retrace your steps to Seventh Avenue South.

On the right, across Seventh, is the **Milwaukee Hotel**, the first establishment in this neighborhood to be built by an Asian. It was constructed around 1911. At the time, Seattle's Chinatown was located elsewhere—closer to Pioneer Square—

deconstructing chinatown: the anti-chinese riots of 1886

WHEN THE FIRST CHINESE CAME to Seattle in the 1860s, they were less than warmly received. They were poor and uneducated, and prejudice was rampant. Yet the white settlers tolerated the Chinese because their labor was needed to help carve a nation from the western wilderness. Chinese men were reputed to work harder for less money than any white man would, making them highly desirable to those who ran the railroads, mines, and salmon canneries.

When the economic depression of the mid-1880s hit, though, whites wanted whatever jobs were available. Laws were passed restricting Chinese immigration, and acts of violence against Chinese people increased across the country. In one famous incident, a large group of Tacomans dragged the town's Chinese residents from their homes in the rain, marched them to a railroad station, and loaded them onto a train bound for Portland. Numerous Seattle-area companies fired their Chinese workers, and some area communities evicted their Chinese residents.

In September 1885, anti-Chinese agitators met in Seattle and demanded that all Chinese leave the area by a certain date. Many did, but others stayed; some had investments, and others were too poor to travel elsewhere. On the morning of February 7, 1886, agitators moved into Chinatown. They barged into Chinese households, told the Chinese their homes were being condemned as health hazards, and hauled their belongings to the waterfront, where the steamer *Queen of the Pacific* was docked.

As it turned out, the ship had room for only 196 Chinese—leaving more than 100 stranded on the docks—and the next steamer wasn't due for several days. As the remaining Chinese were escorted back to their houses by the volunteer Home Guard, a riot broke out between the guard and the angry mob of onlookers, which didn't want the Chinese to return. Shots were fired; one man was killed and several injured.

The agitators were eventually tried for conspiring to deprive the Chinese of their rights, but none were convicted. The Chinese, meanwhile, became a minority in Chinatown: Many left on that next steamer, and by May 1886 only about a dozen were left. Although the Chinese population eventually rebounded, the Japanese, who were less restricted by immigration laws, soon grew to outnumber them. Filipinos and other Asians later immigrated to Chinatown as well, and in the 1950s the area became known as the International District.

In 1996 Washington state elected the first Chinese American governor in U.S. history, Gary Locke. He's also the first Asian American governor on the U.S. mainland. The son of immigrants, Locke grew up in Seattle's Yesler Terrace public housing project. Happily, the people of Seattle and the state of Washington have come a long way toward accepting the Chinese community.

Bing Kung Association Building

South Main Street. On the left, just before South Jackson Street, are the Theatre Off Jackson, home of the Northwest Asian American Theatre, and the **Wing Luke Asian Museum**, which features exhibits on the cultures and history of the International District. The museum was named in honor of the first Asian American elected official in the Pacific Northwest, a Seattle City Council member during the 1960s. The museum is open on weekdays except Mondays, and on weekend afternoons; there's a small admission fee, except on Thursdays, when admission is free.

Main Street ends at an entrance to Kobe Terrace Park, but you'll come to a more formal entrance to the park later in this walk.

❾ Turn left on South Main Street and follow it to Sixth Avenue South. After about half a block, on your right is an entrance to the **Danny Woo International District Community Garden**, which comprises more than 90 small, neatly numbered plots terraced into the hillside as well as amenities such as a pig-roasting pit. Low-income seniors use the garden plots to grow produce free of charge. This is one of the few places in the neighborhood with both a view—of industrial Harbor Island, the skyline, and the Sound—and green open space.

A map near the entrance shows the pathways through the garden and the adjoining Kobe Terrace Park; if you like, take a stroll along

but after the Milwaukee was built, this area gained many more Asian residents, and by the 1920s most of Seattle's Asians lived here.

Wherever Chinatown has moved, its residents have suffered discrimination, but Seattle's first Chinatown endured the most blatant threat: It was all but destroyed in 1886 when agitators drove most resident Chinese out of town. (See "Deconstructing Chinatown: The Anti-Chinese Riots of 1886" on page 63.)

❽ Turn right on Seventh Avenue South and follow it to

the paths, admiring the neatly numbered plots and the added artistic touches, such as the inspirational words carved into the cement steps of one stairway: "May each step you take and each seed you sow bring you closer to prosperity." When you're done, return to the entrance and continue downhill to Sixth.

The corner of Sixth and Main, relatively desolate today, was once the center of a thriving community known as **Nihonmachi (Japantown)**. Nihonmachi's core stretched along Main between Fourth and Seventh Avenues, although clusters of Japanese residents could also be found extending east to about 15th Avenue between Yesler Way and Dearborn Street.

Although the Chinese were the first Asians to immigrate to Seattle, by 1910 the Japanese outnumbered them by more than five to one. A strong Japanese consulate and moderately liberalized immigration laws helped the community grow, and the Japanese came to dominate the retail trade in the International District before World War II.

While most Chinese men lived as bachelors, Japanese men were more likely to bring their families to America, making Nihonmachi more of a traditional community than Chinatown. Every year during Bon Odori, a summertime festival honoring the souls of departed relatives, Main Street was closed off between Fifth and Maynard, a bandstand was erected, and people gathered to dance and celebrate their cultural heritage.

This all came to an end when Japan bombed Pearl Harbor in 1941; Japanese communities throughout the country were suddenly seen as threats. A few months after the United States entered World War II, Seattle's entire Japanese population was shipped off to an internment camp in the Idaho desert; meanwhile, the Yesler Terrace public housing project and area businesses took over large portions of Nihonmachi. Many Japanese returned to

Danny Woo Garden

seattle builds a railroad (or two)

THE RAILROADS OF THE 1860S and 1870s brought instant prosperity to the towns they serviced; on the other hand, once-thriving communities often died after being bypassed by a rail line. So when the small town of Seattle (just over 1,100 souls) received word that the Northern Pacific Railroad planned to build a line terminating somewhere on Puget Sound, the community held its breath.

In a bit of officially sanctioned extortion, Northern Pacific officials asked various Puget Sound towns what they would pay to be the rail line's terminus. Seattle pledged $250,000 in cash and bonds, 7,500 town lots, 3,000 acres of undeveloped land, and half the town's waterfront—an offer accounting for two-thirds of the value of the entire county.

Alas, Northern Pacific decided it would be more profitable to build on undeveloped land; that way, when a prosperous community developed around the terminus, the railroad would own it all. On July 14, 1873, Northern Pacific officials sent Seattle a fateful telegram informing the city that they had chosen Tacoma, which, at the time, was little more than a sawmill and a few cabins clustered around a good harbor.

Outraged, Seattleites held a mass meeting and decided to build their own railroad—to Walla Walla in eastern Washington, where the line could join the Northern Pacific's tracks. Within two months, half a million dollars in Seattle and Walla Walla stock had been sold, but that wasn't enough to build a railroad. Less than a year later, the railroad's investors threw a May Day picnic and invited the entire city.

Seattle's citizens listened to inspiring speeches about how Seattle had to save itself since the Northern Pacific would not, but it was pioneer Henry Yesler who finally goaded the crowd into action, saying, "Let's quit fooling around and get to work." The picnickers then marched out, rolled up their sleeves, and started grading land for their railroad.

A railroad built with volunteer labor was not likely to get very far, of course. Four years after it was conceived, the line consisted of just 12 miles of graded road and four miles of track. It was finally purchased by engineer and entrepreneur James Colman, who extended it to Renton and used it to haul coal. Although very profitable for Colman, the railroad was a great disappointment to Seattle.

Today's Burke-Gilman Trail, a popular cycling/jogging path, runs along the right-of-way of another homegrown upstart rail line: the Seattle, Lake Shore & Eastern, organized by a group of investors headed by Thomas Burke and Daniel Gilman. Their railroad was to run to Canada, where it would connect with a trans-Canada line; although they failed to find enough investors to realize that vision, the railroad was quite successful as a local line, bringing coal from Issaquah and passengers from as far as Snoqualmie.

James J. Hill's Great Northern Railway eventually purchased the Seattle, Lake Shore & Eastern, and Thomas Burke became Hill's attorney. When the Great Northern completed its rail line in 1893 with Seattle as its terminus, the city finally gained the transcontinental rail connection it had so long sought.

Markets on Jackson Street

Seattle after the war, but without a neighborhood to call their own, they scattered across the city.

⑩ Turn right onto Sixth Avenue South, then turn right onto South Washington Street and follow it uphill to the end. Perched on the hillside is the red-brick **Nippon Kan Theatre**. The Nippon Kan, which means "Japanese Hall," was long the principal gathering place for the Japanese community. From 1909 until World War II, gatherings and performances were held here several nights a week—everything from Kabuki theater and movies to judo competitions. Audience members used to bring potluck dishes to theater productions and spread out the feast at intermission. The Nippon Kan is still a venue for plays, concerts, and lectures; it also houses the *International Exam-*

iner, one of the city's several Asian newspapers headquartered in the International District.

At the end of Washington Street, abutting the Danny Woo Garden, is the formal entrance to **Kobe Terrace Park**, featuring a huge stone lantern donated by Kobe, Seattle's Japanese sister city. Beyond the lantern, winding along the hillside, are landscaped pathways set with benches. Enjoy the sweeping view of the International District offered by this vantage point.

⑪ Retrace your steps to Sixth Avenue South, turn left, follow it to South Jackson Street, and turn left again. Near the corner of Sixth and Jackson is a remnant of Nihonmachi, the **Higo Variety Store**, which has been in this

location since 1932. Sanzo Mura-
kami founded the store in the early
1900s, and his daughters currently
run it. Inside is the usual variety-
store merchandise as well as
kimonos, Japanese tableware, and
knickknacks with an Asian flair.

**Stroll along South Jackson
Street for six blocks, passing
under the Interstate 5 freeway,
to 12th Avenue South.** The construction of I-5 in the 1960s
destroyed some of the last remnants of Nihonmachi. Now the
pillars supporting the freeway are
gaily painted with a red and yellow
Asian-inspired design, and the
freeway has become a sort of
dividing line: To the west of it is
the older Chinatown, and to the
east is **Little Saigon**, home to the
more recently arrived Vietnamese
community.

⓬ Sprinkled along Jackson Street,
between the occasional warehouse
or battered old building, are an
assortment of grocery stores, shops,
and eateries. Browse through the
foods and gifts at the **Viet-Wah
Supermarket** (1035 South Jackson Street), whose merchandise is
less upscale but no less intriguing
than Uwajimaya's, encompassing
groceries and wares used by the
Thai, Laotian, Filipino, and Chinese communities as well as the
Vietnamese community. You can

try a bowl of *pho*, the popular
Vietnamese beef noodle soup, at
the supermarket's deli next door
or at many of the nearby eateries.

The intersection of 12th and
Jackson features Vietnamese businesses on all corners. Here Little
Saigon looks slightly suburban,
with businesses in strip malls rather
than along narrow streets as in
Chinatown.

Although few traces of its merry-
making past remain, from the
1920s to the 1950s this corner was
the hub of the **jazz district**. In
those days Jackson Street jumped
24 hours a day, the center of non-
stop music, gambling, and drinking. Sarah Vaughn and Louis
Armstrong were just a few of the
many musicians who performed
in the clubs lining Jackson Street
all the way to the waterfront. (See
"The New Orleans of the Northwest: Jackson Street, 1920–50"
on page 69.)

**Retrace your steps on South
Jackson Street and stroll for
eight blocks to Fourth Avenue
South, where you started this
walk.**

If you prefer, you can return to
Fourth and Jackson (where you
parked your car) or elsewhere
downtown via the bus routes
noted at the beginning of this
chapter.

the new orleans of the northwest: jackson street, 1920–50

TODAY'S JACKSON STREET hardly looks like the center of a hot jazz scene, but from the 1920s to the 1950s it was a flourishing nightclub district where people gathered to drink and gamble. Almost any kind of pleasure was available at any hour, always accompanied by the strains of jazz. Jackson Street was located at a fortuitous junction between the low-rent International District and the Central District, one of Seattle's major African American neighborhoods.

Twelfth and Jackson was the center of the scene, but dozens of clubs stretched along Jackson from 14th Avenue all the way to the waterfront—some of them elegant cabarets, others holes-in-the-wall barely big enough for a few tables and a jazz trio. People would wander down Jackson Street from club to club, serenaded by a different jazz act at every nightspot. The clubs played host to established jazz greats, and also helped develop the careers of Ray Charles, Quincy Jones, and Ernestine Anderson, who lived in Seattle during this time.

The scene flourished in part because of Prohibition—which brought about speakeasies that were also jazz clubs—and police corruption. The police enforced an unofficial "tolerance policy," under which an illegal club could operate as long as it paid a protection fee to the officers on its beat. Prohibition was finally repealed in 1933, but shortly thereafter the state passed the Steele Act, prohibiting the sale of hard liquor by the glass. The speakeasies and jazz clubs became quasi-illegal bars known as "bottle clubs," where patrons could buy liquor by the bottle.

In 1949 the state legislature passed Initiative 171, legalizing the sale of hard liquor by the glass but limiting its commerce to restaurants and hotels, which made the bottle clubs undeniably illegal. Around the same time, musical tastes were shifting away from jazz. The scene began to fade, and by 1960 the last of the Jackson Street jazz clubs was gone. Looking at the street now, it's hard to imagine they ever existed. There are plenty of places to hear jazz in Seattle today, but there aren't any on Jackson Street.

QUEEN OF THE QUEEN CITY:
queen anne hill

Grand houses and grander views

Distance: 2.75 miles   **Approximate time:** 2 hours

QUEEN ANNE HILL LOOKS LIKE almost any other long-established, affluent Seattle neighborhood. Its residential streets are clean, orderly, and tree-lined. It has impeccably maintained bungalows, venerable brick apartments, modern condominiums, and ostentatious mansions. But the "same old thing" is extraordinary on Queen Anne because of its backdrop: Queen Anne has fabulous views.

Seattle has never had a shortage of views, but southern Queen Anne Hill has some of the best. It also has more views per square foot than nearly any place in the city. Few spots here are more than a couple of blocks from a breathtaking vista.

Why is the neighborhood called Queen Anne? Alas, the explanation is rather mundane. The hill was named not for a pioneer woman with delusions of grandeur or an Indian princess with an English name, but for an architectural style. In the late 19th century, prominent citizens built many turreted Queen Anne–style houses on the hill's lower slopes. In fact, the area was known as Queen Anne Town until it was incorporated into the city of

The view from Kerry Park

Seattle in 1891. Regrettably, relatively few of those houses are still around today, which makes the hill's name even more enigmatic.

Note: All the houses on this walk are private; none are open to

parking Street parking is usually easy to find.

bus connections Catch Route 2 (West Queen Anne) on Third Avenue near Union Street downtown; get off on Sixth Avenue West near West Garfield Street, and follow Garfield to Seventh. (To get information on other bus routes serving this area, see the "Getting Around" section in the introduction to this book.)

the public. Please admire them from a respectful distance.

❶ **Start this walk at Seventh Avenue West and West Garfield Street. Descend the stairway, turn left on Eighth Avenue West, and stroll along it.** The **Willcox Wall**, a short, vine-covered wall set with antique streetlights, follows Eighth Avenue. Designed by W. R. B. Willcox and built in 1913, the wall sets off the sweeping view of Puget Sound that unfolds as you stroll along.

The view looked very different 150 years ago, when giant timber

Betty Bowen Viewpoint

covered the area. Below, near where the ship-loading docks (Piers 90 and 91) are today, was the land claim of one of Seattle's early settlers, Dr. Henry Smith. Leaving home one morning headed for Pioneer Square, Smith became lost in the thick forest that thrived on his land. When he at last came upon a clearing, he saw his own cabin below. He had been walking in circles for hours.

The tall timber that so confused Smith was useful to the Native Americans who lived here before him. When the slaving parties of Vancouver Island tribes came

queen anne hill

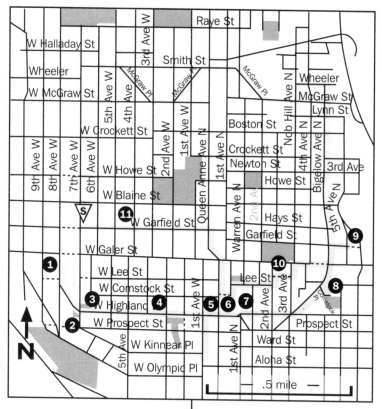

1. **Willcox Wall**
2. **Betty Bowen Viewpoint**
3. **Parsons Gardens**
4. **Parsons house**
5. **Gable House**
6. **Half-timbered mansion**
7. **One of Queen Anne Hill's oldest houses**
8. **Bhy Kracke Park**
9. **Former home of Anna Louise Strong**
10. **Old Queen Anne High School**
11. **Queen Anne Public Library**

Parsons Garden

left, the tiny Marshall Viewpoint, informally known as **Betty Bowen Viewpoint**, presents yet another stunning vista. On a clear day the Olympic Mountains are visible, towering above Puget Sound. Cast into concrete panels in the park's walkway are sketches by several well-known Northwest artists, including Mark Tobey and Kenneth Callahan, in tribute to Bowen, a neighborhood resident who was a friend and patron of many local artists. This innovative homage was designed by Victor Steinbrueck, the local architect best known for leading the effort to save Pike Place Market from redevelopment in the 1960s and early '70s.

❸ Directly across the street is the charming **Parsons Gardens**, which used to be part of a private estate. Stepping through the gate still feels like entering a private garden: Landscaped pathways wind past magnolia trees and flower beds to an arbor at the far end. You may want to linger on one of the benches amid the flowers, trees, and seclusion—unless a wedding is taking place, of course (it's a popular spot).

Immediately past Parsons Gardens is the home to which it was once connected: the **Parsons house** (618 West Highland Drive), a 1905 Dutch Colonial with a slate roof. Reginald Parsons commissioned this home, and his descendants donated Parsons Gardens to the city in 1956.

ashore to conduct raids, local Indians would hide in the forest on this side of Queen Anne Hill, at its base. Years later, another group of refugees sought sanctuary there: During the Great Depression a Hooverville, or homeless camp, was established in Interbay, an area of flats between Queen Anne Hill and Magnolia, inland from Piers 90 and 91.

❷ **Continue following Eighth Avenue West as it curves to the left and becomes West Highland Drive.** As the road curves to the

Stroll along West Highland Drive for about five blocks. Highland

74

Drive has some of the city's best views and consequently some of its nicest homes, most of them from the late 19th or early 20th century. This side of Queen Anne Hill gained a reputation as a wealthy community soon after it was settled.

❹ The 1914 **Prairie-style house** at 222 West Highland Drive was designed by architect Andrew Willatsen, who worked in Frank Lloyd Wright's studio in Oak Park, Illinois, before coming to Seattle. This home has been modified over the years, but Wright's influence is still apparent.

On the right, across from the Prairie-style house, is **Kerry Park**, one of the three best vantage points from which to view Seattle's skyline (the others are Gas Works Park and West Seattle's Duwamish Head). Of the three, Kerry Park is the most popular with sightseers, probably because it's the most easily accessible from downtown. It also has symbolic superiority: This is the only place

A classical revival mansion on Highland Drive

where the three most recognizable symbols of Seattle—the Space Needle, the skyline, and Mount Rainier—are all neatly lined up within the focal range of the average camera. Tourists have their pictures taken here to prove they've been to Seattle.

Kerry Park functions as a picture window in the row of grand houses that otherwise hides Highland Drive's spectacular view from passersby. You can enjoy this lovely panorama today thanks to the limitations of early 20th-century engineering: Albert Sperry Kerry and his wife donated the property to the city in the early 1900s because they considered the hill too steep to build on.

Thick forests once obstructed the view from this spot, but by 1890 most of that timber was gone. One remaining tree was still clearly visible, however: a massive cedar sacred to the Duwamish

the lookout tree

BEFORE WHITE SETTLERS rearranged much of Seattle's landscape, there was a tree on Queen Anne Hill's southern slope that was so massive it took 10 men with their arms outstretched to encircle its trunk. In the late 19th century, the tree was about 600 years old. It had been used as a navigation point by ships in Puget Sound for 200 years. Ship captains called it the Landmark Cedar; sailors called it the Lookout Tree.

The local Indian tribe, the Duwamish, considered the tree sacred. Intertribal councils were held, disputes resolved, issues deliberated, and friendships forged beneath this huge cedar. However, most of Seattle's early settlers were more interested in harvesting timber than preserving native landmarks. By 1890 the thick forests that had once covered Queen Anne Hill were only a memory, but the Lookout Tree remained, too massive to remove easily.

In 1891, Rollin Ankenny purchased the land on which the Lookout Tree stood. In order to build a house for his daughter on the lot, he announced, he would have to cut down the tree. The Duwamish tribe protested, as did some white settlers, but Ankenny had the Lookout Tree removed anyway. In a ceremony, the Duwamish placed a curse on the site of their demolished landmark. Perhaps their curse was effective: It took Ankenny 20 years to finish his house. Nonetheless, it still stands today. Not only that, this house that replaced the Landmark Cedar is now a registered historic landmark itself.

tribe, which stood three blocks from here. In 1891 the tree was felled to make way for an elegant home. If you don't mind a bit of a hike uphill on the way back, take a short detour to see the spot where the **Lookout Tree** once stood. Descend the stairway just past Kerry Park, then continue down Second Avenue West for a few blocks. The unusual house at 912 Second Avenue West stands where the tree once did. Retrace your steps to continue the walk.

❺ Two blocks farther is **Gable House** (1 West Highland Drive). Originally a mansion built for real estate developer H. W. Treat, it was once the most ostentatious dwelling on this street. Treat was one of Seattle's turn-of-the-century nouveaux riches. At the time, a fine mansion could be built for $30,000; Treat spent $101,000 on his. After he died, it was converted into a multi-unit dwelling because no buyer could afford such a large building as a private residence.

Cross Queen Anne Avenue North. In earlier days, Queen Anne Avenue was sometimes referred to as the Counterbalance, after the system of weights and pulleys that was used to haul streetcars along this avenue and up the steep hill. The streetcars ran until 1940; although no longer in use, the tunnels beneath the streets, where the counterweights ran on tracks, are still there.

The intersection of West Highland Drive and Queen Anne Avenue North marks what was the northwest corner of **Thomas**

Mercer's plat. Mercer was one of the hill's early settlers, but before he ever set foot in Seattle, he saw this hill in a dream. (See "Thomas Mercer's Dream: Progress Comes to Eden" on page 81.)

❻ The lovely **half-timbered mansion** at 21 Highland Drive, behind an elegant gate, currently serves as the residence of the Japanese consul. On the wall over the driveway is a gold 16-petaled chrysanthemum relief, the heraldic symbol of Japan's imperial family. Exceptionally light and open for a Victorian-era home, the mansion was originally built for William M. Chappel in 1906, who struck it rich during the Klondike gold rush and invested his fortune in Seattle.

❼ Continue on Highland Drive, staying to the left as the road divides. The 1893 Shingle-style home at 153 Highland Drive is one of Queen Anne Hill's old-est houses. The shingles have been painted white over the years and the home is starting to show its age, but the large back porch still has an enviable view of Seattle's skyline.

Continue on Highland Drive, this time staying to the right as the road divides; turn left onto Bigelow Avenue North and follow it to Comstock Place. Bigelow is one of the few residential streets in Seattle that have no sidewalks. In spite of that seemingly unfriendly characteristic, it looks inviting. The street is lined with oak and chestnut trees. The chestnuts are the edible kind, not the more ubiquitous horse chestnuts. You're free to gather them (fall is the season to come), but

The William M. Chappel house

strong-willed: the story of anna louise strong

ANNA LOUISE STRONG WAS BORN at a time when most women could not even vote, yet she was determined to change the world. She was only in her early 20s when she received her Ph.D. from the University of Chicago, having even taken time off to work in a canning factory in order to gain a better understanding of the problems faced by working people. The welfare of the proletariat would be her lifelong cause.

After moving to Seattle in 1916, Strong was petitioned by progressives to seek a school board seat, which she won easily. She also became involved in the pacifist movement, opposing the draft and military training in the schools. When the United States entered World War I in 1917, she wrote, "Nothing in my whole life, not even my mother's death, so shook the foundations of my soul. . . . 'Our America' was dead! . . . The people wanted peace; the profiteers wanted war—and got it."

After spending a summer in retreat from civilization, climbing on the slopes of Mount Rainier, Strong began writing for the *Seattle Daily Call*, a paper sympathetic to the Industrial Workers of the World (IWW), a prominent radical trade union. She also continued to sit on the school board, but her politics soon raised the ire of some conservative citizens, who pressed for a recall election. She was removed from office by a narrower margin than expected; not too long thereafter, a group of irate citizens broke into the *Daily Call* offices and smashed the presses, closing the paper and putting her out of a job.

Strong soon found work at another leftist paper, the *Seattle Union Record*. She was still writing for it in February 1919 when Seattle workers organized the nation's first general strike, a city-wide labor stoppage joined by unions from virtually every industry. Ignored by governmental officials, the strike

Former home of Anna Louise Strong

ended after several days, and the entire *Union Record* editorial staff was then brought to trial for attempting to "incite, provoke, and encourage resistance to the United States . . . by presenting and purporting to advance the interests of laborers as a class . . . [and] using the post office to distribute indecent and unmailable matters." The charges were based on editorials urging worker solidarity that had appeared in the paper prior to the strike.

Although the case was later dropped after the frenzy had subsided, Strong grew more dissatisfied with the American system. In 1921, encouraged by journalist and friend Lincoln Steffens, she packed her bags and headed to the Soviet Union. She later told a reporter, "There was no further west for me to go, so I went to Moscow."

After several decades in the Soviet Union, Strong fell into disfavor there. The Soviets accused her of spying for the United States and eventually expelled her in 1949; meanwhile, the United States accused her of spying for the U.S.S.R. and had its intelligence services keep her under surveillance. None of the accusations halted her determination. In the late 1950s she moved to China, where she was an honored figure whose friends included Chairman Mao and Premier Chou En-lai. When she died in China in 1970, at the age of 84, her passing was mourned in memorial services held across the world.

they do tend to be picked over. In fact, Seattle's Asian community considers them such a delicacy that the city has felt the need to post a sign here, in Vietnamese, Chinese, and other Asian languages, urging pickers to avoid trespassing on the property of nearby homeowners.

This curving street is part of the **boulevard system** designed by the Olmsted Brothers, the nationally known landscape architecture firm that planned much of Seattle's park system. The Olmsted plan for the city, presented in 1903, recommended a 150-foot-wide, tree-lined boulevard to circle Queen Anne Hill, and in 1906 the city built Bigelow Avenue and Highland Drive.

❽ Turn right onto Comstock Place and follow it until it ends.
Here is a little-known park with an arresting, panoramic view of the city. Donated to the city in 1966 by Werner Kracke, this green spot is called **Bhy Kracke Park** because "by cracky" was Kracke's favorite expression. It eventually became his nickname, which he chose to spell "Bhy Kracke."

The view here nearly rivals that from Kerry Park, and Bhy Kracke Park has some distinct advantages. It offers a view of Lake Union as well as the Space Needle and the skyline, and it's often virtually empty, whereas Kerry Park is usually occupied and often crowded. In addition to its viewpoint, this little park has a winding pathway leading down past landscaped terraces to a playground on the lower level.

One of Queen Anne's oldest houses

and Louise Bryant, a writer and the wife of Communist Labor Party cofounder John Reed. The house has been modified since those days, but its view of Lake Union and the Eastlake neighborhood is still inspiring. (See "Strong-Willed: The Story of Anna Louise Strong on page 78.")

Retrace your steps to Bigelow Avenue North. If you like, from here you can take an extended walk that follows Queen Anne's winding, tree-lined boulevards and takes in some views from the north side of the hill. This extended walk is not described here in the text, but is clearly marked on the map. It adds about 1 mile to the basic walk for a total of 3.8 miles, taking about 3 hours. To begin the extended walk, turn right on Bigelow and follow the route outlined on the map. To continue on the shorter walk, read on.

⑨ Retrace your steps to Bigelow Avenue North, turn right, and follow it for several blocks to Garfield Street. Turn right and follow Garfield for a little more than a block, as it becomes a public walkway. On the left, a short distance down the walkway, is the **former home of Anna Louise Strong** (508 Garfield Street), a tireless activist, journalist, and supporter of workers' rights who lived here from 1916 to 1921. Prominent visitors to her home included Lincoln Steffens, a well-known muckraking journalist; Upton Sinclair, author of *The Jungle*, an exposé of the working conditions in Chicago's meatpacking industry;

⑩ Turn left onto Bigelow Avenue North and follow it to Galer Street, which is a stairway here. Ascend the stairs to the right and continue on Galer to Third Avenue North. On the corner of Third and Galer is the former **Queen Anne High School**, a massive Beaux Arts building that sits on the very top of the hill and is visible from many parts of Seattle. The upper stories have a commanding view of the city, marred only by the nearby radio towers. Queen Anne High School operated from 1909 through 1981; it has since been remodeled into condominiums.

thomas mercer's dream: progress comes to eden

EARLY SEATTLE SETTLER THOMAS Mercer saw his plot of land on Queen Anne Hill for the first time in a dream. He saw himself standing on a forested hill by a clear lake, then walking over the hill to find the sea lapping against its opposite side, and thought how lucky he was to have land with water on both sides.

Mercer was a responsible family man living in Illinois in the 1840s when he had this dream. He came under the spell of "Oregon fever," and in 1852 he and his family joined a wagon train and became part of the popular exodus westward. Unlike most of his fellow travelers, however, Mercer's ultimate destination was not the Oregon Territory's Willamette Valley. Instead, he intended to go the extra distance to Puget Sound, in search of the piece of land he had seen in his dream.

The long trek from Illinois cost Mercer's wife her life—she died of pneumonia en route. But Mercer persevered and made his way to Seattle to stake his claim for a parcel of land on the southern slope of today's Queen Anne Hill, a plot bordered by fresh water to the east and saltwater to the west. He called the spot Eden.

Soon Mercer and his daughters were living in a cabin he had built on the hill. In 1854, he invited Seattle's dozen or so white families to a Fourth of July picnic on the shore of the lake adjoining his property. It was at this gathering that he proposed renaming that lake, known as *tenas chuck* ("little water" in a local Indian dialect), as well as its larger neighbor to the east, *hyas chuck* ("big water"). The rest of the party agreed, and from that time on, the two bodies of water were called Lake Union and Lake Washington. "Lake Union" referred to Mercer's belief that a canal through that lake would one day unite Lake Washington and Puget Sound—a prophecy that would be fulfilled with the creation of the Lake Washington Ship Canal in 1917.

Besides being a prophet and a dreamer, Mercer also was known as a just man. Respect for him among local Indians was such that they spared his house during an attack on Seattle in 1856, when the homes of many others were destroyed. The white community also recognized Mercer's just nature, and he served them as probate judge and county commissioner.

But Mercer's Eden was to undergo drastic changes even during his lifetime. Logging of the densely wooded east side of Queen Anne Hill began soon after it was settled, and when fellow pioneer David Denny established a sawmill on Lake Union in 1880, most of the area's remaining timber quickly disappeared. Mercer subdivided his plat in the 1870s and sold his last lot in the 1880s. By his death in 1898, scarcely a tree was left standing. Today the vista from Queen Anne Hill is still astounding, although the hill itself bears little resemblance to the wilderness in Thomas Mercer's dream.

Turn left onto Third Avenue North, then right into the fountain courtyard of the Queen Anne High School condominiums. Stroll straight through. Turn left onto Second Avenue North. Turn right onto Lee Street and follow it until it ends at First Avenue North. You pass a fire station on the right, on the corner of Lee Street and Warren Avenue. Adjacent to the fire station are two **water towers**, the first of which solved a serious sanitation problem for Queen Anne Hill in the early 1900s. Prior to the tower's installation, 500 families on the hill got their drinking water from Lake Union, which was also a receptacle for city sewage.

Turn left onto First Avenue North and follow it as it becomes a

Water tower on Warren Avenue

sidewalk, then curves to the right and becomes a stairway. Descend the stairs to Queen Anne Avenue North. Queen Anne Hill boasts almost 100 different stairways. This one is rather grand, bordered on both sides by lush trees and banks of ivy as the wide steps proceed down the hill.

Turn right onto Queen Anne Avenue North and stroll along it for several blocks to West Garfield Street. The hill's business district, which runs along Queen Anne Avenue, abounds with restaurants, coffeehouses, bars, markets, and specialty-food stores, so if the walk has made you hungry, you have many options.

⓫ Turn left onto West Garfield Street and follow it for several blocks to Fourth Avenue North. This pleasant but unassuming residential street is lined with tidy bungalows and Colonial Revival homes. The beautiful red-brick **Queen Anne Public Library** (1912–13), on the corner of Fourth and Garfield, is worth a stop. A small Carnegie library, it has an unexpected feature inside: a large stained-glass window that casts an evocative blue light across the room.

Continue on West Garfield Street to Seventh Avenue West, where you started this walk.

HIGH SOCIETY AND COUNTERCULTURE:

CAPITOL HILL HAS TWO DISTINCT temperaments. One is young and rebellious: She campaigns for social justice, reads poetry in coffeehouses, and lives for the moment. She revels in youth culture, tattoo parlors, and body piercing, and may even show you gay men dressed as nuns, white-robed religious fanatics chanting and distributing pamphlets, or dogs begging for change. The hill's other personality is quite different: She's matronly and refined, with impeccable breeding, never a hair out of place. She cherishes the hill's monuments to the city's past, its gracious tree-lined streets, and its wonderful views of water and skyline, which can be glimpsed between its opulent houses.

Fortunately, the hill's two personalities cohabitate peacefully. You can get to know each in turn via the two walks in this chapter. The first route reveals the society-matron side of Capitol Hill, while the second explores the young rebel. If you like, you can join the two for a study in contrasts.

ROUTE 1:

Distance: 3.5 miles
Approximate time: 2.5 hours

Start this walk on the corner of East Galer Street and 15th Avenue East. This is the northeast entrance to **Volunteer Park**, a garden paradise that represents an ideal most city parks can only aspire to: a green respite from a crowded landscape, a place where the community gathers and urban caution is moderated.

This splendid park had a humble beginning. The city bought the land in 1876, but then seemed unsure what to do with it. Officials had it logged, sold the timber, and then let the land sit treeless and vacant for years. In 1884 it became a cemetery, but after only three years the city decided to make it a park, spurred by *Seattle Post-Intelligencer* owner Leigh Hunt, who editorialized that this lovely spot should be "reserved for the enjoyment of the living." The bodies were moved to the adjacent Lake View Cemetery, and the park was named City Park.

starting/ finish point

Volunteer Park, at the corner of East Galer Street and 15th Avenue East

parking Free parking for an unlimited time is usually available in Volunteer Park; if not, it can usually be found on the residential streets to the east. Parking is limited to two hours on streets within several blocks of a business district.

bus connections Catch Route 10 (Capitol Hill) on Pike Street near Third Avenue downtown; get off near East Galer Street and 15th Avenue East. (For more information about bus routes serving this area, see the "Getting Around" section in the introduction to this book.)

In 1893, City Park was almost sold after officials argued that it was too hard to irrigate and too far from town. Fortunately, the city kept the park, and a decade later it was at the center of a prosperous suburb. In 1901 it was renamed to honor the volunteers in the Spanish-American War.

Inside the conservatory

❶ **Enter Volunteer Park and stroll down its drive.** You pass a playground and, a bit later, some quaint cottagelike restrooms; just beyond, on the right, is the glass-enclosed **Volunteer Park Conservatory**, open free to the public every day. This charming Victorian greenhouse, constructed of plates of glass separated by iron and wood mullions, was added to the park in 1912. The conservatory was fashioned after London's Crystal Palace, manufactured in New York, and shipped to Seattle, all for a cost of $500.

Inside, the conservatory is a gardener's fantasyland of bromeliads, breadfruit trees, gardenias, cacti, and exotic plants of all sorts. The prizewinning orchid collection includes more than 800 plants, although not all are on view at any one time; the best time to see them in bloom is fall through early spring. On the way out, notice the etched handblown glass roof of the entryway; it was produced in Germany and installed in the early 1980s.

A **statue of William Henry Seward** stands in front of the conservatory. As U.S. secretary of state, he arranged the purchase of Alaska from Russia in 1867. Some

capitol hill route 1: high society

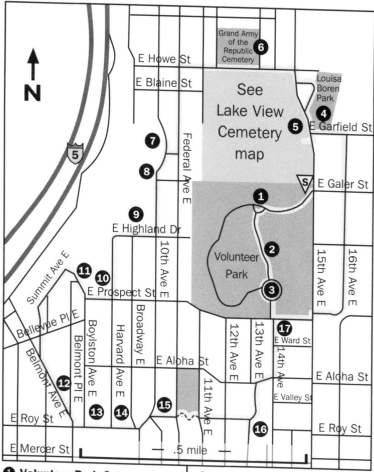

1. Volunteer Park Conservatory
2. Seattle Asian Art Museum
3. Volunteer Park water tower
4. Louisa Boren Park
5. Lake View Cemetery
6. Grand Army of the Republic Cemetery
7. Leary House
8. North campus of Cornish College of the Arts
9. Sam Hill House
10. Estate of Horace C. Henry
11. Tudor Revival homes
12. Anhalt apartment buildings
13. South campus of Cornish College of the Arts
14. Loveless Building
15. More Anhalt apartment buildings
16. Maryland Apartments
17. G.H. Parker house

Volunteer Park water tower

won nationwide acclaim and a design award from the Architectural League of New York. The museum's construction was paid for by Richard Fuller, a local man with inherited wealth who, with his mother, also donated most of the original collection.

The Seattle Art Museum remained in this building until the early 1990s, when it moved its main collection to a roomier facility downtown and established a sister institution here to focus exclusively on Asian art, of which the Fullers were particularly fond. The Seattle Asian Art Museum houses the Fullers' collection of rare Chinese snuff bottles, as well as Asian ceramic and textile arts, religious icons, and paintings. The museum is open daily except Mondays; there's an admission fee except on the first Thursday and Saturday of each month, when admission is free.

Opposite the museum is a large sculpture that's also a favorite photo opportunity (and viewing point for Fourth of July fireworks). Isamu Noguchi's **Black Sun** is a nine-foot-high circle of black granite, with a hole in the center, that perfectly frames the Space Needle.

❸ Beyond the art museum, at a circle in the park's drive, is the 95-foot **Volunteer Park water tower**, nestled amid lush ferns and tall evergreens. The observation deck at the top offers a 360-degree view—including Puget Sound, Lake Union, and Lake Washington—that's well worth climbing the 106 steps to reach. Completed

called the purchase Seward's Folly, but Seattle's citizens were delighted. They made a considerable profit from trade with Alaska, and named Seward Park in his honor as well.

❷ **Exiting the conservatory, follow the park's tree-lined drive straight ahead.** After a few hundred feet, on the left is the **Seattle Asian Art Museum**, located in a building constructed in 1933 for the original Seattle Art Museum. The first American museum built in the Moderne style, the building

Louisa Boren Park

in 1907, the standpipe was made a viewing tower shortly after it was built, at the recommendation of the Olmsted Brothers, the landscape architects who designed much of Seattle's park system. In homage, the observation deck now houses a display commemorating their work. The tower is open daily till dusk and is free.

Exiting the water tower, continue on the park's drive for a short distance. Turn left onto East Prospect Street, following it as it jogs to the left and later curves left to become 16th Avenue East. The predominant architectural style in this neighborhood is the "classic box," or Colonial Revival. A symmetrical boxlike frame, hipped roof, and slightly projecting square bay windows characterize this style, and the houses at 1115 and 1119 16th Avenue East, on the left, exemplify it. As you continue down 16th, the houses on the left, which presumably enjoy a fine view from their ridge, become considerably more grand than their counterparts on the right.

This neighborhood was developed in the early 20th century by James A. Moore, who came to Seattle from Colorado because he believed this city would provide the best return on his investment. He purchased all the land between 16th and 23rd Avenues, and Galer and Roy Streets, and proceeded to build what he called the **Capitol Hill Addition**.

The Addition was indeed a fashionable neighborhood—but not the most fashionable. Moore advertised that no lot was more than a two-minute walk from one of the six streetcar lines that serviced Capitol Hill. That was a selling point for the upper middle class, but the truly wealthy preferred to live farther from the common man (and thus farther from the streetcars).

④ Follow 16th Avenue East for several blocks, until it ends; turn left onto East Garfield Street and follow it to 15th Avenue East. To the right is **Louisa Boren Park**, named for the longest-surviving member of the party that founded the city of Seattle in 1851. Featuring a breathtaking view of Union Bay and Lake Washington, Boren Park owes its design to Victor Steinbrueck, the local architect who spearheaded the campaign to save

Lake View Cemetery

Pike Place Market from redevelopment.

⑤ Cross 15th Avenue East and follow it to the left a short distance. This is the entrance to **Lake View Cemetery**, a burial ground featuring ornate family headstones, lush vegetation, and views of two lakes from the very top of Capitol Hill. This is Seattle's oldest existing cemetery, but it wasn't the first; some of those interred here were exhumed three times before finally being allowed to rest in peace.

Seattle's first cemetery was downtown at Fifth and Jackson, where the International District is now. That graveyard became wet at high tide, so it was moved to what is now Denny Park. When the city decided to put a park there, the bodies were moved to the area that is today Volunteer Park. Just three years later that site was also turned into a park; the graves were moved for a fourth, and hopefully final, time to Lake View Cemetery.

In this cemetery rest many Seattle pioneers as well as a couple of celebrities. The map on page 89 shows the location of some graves you may be interested in visiting. **Ⓐ** Two unassuming headstones mark the most frequently visited plot in Lake View Cemetery, the graves of **Bruce and Brandon Lee**. The headstone of Bruce Lee, a martial artist and movie star idolized by many of his fans, reads: "Your inspiration continues to guide us toward our liberation." Both Bruce Lee and his son,

Brandon, also an actor, died at a young age. (See "Bruce Lee" on page 91.)

B The **Denny family plot** is graced by elaborate marble headstones. Arthur Denny was arguably the most influential of Seattle's founders. He rests here with his wife, father, stepmother, children, and various other family members. (See "The Alki Landing: Where It All Began" in Chapter 12.)

C A massive stone monument marks the final resting place of **Thomas, Nancy, and Hester Mercer**. Thomas Mercer settled the southeast side of Queen Anne Hill. Mercer Island and Mercer Street were named in his honor. (See "Thomas Mercer's Dream: Progress Comes to Eden" in Chapter 6.)

D The grave of **Princess Angeline** features a rough-hewn stone next to the drive. Angeline was the daughter of the Duwamish chief for whom the city of Seattle was named. (See "Her Majesty Kickisomlo-Cud" in Chapter 1.)

E Resting under a giant sequoia tree are the graves of **David "Doc" and Catherine Maynard.** The Maynards' headstones lie flush with the ground and are so eroded they are difficult to read. Doc Maynard was a generous man who did much to promote the advancement of early Seattle. (See "The Good Doctor" in Chapter 2.)

6 **Exiting Lake View Cemetery, turn left onto 15th Avenue East. Turn left onto East Howe Street and follow it a short distance past 14th Avenue East.** A hedge

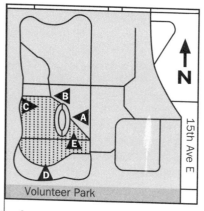

Volunteer Park

forms a circle in the center of the park, and behind that hedge is a somewhat surprising sight in this city so far from the South: a small burial ground for Civil War veterans called the **Grand Army of the Republic Cemetery**. When the Civil War began in 1861, Seattle had been in existence for just 10 years, had a population of only about 250 people, and was not terribly concerned with a skirmish on the other side of the continent. Most of the veterans buried here are war survivors who later migrated to Seattle.

Continue on East Howe Street for several blocks to Federal Avenue East; turn left onto Federal and follow it for several blocks to East Garfield Street. Most of the houses on Federal were built between 1900 and 1920. At first they're relatively modest, but they get larger and more elaborate as you continue down the street. One of the most charming is the home on the right just before Garfield, built in 1909. Seen from Federal, the house looks like a small English cottage (although it's actually more of a mansion, as you see when you round the corner). A small rose garden is out front, and a hydrangea climbs the south side of its entryway.

❼ Turn right onto East Garfield Street, then cross 10th Avenue East and follow it to the right for a short distance. The grand stone mansion enjoying a dramatic view of the city and water below is the **Leary House** (1551 10th Avenue East), named for Eliza Ferry Leary, the daughter of Washington's first governor and one of the state's richest women in her time. She and her husband John, who had interests in lumber, real estate, politics, and manufacturing, wanted their home to be one of

The Sam Hill house

the grandest in Seattle. They copied the design from a house they visited while honeymooning in Ireland, and engaged English architect Alfred Bodley to oversee its construction. John Leary died in 1905, but the house wasn't completed until several years later. The total cost was $250,000, a spectacular sum at the time; most of the classic boxes on 16th Avenue East were constructed for about $5,000.

The completed mansion stood on a 15-acre site that included a deer park and riding stables. The house had a walnut-and-mahogany interior that had taken a team of Belgian woodcarvers a year to complete. Other features included a room finished entirely in gold leaf, windows made by Louis Tiffany, and an impressive stone entrance. Some said the house was more like a church than

bruce lee

ALTHOUGH BRUCE LEE DIED IN 1973, his grave in Lake View Cemetery—and that of his son, Brandon, located alongside it—still receives regular visits from loyal admirers who leave flowers, trinkets, and mementos. The lives of both Bruce and Brandon Lee ended prematurely, a fact that has only furthered the mystique surrounding them.

Although Seattle is their final resting place, neither spent much time here. Hong Kong native Bruce Lee lived in the city between 1959 and 1964, when he studied at the University of Washington, opened his first kung fu school in an International District basement, and married Seattleite Linda Emery. He attained fame only after leaving the city, though, and starring in several martial arts films in Hong Kong that became wildly popular. His striking looks and rebellious persona gave him wide crossover appeal, catching Hollywood's attention and leading to his starring role in the hit film *Enter the Dragon*. Yet although Lee's star had risen, his wife Linda reported, the two looked back on the time they had spent in Seattle as their happiest.

Lee always intended to return to Seattle someday. He did return, but not the way he had imagined. On July 20, 1973, in Hong Kong, while working out ideas for a new movie, he complained of a headache; a colleague gave him a prescription painkiller, and he suffered a severe allergic reaction. He died a short time later, and after a memorial service in Hong Kong that drew 25,000 devotees to the street outside the funeral parlor, his body was flown to Seattle for burial at Lake View Cemetery.

Brandon, only eight years old at the time, idolized his father. He eventually followed in his dad's footsteps to Hollywood—and, sadly, to an early death. In March 1993, in a freak accident during the filming of the movie *The Crow*, he was fatally shot with the fragment of a bullet that had been left in a gun otherwise containing blanks.

The premature deaths of Bruce Lee and then his son naturally provoked speculation. Some said Chinese organized crime had a hand in the deaths, while others believed they were caused by the "curse of the dragon"—a hex placed on Bruce Lee and his progeny by the traditional Chinese martial arts community because he refused to follow their prohibition against teaching non-Chinese students. Those explanations make a compelling story, but the deaths of Bruce and Brandon Lee were tragedies, whatever the cause.

Cornish College

⑧ **Retrace your steps on 10th Avenue East and follow it toward East Highland Drive.** On the right you pass the **north campus of Cornish College of the Arts**, established in 1914 by Nellie Cornish to bring culture to then-backward Seattle. To Miss Aunt Nellie, as her students called her, the importance of arts education lay not merely in technical virtuosity but in spiritual growth and personality development. She had no money, no formal education, and few connections, but she was able to charm her way into the hearts of Seattle's citizens to found what became one of the city's leading cultural institutions.

At first her school simply taught music to primary-school children, but she soon expanded and began to exercise her gift for recognizing talent. She hired internationally renowned painter Mark Tobey and dancer Martha Graham to teach at the school long before they were well known. The school's students have included choreographers Merce Cunningham and Robert Joffrey, anchorman Chet Huntley, and actor Brendan Fraser. You pass its south campus later on this walk.

Just past Cornish is **St. Mark's Cathedral**, a neo-Byzantine box of red brick and poured concrete. Its unusual design came about by accident: The Depression halted the Episcopal cathedral's construction before a decorative facade could be added; in fact, at the dedication the congregation still owed $250,000 on the building. That debt was paid long ago, but the

a home. Today it's actually owned by a church: the Episcopal Diocese of Olympia, which has offices here. Call ahead to schedule a free tour, (206) 325-4200.

The generously sized home to the left of the Leary House, now mostly hidden behind a tall hedge, was constructed around the same time for Eliza Leary's brother, Pierre Ferry, the business partner of John Leary. The Ferrys and Learys were on such good terms that they even have a common family monument in Lake View Cemetery.

plain facade remains.

The interior was extensively remodeled in the 1960s to accommodate the church's new Flentrop organ, but the building's harmonious simplicity was never altered. Inside, the walls are still rough concrete and the ornate ceiling beams are unfinished. A huge rose window over the altar and large arched windows on either side of the chapel bathe the pews in light.

Some consider the perpetually unfinished church unattractive, but it has an earthy grace that more elaborate cathedrals lack. St. Mark's doesn't try to imitate heaven with confectionery terracotta ornament and ethereal flourishes; its unadorned walls and towering windows evoke a more grounded spirituality.

You may be lucky enough to hear a musician practicing on the Flentrop organ when you visit; the church also hosts classical music concerts from time to time, and holds a compline service on Sunday nights that's occasionally followed by a short organ recital. The cathedral is open during the day on weekdays and Sundays.

St. Mark's endeavors to reach out to all in the community, including Capitol Hill's substantial gay population. Its ministers wrote a statement proclaiming church affirmation of gay marriage and gays in the ministry, and presented it to the Episcopal Diocese of Western Washington for several years in a row. It finally passed in 1998.

❾ Turn right onto East Highland Drive. On the right as you round

the corner is the massive cement-clad 1909 mansion known as the **Sam Hill house** (814 East Highland Drive), boasting one of the most enviable views in Seattle, looking out over Lake Union and Queen Anne Hill. Sam Hill, the house's original owner, was the son-in-law of railroad baron James J. Hill. During World War I he was active on behalf of Romania, and when the war ended, Queen Marie of Romania and her children visited him here. Other notables who passed through these doors included Grand Duchess Marie of Russia and Marshal Joffre of France.

View from the Sam Hill house

House on East Prospect Street

Hill built a similarly styled home a little south of Goldendale, Washington: a 40-room concrete mansion with 42-inch walls, standing amid 6,700 acres of land that ran along the Columbia River for five miles. He named the home after his wife, Mary, but it was known among locals as Sam Hill's Folly. Hill never moved into his castle; World War I halted its construction, and it stood half-finished for more than a decade. Maryhill is now open to the public as a museum.

Follow East Highland Drive as it curves and becomes Harvard Avenue East; continue to East Prospect Street. An enclave for wealthy Seattle citizens in the early 20th century, this neighborhood is now known as the **Harvard-Belmont Historic District**. On the right, after the street curves, are two impressive mansions (1147 and 1137 Harvard Avenue East), both from this era: The former was designed to resemble an English country estate, while the latter is a fine Georgian Revival home. ❿ On the right as you near Prospect is an expansive lawn surrounded by a hedge. This spot was once the **estate of Horace C. Henry**. He built a grand house on this land in 1894, but it hasn't survived; a smaller home was built on the property in 1955. The original home was also Seattle's first art museum: Henry was a railroad baron and an art collector who would open the "little gallery" in his home to members of the Seattle Fine Arts Society. He eventually donated his collection to the University of Washington and financed the construction of the Henry Art Gallery.

a butcher, a banker, an apartment house–maker

FREDERICK WILLIAM ANHALT'S eclectic Tudor- and Norman-influenced buildings are some of the most sought-after dwellings in Seattle today, commanding premium prices. How did a man with no formal architectural training manage to produce some of the best-designed apartment buildings in the city?

Anhalt grew up on a farm in North Dakota, worked in a butcher shop during his teens, and went into business selling store fixtures after arriving in Seattle in the 1920s. Finding that it could sell more fixtures if it leased empty commercial buildings and sublet them to retailers, his company gradually started constructing its own buildings and then moved from commercial buildings to luxury apartments. About this time, Anhalt started to design the buildings. He'd leaf through pattern books, choosing features that pleased him, and incorporate them into his projects; architectural draftsmen drew up the actual plans.

Anhalt's plans improved upon standard apartment designs of the time in several ways. Most Anhalt apartments have semiprivate entrances, eliminating the need for long, dark public hallways. Most have both front and rear doors, and all face landscaped courtyards. Anhalt used unusual building techniques such as floating floors and double walls to soundproof his buildings. Their brick facades are constructed of overfired "clinker" bricks, which lend the homes a rustic appearance. Surprisingly, while Anhalt's buildings were all well designed and finely crafted, they were also built very quickly.

When the Depression hit in 1929, Anhalt was holding buildings he had planned to sell to investors. Suddenly investors were hard to find, and his creditors were demanding payment. Anhalt had a 49 percent interest in a mortgage company at the time, but even this was not enough to keep most of his buildings from being repossessed. In 1942 he left the building trades for good and devoted his time to a thriving nursery business. More than five decades later, his contributions to architecture were finally recognized by the profession when he was named an honorary member of the American Institute of Architects in 1993. He was 97 years old.

Turn right onto East Prospect Street and follow it for several blocks as it winds downhill and eventually curves to the left, becoming Summit Avenue East. The brick wall on the right marks the limits of what was once the Henry estate; the entrance gate opposite Boylston Avenue East marks the estate's driveway.

⓫ Prospect Street is lined with trees and grand houses. As you continue downhill, passing Belmont Place East to the left, pause to admire the pair of particularly fine **Tudor Revival homes** surveying the city skyline from the corner of Belmont Place and Prospect. Twin brothers Louis and Michael Beezer designed these strikingly similar houses for O. D. Fisher and O. W. Fisher around

Harvard Exit theater

1909. Shortly after the street becomes Summit, you pass the Fisher estates' charming carriage house—also Tudor Revival, naturally—on the left.

Continue on Summit Avenue East, staying to the left as it divides and then, about a block later, jogs slightly to the right. Summit divides to circle what must be one of the city's largest—and most pleasant—traffic islands, featuring large trees and a pathway.

⓬ **Turn left onto Belmont Avenue East and follow it uphill.** On the left, at first hidden by shrubbery, are two typically distinctive **Anhalt apartment buildings** (750 and 730 Belmont Avenue East), constructed between 1928 and 1930. Although Frederick Anhalt had no formal training

in architecture, he designed some of the most highly regarded apartments in Seattle. Many of his buildings boast features such as steeply pitched roofs, multiple-pane windows, private entrances, fireplaces, and varied exteriors featuring charmingly rough "clinker" bricks. He lived at 730 Belmont Avenue East, one of his favorite buildings, until it was repossessed during the Depression.

Continue on Belmont Avenue East, crossing Belmont Place East. As you cross Belmont Place East, glance to the left to see a third, massive Anhalt apartment building (710 Belmont Place East).

⓭ Turn left onto East Roy Street and follow it uphill for several blocks to Broadway. You pass Kerry Hall on the left, the principal building on the **south campus of Cornish College of the Arts**. The 1921 Mission-style structure is adorned with cast terra-cotta ornaments of young girls dancing. Although Nellie Cornish's school struggled repeatedly with debt—especially during the Depression—it has endured. Today, as Cornish College of the Arts, it enrolls about 650 students a year in music, art, dance, and drama courses and has plans to expand its campus. The college hosts a wide range of well-attended concerts, plays, and art shows throughout the year, and its teachers and students continue to contribute to the cultural life of Seattle. ⓮ Next on the left is a replica of Mount Vernon, designed for the local chapter of the Daughters of the American Revolution in 1925 and now often rented for parties. Beyond it is the enchanting **Loveless Building**, a characteristically English structure with retail space on the ground floor, apartments on the second, and a courtyard in the center. Named for its architect, Arthur Loveless, the building was constructed during the Depression, so cinder-concrete block was used in place of stone to cut costs. Remarkably, this structure built on the cheap has more elegance than many modern buildings constructed in flush economic conditions.

Consider a stop at **Bacchus**, the Greek restaurant on the near corner of the Loveless Building, to sample the souvlaki and view the remarkable interior murals. Depicting a Russian folktale (the original tenant of this space was a Russian restaurant), the murals were created by Russian immigrant Vladimir Shkurkin.

Across the street from Bacchus is a 1926 red-brick building that originally housed the Woman's Century Club, founded in 1891 to prepare women to participate fully in the 20th century (which its members optimistically termed the "woman's century"). In the early 1970s the clubhouse and its Little Theater were converted into the **Harvard Exit** movie theater. Its fare tends toward artier films, which seems appropriate for the setting; a formal sitting room with a piano even graces the theater's first floor.

The G.H. Parker house

Pause on the corner of Broadway and East Roy Street to consider your options. If you want to follow the second walk in this chapter, turn right onto Broadway, where that walk starts. If you'd rather return to Volunteer Park, read on.

⓯ Continue on East Roy Street, following it as it jogs to the left, until it ends at 13th Avenue East. On either side of Roy are more **Anhalt apartment buildings** (1005 and 1014 East Roy Street). The one on the right, completed in 1929, was the first building in Seattle to have an underground parking garage. Past the Anhalt buildings, Roy briefly becomes a charming parklike path that winds past Lowell Elementary School and its playground. The street then continues as a quiet, little-traveled lane.

⓰ Turn right onto 13th Avenue East and follow it to East Mercer Street. On the right is an unusual house (627 13th Avenue East) that's somewhat reminiscent of a blonde wearing a kimono. Built in 1905, the home is essentially a Western bungalow with Japanese-style upturned eaves and an Asian design on its windows. Across the street are the **Maryland Apartments** (626 13th Avenue East), built in 1910–11. The facade of this Romanesque Revival building, a Seattle historic landmark, is constructed of three colors of brick and two colors of stone. It has porches on several levels and looks simultaneously massive and airy.

Turn left onto East Mercer Street, then turn left onto 14th Avenue East. Stroll along 14th for several blocks to East Prospect Street. Fourteenth Avenue soon becomes an elegant tree-lined street bordered on either side with magnificent mansions. This area used to be referred to as **Millionaire Row**, and the term is still appropriate. You can stay in at least one of these fabulous homes without having millions in the bank, though: The opulent Shafer-Baillie Mansion, on the left just past Aloha, is a bed and breakfast. Call ahead to see a room, (206)322-4654.

17 On the right, facing Volunteer Park, is the magnificent white **G. H. Parker house**, a Classic Revival mansion. When it was completed in 1909, it was reported to have five porches, 16 rooms (in addition to its 12 bedrooms and five bathrooms), several interior murals, a coach house, and seven fireplaces. Alas, this showplace was built with ill-gotten gains, and its owner lived in it for only a year before the law caught up with him. As a fiscal agent for the United Wireless Company, George H. Parker was able to sell several million dollars' worth of stock in the company, which at the time represented a new and exciting technology. But United Wireless never made a profit or even met operating expenses, and it made false claims to boost stock sales. Parker may not have known they were false, but when the scandal broke he was sentenced to two years in prison on McNeil Island. (He was later pardoned.)

Retrace your steps along Volunteer Park's tree-lined drive to East Galer Street and 15th Avenue East, where you started this walk.

Pilgrim Congregational Church

starting/ finish point	**getting there**
Corner of Broadway and East Roy Street	**parking** Parking is metered on Broadway but free on the surrounding streets. Much of the area's street parking is limited to two hours, but you can park on the street for an unlimited time starting at East Aloha Street and Federal Avenue East, one block north and one block east of this walk's starting point.

bus connections Catch Route 7 (Broadway or University District) on Pike Street near Third Avenue downtown; get off near Broadway and East Mercer Street, and continue for one block on Broadway to East Roy Street. (To get information on other bus routes serving this area, see the "Getting Around" section in the introduction to this book.)

ROUTE 2:

counterculture

Distance: 2.25 miles
Approximate time: 2 hours

Start this walk at the corner of Broadway and East Roy Street. Begin strolling past the many shops of Broadway, for several blocks, toward East Thomas Street. Broadway is Capitol Hill's main commercial street and the principal gathering place for the neighborhood's colorful personalities. On this street, in between comparatively prosaic stores selling groceries, books, and records, are shops offering such exotica as incense and mandalas, gay-oriented merchandise, and body-piercing services. You'll also encounter independent coffee-houses, bead shops, shoeshine boys, and a vast array of eateries.

In the past decade Broadway has become an increasingly popular area, and its retail trade has spread out in all directions. Franchises have moved into many spaces where straggling startups used to be, but youth culture still reigns. Seattle's lesbian and gay community also congregates here—especially in late June, when a large gay pride parade promenades down Broadway in a spectacular celebration of diversity.

❶ After a few blocks, on the left just before East Republican Street, is the red-brick **Pilgrim Congregational Church**. Since 1905–06, when the church was built, the character of its surrounding community has changed several times over: from streetcar suburb to blighted community to colorful, thriving urban center. The church has changed too, welcoming a large gay contingent into its growing congregation and sponsoring a program to aid homeless youth.

❷ About a half block farther, also on the left, is Dilettante Chocolates, a homegrown purveyor of delectable truffles, sauces, and desserts. On the right, occupying a full block, is the hip emporium called the **Broadway Market**. Decades ago, this building housed independent businesses that catered to the then solidly middle-class neighborhood. The shops included a fish market, two butchers, a creamery, two bakeries, a cafe, and a barber. In 1958, however, the Fred Meyer supermarket bought the building and covered all of the beautiful windows, giving the structure a blank white

capitol hill route 2: counterculture

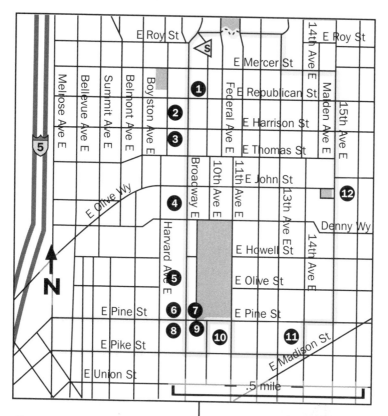

1 Pilgrim Congregational Church
2 Broadway Market
3 Dance steps
4 Dick's Drive-In
5 Seattle Central Community College
6 Broadway Performance Hall
7 Statue of Jimi Hendrix
8 Egyptian Theatre
9 Odd Fellows Hall
10 Value Village
11 Globe Cafe & Bakery
12 Group Health Cooperative

face. Fortunately, in 1984 the building was restored and its glass-roofed atrium added. Many of the tenants are now gift shops, eateries, and outfitters of the young and style-conscious; there's also a movie theater on the top floor.

❸ On the right, a short distance past East Harrison Street, keep your eye on the sidewalk—or you'll miss the **dance steps**, bronze shoeprints illustrating the steps of the mambo, inlaid in the cement. This ingenious public artwork is just one in a series; the steps to seven other dances are

Bustlin' Broadway Market

scattered elsewhere along Broadway, so watch for passersby attempting to dance with the sidewalk. The heels of the prints are decorated with unusual embellishments, everything from parking tokens to foreign coins and coffee beans.

The coffee bean is an apt symbol for Broadway (and just about everywhere else in Seattle, for that matter). The street offers dozens of places to order espresso, and even a place to worship it—at Vivace, an espresso outlet a few feet past the mambo steps. Its minimalist location consists of an open-air service window, some sidewalk tables, and a narrow hallway leading to a staircase, with more tables tucked away on the small top floor. In the hallway is the **Sacred Shrine of Caffeina, Goddess of the Working Day**. The plaque to the right tells you more about her; you may want to pay your respects.

❹ **Continue strolling along Broadway for about a quarter mile to East Pine Street.** After you cross East John Street, Broadway becomes a bit more down-to-earth. A big orange sign on the right heralds **Dick's Drive-In**, somewhat of an anachronism these days with its free parking lot (relatively rare on Broadway) and throwback cuisine. In a city known for innovative fare, the menu at this local favorite still consists of burgers, shakes, floats, fries, cones, and sundaes. The eatery's namesake, Dick Spady, opened his first drive-in in the

queen city of the northwest

SEATTLE'S FIRST GAY COMMUNITY coalesced around Pioneer Square in the 1930s when a couple of gay-friendly bars opened there. Discrimination and prejudice were prevalent during the Depression, though, and gays kept a low profile.

During World War II, things began to change: The community grew as gay servicemen stationed in the area came into the city, and many of them moved here when their military service ended. Seattle's first gay-owned bar, the Garden of Allah, began operating in the basement of a (now-demolished) hotel on First Avenue in 1946; on the bar's opening night, police chaperones watched from the door to make sure same-sex couples didn't touch each other. The Garden enjoyed remarkably few police raids compared to gay bars in other cities—partly due, it turned out, to a system of police payoffs that continued until it was exposed by the *Seattle Times* in 1967.

Seattle's first gay rights organization, the Dorian Society, was formed in 1967. By the 1970s Seattle's gay bars no longer felt they had to hide in basements; instead, they could proudly display their affiliation. A Pioneer Square disco that opened in 1973 had a large sign out front that read, "Shelly's Leg is a GAY BAR provided for Seattle's gay community and their guests."

The community holds a gay pride celebration every year in late June, featuring a lively parade down Broadway. When Seattle's first pride parade was held in Pioneer Square in 1977, a crowd of about 2,000 gathered for the event; in 1998 about 50,000 people gathered, up from 30,000 in 1997.

While Seattle's first gay pride marches were marred by protesters who booed and harassed participants, today's atmosphere is completely different: It's like a giant family reunion—of a somewhat offbeat family, to be sure. There are kids and parents and jubilant crowds, political slogans, bizarre costumes, fantastic floats—and, a perennial highlight, the motorcycle drill team proudly known as Dykes on Bikes.

Broadway Performance Hall

Wallingford neighborhood in 1954; this was his second (opened in 1955). Although Dick's now has drive-ins across the city, the homegrown chain has remained local, resisting franchise opportunities, and retains a loyal following.

❺ A few blocks farther, also on the right, is a rather monolithic red-brick building that houses some of the classrooms and offices of **Seattle Central Community College**. Although nondescript on the outside, it holds a few secrets inside: a little-known garden and a spectacular view. To see them, continue straight ahead on Broadway, passing in front of the long building for almost a full block, until you see a set of doors with "1701 Broadway" above the threshold. There are two sets of similarly marked doors near each other; enter through the ones you

come to first, and take the elevator to the top (fifth) floor. Ahead is the entrance to a balcony, which features an outdoor herb garden that's open to the public; it's actually the Biology Specimen Garden, used by the college's biology and botany classes. On the opposite side of the building, near the elevators, are long windows offering a compelling wide-screen view of the downtown skyline. (Please respect the privacy of classrooms and offices, of course.)

❻ Beyond the classroom building is the **Broadway Performance Hall**, with its tall arching windows, the only historic structure on the community college's campus. It was originally the gymnasium for the majestic Broadway High School, which operated on this spot from 1903 until 1944. When the community college's regents decided to build a campus here in the 1970s, they originally planned to tear down the entire school building. After protests from Broadway High alumni, they agreed to save part of the structure, and transformed the gym into this theater.

❼ On the left, just before Pine, is a **statue of Jimi Hendrix**, silently jamming on the sidewalk for passersby. The legendary guitarist grew up in Renton, southeast of Seattle (he's buried in Greenwood Cemetery there). The statue was installed by AEI Music, whose offices are in the building on the corner. This homegrown Seattle company was founded in 1971 to provide businesses with background music, and today has more than 100,000 customers around the world.

The company owns three other statues of rock-and-roll legends (Bill Haley, Elvis Presley, and John Lennon), all sculpted by Seattle artist Daryl Smith, as well as guitars played by all four artists and a brass belt buckle that belonged to Elvis Presley. To see these sculptures and memorabilia, enter through the unmarked door on Pine Street and inquire at the desk.

❽ Turn right onto Pine Street and walk half a block. On the left is the **Egyptian Theatre**, built in 1915 as the Masonic Temple. Inside, the walls are covered with colorful Art Deco Egyptian motifs that look historic but actually date back only to 1980—when Darryl Macdonald and Rajeeve Gupta oversaw the theater's remarkable transformation from a wrestling arena into a movie palace. Earlier

they had renovated downtown's venerable Moore Theatre, which served as the sole venue for the first, modest Seattle International Film Festival in 1976. Cofounded and still directed by Macdonald, the festival is now a popular annual event that screens more than 250 feature-length and short films at several theaters around town, including the Egyptian.

Retrace your steps to Broadway; turn right and follow Broadway to East Pike Street. Just a few years ago Pine and Pike Streets on either side of Broadway were full

Hendrix jams to the traffic

of dives and empty storefronts, but those days are fading. Now this up-and-coming area even has a name: the **Pike/Pine Corridor**. As the strip of Broadway you've just explored has become more and more popular, the stores there have become somewhat more commercial and conventional, leaving the relatively low-rent Pike/Pine Corridor to nurture the sort of offbeat, one-of-a-kind businesses that once might have set up shop on Broadway.

Development along the corri-

Looking west on Pike Street

dor has been uneven, although it's picking up steam. (One extreme example of the boom is the Harvard Market, which stands before you across Pike. This block-size shopping center brought 90,000 square feet of retail space to the area in 1997, and business is booming.) While a number of blocks along the corridor are still dominated by relatively prosaic businesses such as car dealerships, garages, corner groceries, and printers, other blocks offer surprises like a sex-toy store run by lesbians, a Mexican restaurant adorned with black-velvet paintings, a funky barber shop that offers tattoos as well as low-cost cuts, a gay and lesbian bookstore, and a tavern co-owned by a founder of Seattle's Sub Pop Records (the alternative label that released Nirvana's first album, among many others).

Those treats and more are scattered along Pike and Pine to the right. If you'd like to search for them, and doubtless make other discoveries along the way, take the **extended walk** outlined on the accompanying map. Two particularly rewarding blocks on the extended route are Pike between Belmont Avenue East and Boylston Avenue East, and Pine between Bellevue Avenue East and Melrose Avenue East; both blocks are full of intriguing shops and eateries. The extended walk is a loop that returns you here so you can continue on the basic walk.

If you'd rather continue on the basic walk, read on. From here the route heads to the left, weaving between Pike and Pine to show you a sampling of the corridor's offerings there.

Turn left onto East Pike Street and follow it to 10th Avenue East. While a few parts of the corridor have gone upscale, some Pike Street businesses determinedly retain their pre-boom edge. Witness the smoky **Comet Tavern**, which has been serving liquor (but no food) from a musty, graffitied bar on the corner of 10th and Pike since 1936.

❾ Turn left onto 10th Avenue East and follow it to East Pine Street. On the left as you near Pine is the **Odd Fellows Hall**, a grand edifice whose several floors are home to theater companies, performance spaces, and a wide variety of other arts-related enterprises. On the second floor is the Century Ballroom, exuding an aura of faded elegance; it's a popular spot for dances and has its own cafe too.

❿ Turn right onto East Pine Street, turn right onto 11th Avenue East, and follow it to East Pike Street.
Whether by accident or by design, this block of 11th Avenue is lined with thrift stores, the most prominent being **Value Village**—the legendary chain that some say was the source of the original "grunge" fashion. This store has three levels of well-organized bargains. Across the street is the far smaller but equally beloved thrift store run by the Chicken Soup

cinema culture

BOASTING THREE MOVIE THE-aters—the Harvard Exit, the Egyptian, and the Broadway Market—within a half mile of each other, Capitol Hill is the favorite neighborhood of many in this cinemaphilic town, which sees more movies per capita than any other city in the United States. Seattle filmgoers have a reputation for being appreciative of good cinema while not as highbrow as New York, which may be one reason Hollywood producers consider the city a good launching point for new releases. The blockbuster *Braveheart* even had its U.S. premiere in Seattle, at the Seattle International Film Festival.

Seattle's annual film festival, which takes place in May and June, was founded in 1976 and has since grown to become the nation's biggest and best-attended. Its three-week run in 1998 drew 132,000 attendees to a typically vast and diverse selection of more than 250 feature films and shorts. Each year, festival programmers review thousands of submissions and attend film festivals all over the world in their quest for celluloid gems.

One of SIFF's most popular features is the Secret Festival, a four-film series within the festival. Secret Festival ticket buyers must sign an oath of silence in which they pledge never to reveal the movies they see at the Secret Fest. The works shown range from films that cannot be publicly shown because of legal battles, to unreleased works and forgotten treasures, to world premieres. The Secret Fest usually sells out soon after the SIFF box office opens.

Brigade, which provides meals and
other services to those living with
HIV/AIDS.

Just before Pike, on the left, is
Northwest Actors Studio,
where you can both see plays and
take classes in the dramatic arts. It's
just one of the many theaters based
on Capitol Hill.

**Turn left onto East Pike Street
and follow it for several blocks
to 14th Avenue East.** As Pike
heads farther from Broadway, the
pace of development slows; here
you'll see a fair number of battered
old buildings waiting for someone
to discover their potential. A few
pubs and eateries have moved in,
though. At 13th Avenue East,
for instance, the relatively new
Elysian Brewing Company, an
airy, sparkling-clean brewpub with
full-length plate-glass windows and
an outdoor deck in back, stands in
sharp contrast to the venerably
dingy Comet Tavern you passed
earlier.

🕚 **Turn left onto 14th Avenue
East and follow it to East Pine
Street.** Just before Pine, on the
left, is the **Globe Cafe & Bakery**,
a funky eatery serving only vegan
food (no dairy products or meat).
If you're so inclined, stop for a
bite; while you wait for your food,
you can check your e-mail at a
remote-access computer terminal
or browse through a book from
one of the shelves along the wall.

🕐 **Turn right onto East Pine
Street, turn left onto 15th
Avenue East, and stroll for sev-**

eral blocks to East John Street.
Fifteenth Avenue is residential for
a few blocks before it segues into a
business district. The first and
largest commercial enterprise you
pass is **Group Health Cooperative**, occupying several buildings
on the right. While it may look
like an ordinary American health
care facility, Group Health pioneered some radical concepts:
cooperative medicine, prepaid
medical service, and preventive
care. Members of the cooperative
paid a flat fee for access to the
services of Group Health's hospital, doctors, and pharmacy, and
Group Health's doctors and other
staff members were paid a salary by
the cooperative.

When Group Health incorporated in the 1940s, Seattle's mainstream, fee-for-service physicians
were alarmed, viewing cooperative
medicine as a threat to private
practice. The King County Medical Society effectively barred
Group Health's doctors from
admitting patients to most area
hospitals and attempted to block
the cooperative's accreditation
with the American Medical Association. In response, Group Health
sued the medical society for
monopolistic conspiracy and won.
Today the cooperative has more
than 650,000 enrollees and is the
largest consumer-governed health
care establishment in the United
States.

**Continue strolling along 15th
Avenue East for several blocks
to East Mercer Street.** Fifteenth
Avenue here is lined with an easy-

going mixture of eateries, shops, and markets. The businesses have a slightly different character than those on Broadway or Pike, more of a melange of "high society" and counterculture. The ambience is less crowded and hectic, making 15th a more inviting place to stop for a leisurely lunch or coffee if you haven't done so already.

Turn left onto East Mercer Street and follow it for several blocks, then turn right onto 13th Avenue East and follow it to East Roy Street. Thirteenth is lined with trees and eclectic homes. On the right you pass the **Maryland Apartments** (626 13th Avenue East), a Seattle historic landmark; across the street is a curious Asian bungalow (627 13th Avenue East). These will be familiar sites if you've already taken the first walk in this chapter.

Turn left onto East Roy Street and follow it to Broadway, where you started this walk. Roy Street here is first a quiet, little-traveled lane and then a charming parklike path that winds past Lowell Elementary School and its playground. As Roy again becomes a street, admire the elegant **courtyard apartment buildings** on

Shops on 15th Avenue East

either side (1005 and 1014 East Roy Street). They were built in the late 1920s and early 1930s by Frederick Anhalt, a man with no formal architectural training who nonetheless designed some of Capitol Hill's most sought-after apartments.

SEATTLE'S LEFT BANK:

Distance: 1.5 miles   **Approximate time:** 1 hour

"FREMONT IS A STATE OF MIND, not a foreign nation but an Imagination."

—*From the "Republic of Fremont Proclamation," posted on the side of a Fremont building*

Fremont is the home of many great works. It's known for its unconventional artworks, its public works, and its beer works. But playing is what Fremont does best. Its official motto is *De Libertas Quirkas*, which it translates as "Freedom to Be Peculiar." Residents dance through the streets in strange costumes to celebrate the summer solstice. They gather at the neighborhood's open-air market on weekends, lounge in a parking lot on Saturday nights watching old movies, and congregate in brewpubs and coffee shops all week long, drinking fashionable beverages and planning the artistic conquest of the world.

Fremont did not just happen upon its image as fun-loving art center; it consciously constructed that persona. This area may have more neighborhood pride and active participation than any other in the city. Its many community organizations include the Fremont Neighborhood Association, which

A wedding, Fremont style

guards the local quality of life; the Fremont Arts Council, which promotes all forms of the arts; and the Fremont Public Association, which watches out for the little

starting/ finish point

Corner of North 34th Street and Aurora Avenue North, underneath the Aurora Bridge

parking Street parking is available in the Fremont business district, but it's limited to two hours and can be hard to find; look on North Canal Street near Phinney Avenue North, by Fremont Canal Park.

bus connections Catch Route 26 (East Green Lake) on Fourth Avenue near Pike Street downtown; get off on North 35th Street near Aurora Avenue North, and follow Aurora downhill to North 34th Street. (To get more information on bus routes serving this area, see the "Getting Around" section in the introduction to this book.)

guy. Over the years, its dedicated residents have transformed Fremont from a dicey neighborhood into the self-proclaimed Center of the Universe.

Fremont fans, especially would-be residents, have at least one regret about the transformation: dramatically rising housing costs. Between 1990 and 1997, the average price of a home here went up 50 percent, and rents increased at a similar rate. But Fremont still makes an effort to keep its small-business retail trade. Its business

Gas Works Park

district is populated with one-of-a-kind art galleries, antique shops, used bookstores, and coffeehouses.

❶ **Start this walk on the corner of North 34th Street and Aurora Avenue North, underneath the Aurora Bridge.** On the corner of 34th and Aurora, behind a whimsical metal fence and gate adorned with colorful flowers, birds, stars, and more, is **History House**, a small museum showcasing the history of Seattle's neighborhoods. The museum offers rotating

fremont

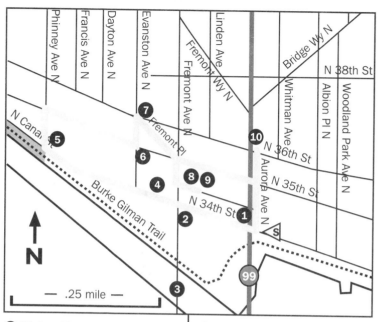

① History House
② People Waiting for the Interurban
③ Fremont Bridge
④ Fremont Sunday Market
⑤ Redhook Ale Brewery

⑥ Fremont Rocket
⑦ Statue of Lenin
⑧ Garden of Everyday Miracles
⑨ Still Life in Fremont Coffeehouse
⑩ Fremont Troll

Statue of Lenin

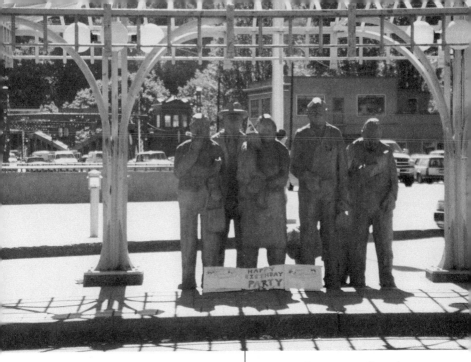

People Waiting for the Interurban

exhibits on different Seattle neighborhoods and features a 120-foot mural, a sort of collage of historic photos of Seattle, that stretches around the main exhibition room. History House is open Wednesday through Sunday afternoons and is free.

❷ With History House on your right, follow North 34th Street to Fremont Avenue North. The traffic island on the corner of 34th and Fremont is the home of the much-beloved, much-adorned sculpture entitled *People Waiting for the Interurban*. Ever since their installation in the late 1970s, the aluminum people have been regularly festooned with hats, T-shirts, signs, banners, and similar accessories by anonymous decorators. Unless you visit Fremont daily, you'll probably never see them

wearing the same outfits twice.

Look closely at the dog peering out from between the legs of the people. His curiously bearded face is a reminder of a 1970s dispute between sculptor Richard Beyer and Armen Stepanian, the former honorary mayor of Fremont, when both were serving on a committee charged with choosing an artwork to commemorate the neighborhood's centennial. The committee ultimately chose Beyer's inspired *Interurban* design, and Beyer put Stepanian's face on the dog as a reminder never to annoy a sculptor.

Beyer's people are made of recycled aluminum because Stepanian, who ran a Fremont aluminum-recycling program (the city's first), felt that would celebrate Fremont's progressive spirit. The Interurban they're waiting for was a railway that once passed through Fremont on its way between Seattle and its northern neighbor, Everett. The Interurban ended its service in the 1930s, after highways had drained off much of its business; ever since, the entire city of Seattle has been waiting for the Interurban. It should finally be arriving in the first decade of the 21st century, when the new commuter rail system approved by voters is projected to be operational.

❸ Just beyond the *Interurban* sculpture, look to the left to see another artwork of sorts: the blue-and-orange **Fremont Bridge**. It began its life in 1916 painted an unassuming green, but in 1972 the city painted it with orange primer in preparation for a fresh coat of green paint. The ubiquitous Armen Stepanian liked the orange color and successfully petitioned the city to keep it. Some loved it; some hated it.

In 1985, when the bridge needed a fresh coat of paint, those who detested the orange color held a vote on the matter at the annual Fremont Street Fair, but the color orange was not on the ballot. The winner was a tasteful blue, but that didn't have enough pizzazz for a few anonymous locals, who sneaked in behind the city's back and painted orange accents on the blue bridge. The bridge has since been repainted in the blue-and-orange combination without a vote or controversy.

❹ **Continue on North 34th Street for several blocks to Phinney Avenue North.** Just past the corner of 34th and Fremont, on the right behind the Red Door Alehouse, is a sizable parking lot

Chic junk in Fremont

the brewpubs at the center of the universe

IN ITS EARLY DAYS, FREMONT was a teetotaling community. When the University of Washington moved to its present site in 1895, a four-mile "circle of sobriety" was declared around it. Fremont's working-class residents were forced to abstain from alcohol in order to keep the souls of the students clean. Several years later the buffer zone between alcohol and the student body was reduced to two miles, and Fremont was freed from the tyranny of sobriety.

Fremont citizens have enjoyed their libations ever since. Finely crafted microbrews, the current favorite, are served up at Redhook's Trolleyman Pub (3400 Phinney Avenue North), Dad Watson's Restaurant and Brewery (3601 Fremont Avenue North), and Hale's Brewery and Pub (4301 Leary Way Northwest). These are just a few of the more than 60 breweries—most of them small operations—in Washington state.

Microbrews have become so popular that several small beer producers have outgrown the term "micro." Officially, a microbrewery produces less than 15,000 barrels (or 465,000 gallons) per year. A regional specialty brewery may produce up to 500,000 barrels (15.5 million gallons), but "regional specialty brew" doesn't have the same ring as "microbrew," so most brewers in this category call themselves "craft breweries," which means a brewery that uses only the classic ingredients of malted grains, hops, yeast, and water.

that plays host to the **Fremont Sunday Market**, a lively outdoor market/street fair, every Sunday between May and October. The market offers produce, crafts, antiques, and a smattering of junk; it's a great place to watch people and get to know Fremont.

On the far side of the parking lot is a building whose cement-block wall has been painted with stage curtains, so it can serve as a proper screen for the festive summer tradition known as the **Fremont Outdoor Cinema**. On Saturday nights from June through August, this patch of asphalt is full of people who bring their own chairs and watch popular classics, from *Casablanca* to *Saturday Night Fever*, projected on the wall (there's a small admission fee). Costume contests, comedic hosts, and other unpredictable revelry further enliven the proceedings before the show and between double features.

On the left, just past Phinney, is the beginning of **Fremont Canal Park**, a lovely strip of lawn, trees, and inviting benches that stretches along the Lake Washington Ship Canal for several blocks. If it's a summer weekend, you can watch the continuous parade of passing boats heading for the Ballard Locks on their way to Puget Sound.

❺ On the right, the large brick building on the corner of 34th and Phinney used to be a trolley-car storage barn for the West Coast's first electric railway, which ran through Fremont (See "A Short History of the Center of the Universe" on page 120.) Today it

houses the **Redhook Ale Brewery** and its appropriately named Trolleyman Pub (inquire here about free brewery tours). Now one of the big names in microbreweries, Redhook was started by Gordon Bowker and Paul Shipman in a warehouse in Ballard, the neighborhood just northwest of Fremont. Bowker was also one of the founders of Starbucks; apparently everything he drinks turns to gold.

❻ Turn right onto Phinney Avenue North, then turn right onto North 35th Street and follow it to Evanston Avenue North. Affixed to a building on the corner of 35th and Evanston is another piece of public art: the neon-enhanced **Fremont Rocket**, eternally awaiting lift-off and glowing with the confidence of an upwardly mobile spacecraft. Originally part of a 1950s Cold

Artwork on 35th Street

War implement of destruction, the Rocket spent the first part of its retirement years on the facade of a surplus store in Belltown. When the store went out of business, the Fremont Business Association sensed the Rocket's potential as a landmark monument and snapped it up.

A coin box on the wall beneath the Rocket invites you to "launch" it for only 50 cents. It doesn't actually go anywhere, but steam shoots impressively out of its jets, and your coins help fund its upkeep.

❼ Turn left onto Evanston Avenue North and follow it to Fremont Place North. On the corner plaza is an incongruous sight: a 16-foot **statue of Lenin**, the former communist leader. As with most Fremont public art, there's an interesting story behind

The Garden of Everyday Miracles

about selling the statue for scrap bronze, but instead the foundry expressed interest in putting it on display. The statue is actually for sale (asking price: $150,000), but thus far no one has snapped it up.

Turn right onto Fremont Place North and follow it to Fremont Avenue North. Cross Fremont, turn right onto it, and follow it for half a block to an alley. Just before the alley, metal-junk sculptures of a bride and groom greet you outside **Glamorama**, advertising perhaps its most exceptional feature: low-budget personalized wedding ceremonies, performed underneath an upside-down wedding cake suspended from the ceiling. Various Glamorama staff members are ordained ministers of the Universal Life Church (which advertises ordination by mail in the back of *Rolling Stone*), so their weddings are entirely legal. The store also sells kitschy cards, gifts, and T-shirts; if you're looking for a Lava lamp, a lunchbox with cartoon characters on it, or Elvis memorabilia, this is the place to come.

❽ Turn left into the alley and follow it to a parking lot on the left. On the hillside adjoining the parking lot is a little-known public artwork called the **Garden of Everyday Miracles**, if it hasn't yet been demolished for a planned construction project. The longer you look, the more you'll see: Various ceramic artworks, a cluster of pink flamingos, cheerfully twirling pinwheels, and an array

this curiosity. The seven-ton statue is the work of Emil Venkov, a widely exhibited Slavic sculptor. Lewis Carpenter, an American teaching English in Slovakia, found the statue in the town dump there sometime after the 1989 revolution. Sure he could find a buyer who would value the sculpture's aesthetics over its politics, he mortgaged his house to transport the statue back to the States.

After Carpenter's untimely death in 1994, his family contacted the Fremont Fine Arts Foundry

of old television sets and computer monitors are just a few of the features of this ever-evolving collection.

⑨ Exiting the alley, turn right onto Fremont Avenue North, then turn right onto North 35th Street and follow it for several blocks to Aurora Avenue North. On the right is the casual, eclectic **Still Life in Fremont Coffeehouse**, whose big windows, reasonably priced food, and array of mismatched wooden chairs fit right into the laid-back Fremont aesthetic. A few steps farther is the charming Mission-style **Fremont Public Library**, with a red barrel-tile roof. Opened in 1921, this library is one of more than 2,500 built across the United States, Canada, and Great Britain with funds from the Carnegie Foundation, established by wealthy industrialist Andrew Carnegie in the early 20th century. (Other Carnegie libraries are in Ballard, the Central District, Green Lake, and Queen Anne.)

⑩ Turn left and walk up Aurora Avenue North for several blocks. Where the span of the Aurora Bridge meets the ground, you'll come face to face with the neighborhood's largest work of art: the 30-foot-wide cement **Fremont Troll**, who clutches a VW Bug threateningly in his left hand and scowls at the many people who come to snap his picture. (Yes, it's a real Bug; in fact, vandals once broke into its trunk looking for hidden treasure. They didn't

festive fremont

FREMONT MAY HAVE MORE festivals and events than any other neighborhood in Seattle. In addition to the regularly occurring Sunday Market and Outdoor Cinema, described in the accompanying walk, Fremont offers some spectacularly unique once-a-year events, including Trolloween and the Solstice Parade.

Fremont's traditional Halloween celebration, known as Trolloween, features the most creative Halloween costumes in town along with flamboyant performance art. The festival's main event is a candlelight procession beginning under the Aurora Bridge in the lair of the Fremont Troll. As they parade through the streets, Trolloween participants are entertained by ghoulish antics and dance to ghostly music. The costumed procession is usually followed by Troll-a-Go-Go, a dance where prizes are awarded for the best costumes. In preparation for the holiday, the Fremont Arts Council sponsors events such as pumpkin-carving and costume-making workshops.

Fremont's Solstice Parade, the quintessential Fremont celebration, is held on the Saturday nearest the summer solstice (June 21). The parade has only a few simple rules—no printed words, logos, animals, or motors—resulting in an abundance of wacky people-powered floats portraying such visions as a pope on a bicycle, seahorses on a trapeze, and butterflies on stilts. A bicycling streaker also generally makes an appearance. The parade never fails to draw a crowd, and parking anywhere near its route is impossible.

a short history of the center of the universe

FREMONT'S RAINBOW-HUED MOD-
ern persona sprouted from a mono-
chromatic working-class past. The
neighborhood is named after Fremont,
Nebraska—the hometown of its
founders, Edward and Carrie Blewett
and Luther Griffith, who purchased the
townsite for $55,000 in the late 19th
century. Griffith was only in his 20s,
but that same year he won the franchise for the West Coast's first electric railway. He naturally routed it
through his real estate in Fremont.

Seattle annexed Fremont, then a
village of 5,000, in 1891. Most of its
residents worked in nearby mills, and
Fremont remained an industrially
strong, blue-collar area for the next
several decades. But in the 1930s,
the combined effect of the Great
Depression and the completion of the
Aurora Bridge, which made it possible
for people to zoom across Lake Union
without passing through Fremont,
sent Fremont into a decline. The suburban exodus that followed World War
II drew more residents away.

Fremont gained an unsavory reputation in the 1960s and 1970s. Its
streets were lined with vacant storefronts, warehouses, funky antique
shops, and biker bars, and the neighborhood was favored by hippies and
artists in search of cheap studio
space. Comedians quipped, "Why do
they call it Fremont? Because they
couldn't call it Freeload." An article in
the 1977 *Seattle Times* opined, "Fremont has no grocery, no drugstore, no
boutique, no park, no benches, no
statue. It is not likely to get any of
them in the future." (Today, of course,
Fremont has every one of these
amenities, and many more.)

The 1970s were a turning point for
Fremont. In 1972 the first Fremont
street fair was held. In 1974 the Fremont Public Association was formed
to provide food, shelter, and practical
advice to disadvantaged citizens.
Armen Stepanian began actively campaigning for a curbside recycling program, and the Fremont Arts Council
was formed to coordinate community
events and fund art installations.

The area was gradually transformed into the thriving, free-spirited
community you see today, while
retaining some elements of its humble, countercultural past. Its funky
antique shops and coffeehouses have
not yet been crowded out by newer
developments like Adobe software's
office complex (adjacent to the Fremont Bridge). Nowadays, though,
artists are more likely to show their
work in Fremont's upscale galleries
than to rent cheap studio space here.

The famous troll

find anything, but who could blame them for trying? Trolls are known to have a lust for precious metals, and just look at that guy—he has to be hiding something.)

Conjured by the artistic team of Steve Badanes, Will Martin, Donna Walter, and Ross Whitehead, the Troll was the winning entry in a competition sponsored by the Fremont Arts Council. He's made of two tons of ferro-cement and took seven weeks to complete.

Installed in the early 1990s, he quickly became an intrinsic part of the neighborhood's image. He presides over Fremont's annual Halloween celebration, "Trolloween."

From the Troll, follow Aurora Avenue North downhill to North 34th Street, where you started this walk.

it's a gas: gas works park

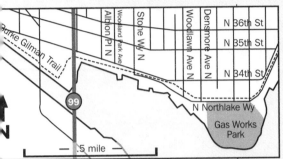

JUST A SHORT HOP FROM FRE-
mont is one of Seattle's most spectacular skyline viewpoints: Gas Works
Park. Gas Works is a perfect complement to Fremont, its inspiring views
and industrial refuse going well with
Fremont's quirky art. The park is
located on the northern shore of Lake
Union, and across its grassy expanse
is scattered the machinery of a gasifi-
cation plant that once powered much
of Seattle, from 1907 until the
1950s. It is the largest remnant of
the 1,400 such plants that once
existed across the United States. The
old gas works produced methane gas
by heating coal, and showered northern Lake Union with soot and sparks
24 hours a day in the process.

After the plant closed, the city
bought the land and made plans to
turn it into a park. With its astounding
views, the site seemed like a perfect
location, but it also had drawbacks:
The soil was layered with hydrocarbon
contaminants, soot, and petrochemi-
cal waste. The city considered several
proposals for the park's design before
choosing one by landscape architect
Richard Haag. He observed that the
site "resists becoming a traditional
park," and wisely designed a park
that is anything but traditional.

However, not everyone has appre-
ciated Gas Works Park's
strange juxtaposition of recreation and rusting refuse. The
park was originally to be
named Myrtle Edwards Park,
after a city council member
who worked to make it a reality, but her family didn't want
her name attached to any-
thing so "ugly." A waterfront
park in downtown Seattle was named
in her honor instead.

Gas Works Park is much less pol-
luted then it once was, but its industrial past still haunts it. In 1984 the
city temporarily shut it down to study
the threat posed by cyanide and other
carcinogens found at low levels in the
soil. A committee concluded that the
contamination was not a significant
health risk—unless large quantities of
dirt were eaten over a long period of
time. However, in late 1998, the city
was considering a multimillion-dollar
project to clean up tar and benzene
contamination in the park.

Gas Works has a playbarn/picnic
shelter that houses machinery on its
east side, and on its west side is a
small hill topped with a 28-foot-wide
concrete sundial inlaid with cast
bronze, shells, ceramics, and miscellaneous objects. Stand in the center
and let your body cast a shadow to
read the time from this solar clock.
You can reach Gas Works Park on
foot starting in back of the Adobe
office complex and following the
Burke Gilman Trail east for 1.25
miles. To reach the park by car from
Fremont, drive east on North 35th
Street to Meridian Avenue North. Turn
right on Meridian and drive two blocks
to the park.

THE U-DUB AND THE U DISTRICT:

Distance: 2.25 miles   **Approximate time:** 2 hours

THE ORIGINAL CAMPUS OF THE University of Washington (or UW, usually referred to as "U-Dub") was located downtown, near University Street and Fourth Avenue. When the university moved to its current location in 1895, the only thing nearby was a tiny working-class community called Brooklyn; the school's 600-acre campus consisted of one building amid a forested wilderness.

The peaceful arts quad

The campus has since expanded to fill those 600 acres, but it is still extraordinarily scenic, with dignified Gothic structures, mountain and water views, gardens, promenades, and a picturesque fountain. The surrounding community has changed a lot since 1895. Now called the U District, it has left behind its working-class roots and become youth-oriented, unkempt, and energetic.

The result is quite a contrast. While the campus is venerable,

starting/ finish point

North gate of the University of Washington, on the corner of Northeast 45th Street and Memorial Way

parking Street parking is extremely scarce and limited to two hours. To park on campus, enter the university's north gate and tell the guard you want to park near the Burke Museum. The museum charges a flat fee to park (it's free after noon on Saturday and all day Sunday). If no parking is available there, the guard can tell you where to find a space. Don't try to park, or drive, anywhere near the U District if there is a football game at Husky Stadium.

bus connections Catch Route 7 (University District) on Third Avenue near Union Street downtown; get off near Northeast 45th Street and 15th Avenue Northeast, and follow 45th alongside campus to Memorial Way. (For more information about bus routes serving this area, see the "Getting Around" section in the introduction to this book.)

To return to your car via bus if you shorten the walk to one direction only: Catch Route 25 (Laurelhurst), 44 (Golden Gardens), 48 (Loyal Heights), or 271 (U District) on 15th Avenue Northeast near Northeast Pacific Street; get off at Northeast 45th Street and follow it for a block to Memorial Way.

To return downtown via bus if you shorten the walk to one direction only: Catch Route 25 or 43 (both Downtown) on 15th Avenue Northeast near Northeast Pacific Street.

green, and majestic, the U District is brash and opinionated. Like estranged sisters, the two are nothing alike but they have a lot in common. This walk leads you down a peaceful tree-lined drive and onto a winding route through campus, veering off the beaten path now and again to explore little-known garden spots

Denny Hall

and venture inside intriguingly designed structures. You conclude by strolling "The Ave," the university's bustling business district. If you want a shorter, one-way route of about 1.75 miles, you can end the walk at the Physics/ Astronomy complex and catch a bus back to your starting point or elsewhere in the city, via bus routes described in "Getting There."

Note: When entering campus buildings to see various features mentioned in this walk, please don't disturb classrooms or offices, and be aware that throngs of students may suddenly appear during breaks between classes. Most buildings are also open on weekends, though some may not be.

Start this walk at the university's north gate, on the corner of Northeast 45th Street and

university of washington

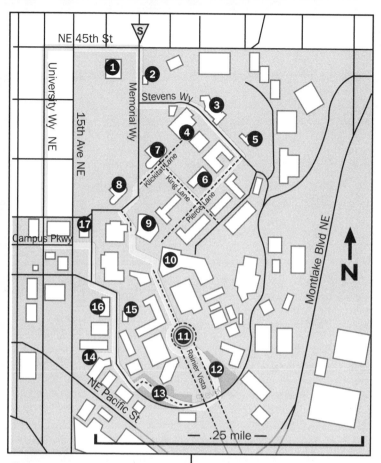

1. **Burke Museum of History and Culture**
2. **Observatory**
3. **Hutchinson Hall**
4. **Balmer and MacKenzie Halls**
5. **Lewis Hall**
6. **Raitt Hall**
7. **Denny Hall**
8. **Parrington Hall**
9. **Kane Hall**
10. **Suzzallo Library**
11. **Rainier Vista**
12. **Sylvan Theater**
13. **Medicinal Herb Garden**
14. **Physics/Astronomy Complex**
15. **Cunningham Hall**
16. **Architecture Hall**
17. **Henry Art Gallery**

Parrington Hall

Memorial Way. Follow Memorial Way to Stevens Way. Memorial Way is lined with 58 **sycamore trees**, each commemorating one of the 58 University of Washington students killed in World War I.
❶ Just past the entry gate, on the right, is the **Burke Museum of History and Culture**, a natural history and anthropology museum established in memory of Judge Thomas Burke. Burke collected Indian artifacts and devoted an entire room in his home to their display. Appropriately, the Burke Museum features exhibits on Northwest Native American tribes and other Pacific Rim cultures as well as the more standard bones and fossils. On the far side of the museum, around the corner, is a separate entrance to the Burke's cloistered and elegant cafe, which features 18th-century waxed-pine

paneling from the music room of a Seattle mansion. The museum is open daily; there's an admission fee, but an additional dollar admits you to the campus's Henry Art Gallery (a later site on this walk) as well.
❷ On the left, across from the Burke Museum, is a tiny stone **observatory** (1895), the second structure built on campus. The observatory still has its original six-inch refractor telescope and is open to the public for free viewing of the stars on Monday and Thursday nights, although the hours change with the seasons; call (206) 543-0126.

❸ **Turn left onto Stevens Way and stroll along it, passing through a parking area.** The first building on the right is the modern red-brick Seafirst Executive Education Center. The Gothic brick structure on the left is

Hutchinson Hall (1927). This building was named for Mary Hutchinson, a longtime executive officer in the physical education department, and was a gymnasium until the 1980s. Just inside the main entrance is a striking tribute to Hutchinson, a relief of a lithe, beautiful figure in a diaphanous dress, gazing into the distance, an unusual tribute to an administrator. The relief seems appropriate to the building's current occupant, the school of drama.

❹ On the right, just beyond the Seafirst Center, are **Balmer Hall** and **MacKenzie Hall**, among the least attractive structures on campus. They're notable only as an illustration of a period in the campus's history; during the 1960s and 1970s the UW's student population doubled in size. Unfortunately, this growth took place at a time when stark, cold architecture was in vogue.

❺ The next building on the left, just past the tennis courts, is the stately brick **Lewis Hall** (its companion, Clark Hall, is down the road a bit). Built as dormitories in 1896, these two structures honoring the famed Northwest explorers constituted the third building project on campus.

Turn right onto the paved pathway opposite Lewis Hall, follow it down a stairway, and walk halfway through the quadrangle. You pass between the **Music Building** and the **Art Building** (1949–50) on the way into the **Liberal Arts Quadrangle**, usually just called the Quad. This is a pic-

turesque square featuring ornate, gargoyled Gothic buildings amid a plush green lawn crisscrossed by footpaths and cherry trees. Designed by the Olmsted Brothers, the landscape architecture firm responsible for much of Seattle's park system, the Quad is especially photogenic in the spring, when the trees are bursting with pink cherry blossoms.

❻ On the right is **Raitt Hall** (1916), the Quad's oldest building, which has had some of its ornamentation altered to suit the changing times. In its original incarnation as the home econom-

Relaxing on Suzzallo's steps

the stolen university: the uw's humble origins

TODAY THE UNIVERSITY OF Washington is a formidable institution with more than 30,000 students, faculty members who've won Nobel Prizes and MacArthur Foundation "genius grants," and graduate studies programs ranked among the best in the country, but it was not always so imposing. When it opened in 1861, the university was more of a grade school with delusions of grandeur and a shady origin.

After Washington became a territory, various towns began to jockey to become the sites of territorial institutions such as the capital, the university, the penitentiary, and the customs house. Seattle founder Arthur Denny wanted the capital for Seattle, but the Reverend Daniel Bagley persuaded him the university was more important. Bagley was a Methodist minister who had migrated west when his anti-slavery views made him unpopular in Illinois; in Seattle, the university became his cause.

The legislators agreed to designate Seattle as the site of the university in 1860. It was a prize granted freely because they didn't expect the town to be able to build it, given the conditions of the designation. The university had to be built on at least 10 acres of land donated by citizens for that purpose, the legislature provided no money to pay for its construction and required that it be completed within a year. The university was a political prize that had been granted to several towns in the past; as each town found it impossible to meet the conditions, the prize would once again revert to the legislature, which then would dole it out to a different town.

At first it looked as if Seattle would fare no better than its predecessors. It seemed preposterous to think that a town of 200 in the middle of nowhere could support a university, or that anyone would be willing to donate a sizable portion of land to such a dubious enterprise. But Arthur Denny gave more than eight acres of his best property—on a knoll near the present site of the Four Seasons Olympic Hotel—for the campus, and others made up the balance.

Bagley and Denny then turned their attention to the issue of financing the campus's construction. Congress had reserved for the Washington Territory two townships of land—about 46,000 acres—"for university purposes." Denny, a member of the state legislature, introduced a bill that, when passed, had the effect of giving Bagley the authority to sell the township land, which he did in order to pay for labor and materials.

By the fall of 1861 the university was complete. The legislature was surprised—and not particularly pleased. Legislators questioned whether it was legal for Bagley to have sold the township land; while the territorial law instigated by Arthur Denny allowed it, federal law did not. Bagley endured years of investigation before his name was cleared. In later years he enjoyed referring to himself as "the man who stole the university."

The university's first session didn't inspire confidence, either. Bagley's son Clarence was the only college-level student; most of the other pupils were grade-school children. (Since people qualified to enter college had proven scarce in the new territory, the university was offering education to the lower grades as well.) The university's president, Asa Mercer, was only 22 and had just graduated from college; he'd recently moved from Ohio to Seattle to join his brother Thomas, who had settled on Queen Anne Hill.

The university didn't see its first graduating class until 1876, more than a decade after it opened—and that class consisted of one student. Eventually, however, both the university and the city around it grew, prompting a move to its more expansive present location in 1895. The university retained its original downtown property, and the rents from this now-prime real estate (roughly from Seneca to Union Streets and Fourth to Sixth Avenues) bring in millions of dollars a year.

ics building, the hall had friezes around its cornice depicting women engaged in various domestic chores, supervised by a bearded male figure holding a tablet. As women achieved greater equality, this decoration grew more controversial and was eventually removed.

In the late 1960s and early 1970s the Quad, along with the rest of campus, was often witness to changing social values. In March 1970, students gathered to present a variety of grievances to the university president. When they received no response, about 200 protesters invaded the Quad and left a trail of destruction.

One of the most famous and spectacular protests at the university, the Freeway March, occurred a couple of months later, in response to two shocking events: U.S. expansion of the Vietnam War into Cambodia, and the shootings of four Kent State University students by National Guard troops. Across the country students went on strike, and this campus was no exception. On May 5, 1970, several thousand students marched from campus through the U District and spontaneously surged onto the I-5 freeway, where they brought all southbound traffic to a halt. The following day 10,000 came out to protest, although this time those who attempted to take the freeway were met with police equipped with tear gas. Two days later, Seattle's mayor closed the freeway express lanes to allow their use by 15,000 marchers attending a rally downtown. Meanwhile, the strike coalition took over a campus building, while others attempted to establish a "free university," and students turned the campus radio station, KUOW, into Radio Free Seattle. Eventually, however, the strike dissolved as the police exerted greater force in response, and students came under increasing criticism.

Today the Quad is much more peaceful, almost idyllic. Students read on the grass, flirt with one another, and gather in small groups to discuss weekend plans. The gargoyle in a gas mask on the nearest

Broken Obelisk, in Red Square

corner of Smith Hall, catycorner from Raitt Hall, is usually the most belligerent-looking creature here. He's actually an allusion to World War I, not 1960s protests; sculptor (and faculty member) Dudley Pratt intended him to evoke the power of Europe, and he's part of a grouping representing the continents. Other gargoyles on Smith Hall relate to themes including the weather, human needs, and Seattle's history. If you like, take a short detour to examine the gargoyles in more detail; then retrace your steps to this spot.

❼ Exit the Quad by turning right onto the pathway just beyond Raitt Hall (the path's official name is King Lane). This pathway leads directly to the university's oldest building, **Denny Hall** (1894–95), which resembles a French Renaissance chateau with a belfry. While the hall's exterior is lovely, the interior is a disappointment. It's cold and institutional, and even the large, colorful paintings in the foyer can't brighten the atmosphere. (Sadly, the interiors of most of the buildings on the Quad have received similarly unsympathetic remodels.) It could've been worse, though: Denny Hall was almost demolished in the 1950s. Fortunately, it's still standing and still beautiful, at least on the outside.

❽ Exiting Denny Hall, turn right onto the pathway in front of it (Klickitat Lane), and follow it, crossing a street and continuing a short distance. To the right is

Suzzallo Reading Room

the Romanesque-derived **Parrington Hall** (1904), all red-brick curves with its round-headed main entrance and arching windows. The second classroom structure built on campus, it was originally a science building but was later transferred to the English department. In 1931 it was posthumously named for Vernon L. Parrington, a popular and Pulitzer Prize–winning English professor—a somewhat curious match since Parrington hadn't thought much of the building, once calling it "the ugliest I have ever seen." Even though the hall's exterior has since been painted and a large front porch removed, it's hard to imagine living in a world where this building could be considered the ugliest—especially given the example of modern-day mistakes like Balmer

and MacKenzie Halls.

Behind the hall is an expansive green space graced by a stand of madrone trees, known in the 1960s as Hippie Hill. This was once a popular gathering spot for pot smokers and counterculture advocates.

Cross the street in front of Parrington Hall, walk around the World War II memorial, and descend the stairs between two modern buildings onto a large plaza. This vast red-brick plaza, officially named Central Plaza but nearly always called **Red Square** (1972), is part of a bizarre landscape dominated by *Broken Obelisk*, a steel sculpture by Barnett Newman, best known for his abstract paintings. Surrounding the plaza is a strange combination of Gothic and modern buildings.

❾ The building on the left, **Kane**

131

Hall (1971), has a distinctly industrial face with monumental squared concrete pillars across the front. However, its interior has an almost medieval charm, with spacious promenades and high windows that let in light but keep the space enclosed, as in an old stone castle. On the second floor is an oddly shaped fresco, by Pablo O'Higgins, which originally graced the walls of the Shipscalers, Drydock, and Miscellaneous Boatworkers Union, Local 541. When the union hall was razed in 1955, the fresco was donated to the university, where it sat in storage for 20 years before being restored and rehung.

The slogans splashed across the

Drumheller Fountain and Rainier view

workers' signs in the painting— "Build a free world / No masters, no slaves / Workers of the world unite!"—are an allusion to the past. Such rallying cries were often issued in the early decades of the 20th century, when Seattle was the center of a sizable left-leaning labor movement that even shut down the city in a general strike in 1919.

The university was no haven from the fear of leftist influence and communism that swept the United States in the 1940s and 1950s. The Washington State Joint House-Senate Committee on Un-American Activities, better known as the Canwell committee (after its chair, Rep. Albert Canwell), began holding hearings in 1948, aiming to determine how far communism had "infiltrated" among the university's faculty. Ultimately, six professors were dismissed or suspended for being or having been members of the Communist Party, and the chilling effect continued for years. Such a political climate may help explain why an artwork dealing with a "radical" topic—workers' struggle—was kept in storage for so long.

To the right of Kane Hall is **Odegaard Undergraduate Library** (1972), and **Meany Hall** (1974), a performing arts theater. Both are simple, cold, modern buildings. These buildings (along with the modestly gothic **Gerberding Hall**) face the most ornate and Gothic of all the buildings on campus.

❿ The monarch of Red Square is **Suzzallo Library** (1923–27), former university president Henry

asa mercer's vision: eve comes to eden

AT THE AGE OF 22 ASA MERCER became the Washington Territorial University's first president. However, by the age of 25 he had abandoned his university post and taken on a more infamous undertaking: the importation of brides for Seattle's bachelors. In the 1860s Seattle was nine-tenths male. Meanwhile, the East Coast had a surplus of unmarried women, largely because the Civil War was decimating the male population. Many people bemoaned this situation, but Asa Mercer was the only one energetic and ambitious enough to do something about it.

Mercer came up with a plan to bring respectable, marriageable Eastern women to the West en masse. Mercer would make two woman-gathering journeys. He returned from the first in 1864 with a modest cargo of 11 single Massachusetts women. A year later nearly all were married to area bachelors, and Mercer began contemplating a second trip—this time he was thinking big, planning to import hundreds of potential brides.

To help finance this sizable undertaking, Mercer sold shares in his enterprise to local men for $300 each. He then headed east, planning to ask President Abraham Lincoln, who was a family acquaintance, to lend him one of the government ships that lay idle at the end of the civil war. His timing was disastrous: En route to Washington in April 1865, he received word that Lincoln had been assassinated. Mercer no longer had friends in high places.

Mercer had no trouble rounding up about 500 respectable single women who were interested in moving to Seattle, but he was unable to convince Washington officials to lend him a war ship. Mercer was forced to buy passage for his charges aboard the vessel *Continental*. Then his endeavor was dealt a second, near-fatal blow; the *New York Herald* published an article charging him with recruiting respectable girls to be sold into slavery in Seattle brothels. When the *Continental* sailed from New York in January 1866, fewer than 100 marriageable women were on board.

After more than three months at sea, the ship arrived in San Francisco, and the by-now-penniless Mercer was forced to send his charges north on lumber schooners. The women were graciously received by Seattle's citizens, but returning flat broke and having delivered considerably fewer women than he'd promised, Mercer was fortunate to escape serious injury. Not long thereafter, he married one of his recruits and left Seattle, eventually becoming a cattle rancher in Wyoming. Over the years the story of the Mercer Girls became the stuff of legend, even inspiring a television series (*Here Come the Brides*) in the 1960s.

133

suzzallo vs. hartley

SUZZALLO LIBRARY WAS NAMED for former university president Henry Suzzallo and epitomizes his approach to governing the university. During his presidency, which began in 1915, Suzzallo oversaw the construction of the liberal arts quadrangle and the university's first stadium, doubled the student population, and changed the university's mascot to the Husky.

Many of Suzzallo's projects were carried out over the opposition of his archrival, Washington state governor Roland Hartley, who called the proposed cathedral-like library "Suzzallo's extravagance" and tried to stop it from being built. While Suzzallo spoke of investing in the future and building a "university of a thousand years," Hartley sought to conserve resources and often vetoed what he considered excessive university appropriations. A skilled politician, Suzzallo was usually able to persuade state legislators to override the vetoes, but eventually Hartley retaliated with a more drastic action. He stacked the board of regents with his own supporters, and it fired Suzzallo in 1926.

Students went on strike in protest, but they were unable to prevail. Suzzallo went on to become president of the Carnegie Foundation, and the regents named Suzzallo Library for him after his death in 1933. The library stands today on Red Square, emblematic of his vision and legacy.

Suzzallo's grandest physical contribution to the campus. When the library first opened, students called it a "cathedral of books." Its facade features eleven 36-foot windows in a row 240 feet long. When it opened it had a compressed-cork floor that absorbed the sound of footsteps, adding to the sense of hushed awe students felt as they entered. At that time only the outer walls of the library were lined with bookshelves; the rest of the space was filled with chairs and tables and reverent students admiring the building's vast open space and academic spirituality.

Suzzallo's interior has suffered a few changes since those early days, the worst offender being a 1960s addition. The library's majesty stops abruptly where the addition begins—it's like walking through a cathedral and suddenly finding yourself in a hospital. But the grandeur remains in the **Suzzallo Reading Room** on the second floor, a must-see with its vaulted ceiling, leaded-glass windows, and ornately carved bookshelves.

⓫ Exiting Suzzallo Library, make a sharp turn to the left, descend the stairs, and walk straight ahead to the fountain. The long, open pathway leading to a breathtaking view of Mount Rainier (on clear days, when "the mountain is out") is appropriately called **Rainier Vista**. Directly ahead is the **Drumheller Fountain** with its vast pool providing a majestic foreground for the mountain view. The pool acquired the nickname Frosh Pond soon after it

Sylvan Theater

was built, when upperclassmen began tossing freshmen into it.

Like many of Seattle's finest parks and tree-lined boulevards, Rainier Vista is a legacy of the Olmsted Brothers firm. The noted landscape architects designed this particular feature—along with a similar pool, then known as Geyser Basin—as part of their work on the grounds for the 1909 Alaska-Yukon-Pacific Exposition (AYP), a world's fair on this site that drew four million visitors. (See "Seattle Throws a Party: The Alaska-Yukon-Pacific Exposition" on page 139.)

⑫ Walk a few hundred feet past the fountain and take the small, unofficial-looking footpath to the left, leading into the woods. You emerge at the **Sylvan Theater**,

actually a clearing amid a small patch of woods that feels like a secret garden in the center of a bustling campus. When martial artist and future movie star Bruce Lee attended the university, he would host informal kung fu practice sessions here.

Standing a bit mysteriously on the clearing are four white Ionic pillars that once supported the university's original downtown building and have now outlasted it by more than 100 years. The first university president to govern beneath these cedar pillars was young Asa Mercer, fresh out of college himself. He served for only a few years and then embarked on a project for which he became far better known: bringing single women to Seattle. (See "Asa Mercer's Vision: Eve Comes to Eden" on page 133.) After the university left its downtown building, the pillars

Medicinal Herb Garden

were placed here to provide a backdrop for commencement ceremonies, which were held in the Sylvan Theater until the student population outgrew it.

⓭ Exiting the Sylvan Theater, turn left and follow Rainier Vista. Just before Stevens Way, take the footpath heading to the right and follow it a few feet. This is the **Medicinal Herb Garden**, established by the department of pharmacy in 1911 to aid its study of herbs and plants, which at that time were the principal ingredients of most pharmaceuticals. All of the roughly 600 plant varieties in the garden are labeled, although their medicinal value is not explained. The Friends of the Medicinal Herb Garden, (206) 543-1126, offers periodic lectures and tours in addition to maintaining the garden.

Stroll the length of the herb garden, following the path across a street as it jogs to the right around a bus shelter. Notice the two monkeys adorning the poles that mark the garden's boundary. Monkeys were a traditional symbol of medicinal herb gardens in medieval Italy.

⓮ Rejoin Stevens Way and follow it past several buildings. On the left is the imaginatively designed red-brick **Physics/ Astronomy complex** (1996), actually two buildings facing each other across a courtyard dominated by *Everything That Rises*, a sculpture by noted artist Martin Puryear. The taller building, which houses the physics department, has scientific formulas carved at eye level in its exterior stone.

Enter the courtyard, step inside the building to the left, and pass through the brick arch to the right. This is the glass-roofed atrium of the **Astronomy Building**. Its light and openness is quite a contrast to the dark, partitioned space in most other modern campus buildings. Suspended from the building's glass dome high above is a large, golden Foucault pendulum, swinging silently and steadily, demonstrating the Earth's rotation.

To shorten this walk by about a half mile, descend the steps at the far end of the Physics/ Astronomy complex and emerge on 15th Avenue Northeast, near Northeast Pacific Street. From here you can return to the university's north gate, where you started, or travel elsewhere in the city, via the bus routes noted at the beginning of this chapter. If you do choose to end your walk here, you'll skip the last four sites: Architecture and Cunningham Halls, the Henry Art Gallery, and The Ave. If you want to continue the loop route, which will lead you back to the university's north gate, read on.

⓯ Retrace your steps, turn left onto Stevens Way, and continue on. Here are the only two campus buildings constructed for the Alaska-Yukon-Pacific Exposition

The Ave

that survive today. On the right is **Cunningham Hall** (1909), built as the Women's Building for the AYP. Considered a temporary structure then, it somehow survived until 1979, when it was rehabilitated. It now serves, appropriately enough, as the campus Women's Center. The hall is named for noted photographer and University of Washington alumna Imogen Cunningham (class of 1907).

⓰ On the left is the Beaux Arts **Architecture Hall** (1909), whose student-run coffee shop on the second floor has an unusual history. Students opened it in the 1960s despite the disapproval of university administrators, who felt it would compete with the student union building's food services. But with conflicts between students and administrators so common in those turbulent times, the adminis-

tration eventually decided to approve this coffee concession as a peace offering. Today there are several student-run coffee shops on campus.

⑰ Continue on Stevens Way as it curves left. Turn right onto the driveway just past Meany Hall and a bus shelter, and follow the driveway to the Henry Art Gallery. The red-brick, Gothic portion of the **Henry Art Gallery** was constructed in 1926 to house the art collection of real estate and railroad baron Horace C. Henry. (Before this gallery was built, Seattle had no art museum at all, and Henry used to open his home to people interested in viewing his collection.) The modern aluminum and glass annex was added in 1996, giving the gallery an extra 30,000 square feet of space to display its nationally recognized collection of cutting-edge contemporary art. The gallery is open daily except Mondays; there's an admission fee except on Thursday evenings, when admission is free.

Walk across the pedestrian overpass near the Henry Art Gallery. Descend the stairs, turn left, follow Campus Parkway to University Way Northeast, and turn right. University Way, usu-

ally referred to as **The Ave**, is the main shopping street in the U District, lined with small businesses catering to student needs: low-cost eateries, book and record stores, copy shops, and the like. Strolling The Ave reveals a different side of the university's culture, one that's less orderly and decorous than the campus you've just toured. While walking here, you're likely to be panhandled, proselytized, and/or exposed to a proliferation of pierced body parts. The smells of a dozen different ethnic cuisines mingle with the scents of coffee and the city.

The U District was once home to people of many different ages and occupations. As the university grew, the number of students living in the U District increased, and families and retirees now find themselves seriously outnumbered. Today the university has more than 30,000 students, and most of them shop on the Ave. On some afternoons it feels as if they're all shopping here at the same time.

Stroll University Way Northeast for several blocks to Northeast 45th Street; turn right and follow 45th to the university's north gate, where you started this walk.

seattle throws a party: the alaska-yukon-pacific exposition

IN THE MID-1900S SEATTLE WAS a major port city of well over 100,000 people, its population having tripled in the last decade, and it had established profitable trade links. Seattle had become Queen City of the Northwest, as it immodestly referred to itself, and its citizens wanted to celebrate. Local business interests began organizing the Alaska-Yukon-Pacific Exposition (AYP), a sort of coming-out party for a rough frontier town turned cosmopolitan.

Organizers chose Alaska as the exposition's theme because of the major role the Klondike gold rush and trade with Alaska had played in the city's development. They persuaded University of Washington president Edmond Meany to host the AYP on his still largely vacant 600-acre campus, constructed a host of ornate buildings there to house it, and hired the Olmsted Brothers firm to design the grounds.

The result was a visual feast. Although considered temporary structures, most of the AYP's buildings were monumental plaster confections. Inside were elaborate displays sponsored by hundreds of cities, states, and foreign countries. Outside, floral displays changed periodically throughout the exposition. At night, the buildings sparkled with over 20,000 electric lights. One visitor enthused, "A gorgeous spectacle met my eyes. . . . I have dreamed often of heaven. My heart thrilled with a sensation that I had passed through the celestial portals."

This visual splendor was not the main attraction, though. The largest crowds congregated at the Pay Streak, which featured carnival rides, games, and sideshows. Visitors could gawk at belly dancers from Cairo, watch mock Civil War battles, and even see a human zoo in which members of a Filipino tribe lived on display in a replica of their village.

The total cost of the AYP was $10 million, a staggering sum at the time, but it turned out to be money well spent. One-quarter of Seattle's residents attended the AYP's opening-day festivities on June 1, 1909, and by the time the exposition concluded in mid-October, almost four million people—including President William Howard Taft—had passed through its gates. The university's Architecture and Cunningham Halls, along with Rainier Vista, remain as reminders of the glorious Alaska-Yukon-Pacific Exposition of 1909.

THE UNIFIED LAKE:

lake union

The working waterfront

Distance: 2.5 miles (one way)   **Approximate time:** 2.5 hours

Looking across Lake Union toward Capitol Hill

IF YOU WERE ROW A BOAT TO the middle of Lake Union, you would behold a breathtaking sight in every direction. The city's skyline gleams to the south; urban structures meld with a verdant landscape on the surrounding hills. Boats and floating homes cluster along the shoreline, and arched bridges add a picturesque touch.

The view from land is a bit different. Lake Union's shoreline is dominated by unabashed commerce and industry. A plethora of parks are scattered along the lake, but most are just tiny sections of shoreline from which you peek out at the water between warehouses and moorages. The scenery is spectacular in some places, unsightly in others.

Yet despite its industrial aesthetic, the shore of Lake Union has its charms. It offers fine dining, historic ships, and charming old houseboats. The lakeshore illustrates Seattle's maritime heritage, its history, and its industry. It's not always beautiful, but it's nearly always interesting.

❶ **Start this walk on the corner of Westlake Avenue North and Aloha Street.** The small green lawn near the lake is **South Lake Union Park**, with benches and picnic tables overlooking its tiny inlet. About 100 years ago, this was the entrance to a bay on the

starting point

South Lake Union Park, at Westlake Avenue North and Aloha Street

finish point

East Roanoke Street and Eastlake Avenue East

parking Parking is available in a lot at South Lake Union Park.

bus connections Catch Route 17 (Loyal Heights) on Fourth Avenue near Pike Street downtown; get off near Westlake Avenue North and Aloha Street. (For more information on bus routes serving this area, see the "Getting Around" section in the introduction to this book.)

To return to your car via bus: Catch the local (not express) Route 70, 71, 72, or 73 (Downtown) along Eastlake Avenue East; get off near Eastlake and Valley Avenue North (it's not well marked, but it's where the bus takes a sharp left turn away from the lake). Follow Valley several blocks to Westlake Avenue North, turn right, and walk one block to Aloha Street.

To return downtown via bus: Catch Route 66, 70, 71, 72, or 73 (Downtown) along Eastlake Avenue East.

far side of Westlake Avenue. (The avenue was originally built on trestles over the lake's marshy shoreline.) The bay was used as a swimming hole and also served as an ice-skating rink when Lake Union froze over in the winters of 1861 and 1875. The old swimming hole has long since been filled in, and the area is now home to offices and light industry.

The shores of this now-vanished bay were the true birthplace of Lake Union, or at least of the name by which we know it. Seattle's early citizens had called the lake *tenas chuck* ("little water" in a local Indian dialect), but at settler Thomas Mercer's Fourth of July picnic near here in 1854 they decided to rename it Lake Union, after Mercer's prophetic vision that a canal through the lake would one day unite the waters of Lake Washington and Puget Sound.

❷ **With the inlet to your left, follow the train tracks as they curve to the left.** The tracks aren't currently in use, so you needn't keep an eye out for oncoming trains. On the left is a large building set back from the road: the **decommissioned U.S.** Navy Reserve Center, now owned by the city of Seattle. Northwest Seaport, the Center for Wooden Boats, and the Maritime Heritage Center hope to open a maritime heritage museum here.

Continue along the tracks to a parking lot on the left, and follow the gravel pathway heading left from the lot. At the very end of the pathway, to the right, is a wooden footbridge leading you into the historic **schooner *Wawona*** (1897), open daily though often covered with tarpaulins. Brochures inside offer a self-guided walking tour of the schooner, which has three masts but no sails or rigging. At 156 feet, she's the largest three-masted sailing schooner ever built in North America, and in her prime she had a reputation for speedy runs up and down the coast. The only survivor of the vast fleet of commercial sailing vessels that formerly plied the Pacific coast, the *Wawona* was the first ship ever listed on the National Register of Historic Places.

lake union

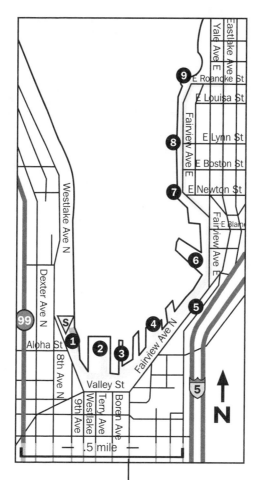

1. **South Lake Union Park**
2. **Decommissioned U.S. Navy Reserve Center**
3. **Center for Wooden Boats**
4. **Puget Sound Maritime Museum Exhibit**
5. **Old Lake Union Steam Plant**
6. **Lake Union Drydock Company**
7. **Terry Pettus Park**
8. **Lynn Street Park**
9. **Roanoke Street Mini Park**

Decommissioned Navy Reserve Center

A nonprofit organization called Northwest Seaport purchased the *Wawona* in 1964 to restore her, but this has proved a slow process. Restoration has started and stopped several times, and the natural forces of decay have taken their toll during every period of neglect. Northwest Seaport is currently attempting to raise the estimated $1.5 million it will take to complete the renovation, so your donations are greatly appreciated.

❸ **Exiting the *Wawona*, follow the gravel pathway to the left along the lakeshore for a short distance.** The wooden gazebo marks the entrance to the **Center for Wooden Boats**, a unique, free working museum whose exhibits are the small wooden sailboats moored along its dock. Each boat has a plaque that describes its history; if you're particularly inspired by one of the museum's exhibits, you can rent it and take it out on the lake. The center also offers sailing lessons, marine skills workshops, and boatbuilding classes. It's open every afternoon except Tuesdays.

Follow the pedestrian pathway—sometimes a sidewalk, sometimes a wooden deck—for about half a mile as it winds along the lakeshore side of various piers. Most of the piers hold restaurants, shops, and yacht brokers, and pleasure boats line the docks, making for a lively nautical scene on summer days. Not that long ago, however, this area was primarily industrial. Sawmills thrived on Lake Union until after World War I; they even changed the lake's shoreline by filling it with sawdust.

Other prominent early businesses included a rug factory, a brewery, a tannery, and a varnish

flying into history: the story of bill boeing

THE FORTUNES OF THE BOEING aircraft company have long had a dramatic effect on the economy of the Puget Sound region. In the early 1970s, when government project cancellations and other factors forced the company to lay off thousands of workers, an anonymous wag erected a billboard on a prominent Seattle thoroughfare reading, "Will the last person leaving Seattle turn out the lights." The city never went dark, though, and today Boeing is stronger than ever: Its jetliners carry 2.5 million passengers a day, and the company's name is known around the world.

This financial leviathan began as a rich man's dalliance. The son of a wealthy Minnesota businessman, the young William Boeing came to Seattle in the 1900s after establishing a successful lumber operation in Hoquiam. He built a 30-room mansion in an exclusive gated community north of the city. One fateful day in 1914 he and his friend Conrad Westervelt went to Leschi Park on Lake Washington, where rides in a rickety Curtiss seaplane were being offered.

Boeing was already an airplane devotee, but the experience changed his life. After taking several flights, he examined the plane and declared that he could build a better one. A short time later he and Westervelt hired an engineer, bought a warehouse on Lake Union, and began working on their first floatplane, which they finished in 1916 and called the B & W, for Boeing and Westervelt.

World War I gave Boeing a unique opportunity to make his airplane-building hobby profitable. His third plane, known as the Model C, won the firm—now known as the Pacific Aero Products Company—a sizable government contract, and the operation moved its headquarters to a former shipyard on the Duwamish River in south Seattle. In 1917 the firm changed its name to the Boeing Airplane Company.

The company continued to operate after the war, suffering during the Depression but keeping its doors open by diversifying, for a time manufacturing household products and furniture. During World War II, Boeing's financial picture brightened as government contracts rolled in for B-29s and other planes. Today Boeing manufactures passenger jetliners such as the familiar 747 and 777, as well as military aircraft and systems used in space exploration.

Boeing's modern headquarters are still located on the Duwamish. The building where the Model C was constructed, affectionately known as the Red Barn, still stands too; it's now an honored part of the Museum of Flight (9404 East Marginal Way South) near Boeing Field.

manufacturer. After the Lake Washington Ship Canal was completed in 1917, providing a way for boats to travel between Lake Union and Puget Sound, Lake Union became a shipbuilding center because of its perfect location: a sheltered freshwater harbor with saltwater access and an abundant supply of timber.

4 Two piers beyond the Center for Wooden Boats, the pier known as Chandler's Cove begins (note the banners). Toward its center is the **Puget Sound Maritime Museum exhibit**, a preview of the maritime heritage museum that proponents hope will one day inhabit the former U.S. Navy Reserve Center you saw earlier. The exhibit features wooden ship models and black-

The old Lake Union Steam Plant

and-white photos of historic ships. Related books and souvenirs are also available. A tour boat is located on the far eastern end of this pier; if you like, you can explore the area's waterways by boat for a while.

At the end of the next pier (called Yale Street Landing) is a tiny circular playground and, just past it, a gate that looks locked but is usually open. At the end of the dock beyond the gate is one of the city's most unusual lodging options: the red-and-white **MV Challenger B&B**. A 1944 Army tugboat whose tugging days are behind it, the MV *Challenger* has been renovated into a floating "bunk and breakfast" hotel. You can tour the boat for a small fee if you call ahead, (206) 340-1201; otherwise, admire it from behind a second gate (which *is* locked).

Leaving the lakeshore, cross the parking area; turn left onto Fairview Avenue North and follow it for several blocks until it becomes a floating sidewalk. This area is undergoing rapid development; its many recently constructed or renovated buildings include a large hotel and the internationally respected Fred Hutchinson Cancer Research Center, both across the street.

South Lake Union used to be much more residential. As you pass the hotel, look up at the hill to your right; the wooden houses just this side of the freeway are the remnants of one of Seattle's oldest neighborhoods, one of the first to be developed when the city began to spread beyond Pioneer Square. It was home to working-class Norwegian, Swedish, German, and Russian immigrants as well as a few wealthy citizens. When the ship canal was completed in 1917, though, this area became increasingly industrial.

❺ On the right is the **old Lake Union Steam Plant**, with its signature smokestacks. Constructed in the early 1900s, the structure was adapted in the 1990s for use as an office building by ZymoGenetics, a biotechnology research firm. The facsimile smokestacks recall the building's days as a coal-powered 10,000-kilowatt steam plant; the decaying wooden dock opposite the building was once used to unload coal and, later, fuel oil. Today it's a favorite resting spot for cormorants, grebes, and the occasional blue heron and bald eagle.

Houseboat dock on Fairview Avenue

❻ Cross the floating sidewalk, turn left onto Fairview Avenue East almost immediately, and stroll along it for several blocks to East Blaine Street.

Fairview Avenue East becomes a little-traveled back road that later grows narrow and a bit rutted. The **Lake Union Drydock Company**, one of the oldest businesses on the lake, occupies a 12-acre complex here. The company used to build yachts and Coast Guard cutters (and also made the first water skis in the United States), but today it specializes in ship repair.

Lake Union Drydock first opened its doors in 1919—a particularly bad year for the shipbuilding industry, since World War I

Houseboats on Lake Union

had just ended and orders were drying up. When wages for shipyard workers were cut, most of Seattle's unions joined together to declare the nation's first general strike, which brought the city to a halt for several days—just one of the many events of the era that furthered Seattle's reputation as a left-wing town.

The company survived that turbulent period, and was one of the few shipbuilders that were able to do so. In its first years, the operation had a clear view of Lake Union's "ghost ships": rotting wooden hulls of unfinished warships left floating in the lake, abandoned, at the end of World War I. They were eventually salvaged for scrap metal at the beginning of World War II.

On the right, just past East Blaine Street, is a restaurant housed in a peculiar structure that looks somewhat like an old farmhouse with strange appendages. The appendages are actually **boxcars**, reminders of the railroad-themed eatery that occupied this site many years ago.

Opposite the boxcar restaurant are the buildings of the **National Oceanic and Atmospheric Administration Pacific Marine Center**, the headquarters for a fleet of ships that travels the world gathering information on oceans, climate, and atmosphere. The center isn't open to the public, but during the winter you may be able to schedule a tour of the ships in advance; (206) 553-7659.

❼ Contine strolling along Fairview Avenue East for several blocks to East Lynn Street. On the left, at East Newton Street, is one of the Eastlake neighborhood's numerous street-end parks. Most are so small you can walk right by without noticing them,

living on water

TOURISTS HAVE LONG CONSID-
ered Seattle's houseboat communities a charming dash of local color.
Unfortunately, the communities have
never enjoyed such wide acceptance
among local landlubbers.

In the early 1900s there were
houseboats on Lake Union, Elliott
Bay, the Duwamish River, and Lake
Washington. At that time most houseboaters were laborers and tramps
who found they could pay little or no
rent by living in makeshift homes
placed on real estate of uncertain
ownership: the water. Their more
respectable neighbors on solid ground
often resented having this supposedly
unsavory lot living so near.

Living aboard boats encouraged
hospitality and bonding between
water dwellers. Houseboat communities were known to be both more hospitable and more indulgent than
land-based neighborhoods. Music,
dancing, and drinking predominated,
much to the consternation of nearby
homeowners. A 1908 *Seattle Post-
Intelligencer* article described houseboaters thus: "They're a lazy crew, the
houseboat mariners. They idle away
precious hours, forgetting that the
real object of life is to make money,
and that time is money." Of course,
houseboaters might have responded,
when your neighbors are your friends,
you have no rent to pay, and the lake
is your front yard, what need do you
have to spend time making money?

Over the years most of Seattle's
houseboat communities have been
eliminated one by one. In the 1930s,
for instance, the city shut down most of
Lake Washington's houseboats on
health grounds. Today the only surviving

communities are on Lake Union.

Houseboaters are still a somewhat
bohemian element; waterfront living
attracts poetic and artistic souls,
those unconventional enough to
choose a compact floating home over
a suburban ranch-style with four bedrooms and a manicured lawn. But
houseboats are no longer a cheap
housing alternative for the working
class; most have been remodeled or
expanded, and some even have sky-
lights and hot tubs. The movie *Sleep-
less in Seattle* romanticized the
modern Seattle houseboat lifestyle,
and the romance is still undeniable—
but securing it nowadays usually
requires a hefty paycheck.

View from Lynn Street Park

and many are unmarked, but each provides a unique viewpoint on the lake. **Terry Pettus Park**, with its picnic table and floating dock, was named for the journalist who led a successful campaign to preserve Seattle's houseboat communities.

A short distance farther, also on the left, is one of those **houseboat communities**. Houseboats first appeared on Lake Union in 1911–17, as cheap and convenient housing for the workers who were building the ship canal. Most early houseboats were thrown together with scrap lumber, but today they're considerably more upscale. (See "Living on Water" on page 149.)

You'll see the entrances to a number of houseboat communities

on the left as you continue along Fairview. You'll also see signs reminding you that the long piers at which the boats are tied are private property. Houseboats have a definite allure, and some of their residents have grown a bit weary of all the attention.

❽ Several blocks farther, on the left at East Lynn Street, is the small **Lynn Street Park**, which has benches and a tiny beach. Just beyond the park, built on a pier over the water, are the five-story Union Harbor condominiums, whose construction led the city council to pass the Shoreline Management Act in 1972 to prevent further overwater development. Eastlake residents feared that similar structures would be built all along the lake, walling it off from view and access.

Continue on Fairview Avenue East for several blocks, following it as it curves to the right and ends at Roanoke Street.
❾ On the corner of Fairview and Roanoke is **Roanoke Street Mini Park**, bordering the lake. On this site in 1916, in a wooden hangar 188 feet long, **the first Boeing airplane** was built. After Boeing received a government contract to build planes for World War I, it moved its principal operation to a factory on the Duwamish River in south Seattle.

In 1973, Boeing's historic wooden hangar was razed by developers who envisioned a 112-unit condominium on the site. After the Shoreline Management Act thwarted their plans, a community of spacious, relatively uniform houseboats was built here instead; to see them, cross the small parking area. (You'll also see the slightly larger other half of the Roanoke Street Mini Park.) The dock used by these houseboats was constructed for the condominiums before that project was abandoned.

Turn right onto East Roanoke Street and follow it for several blocks to Eastlake Avenue East. The Eastlake neighborhood's character was permanently altered in the 1960s when Interstate 5 was built through its center, destroying hundreds of homes and businesses.

Eastlake Avenue marks the end of this walk. From here you can return to South Lake Union Park (where you parked your car), or

Fishing boats

travel elsewhere in the city, via the bus routes noted at the beginning of this chapter.

Alternatively, you can walk back to the park via Eastlake Avenue, following the loop route outlined on the accompanying map. Eastlake is the major arterial of this neighborhood, but it's not the best for walking: Cars tend to zoom by, and the street is dotted with unpicturesque office buildings and condominiums. On the other hand, strolling Eastlake gives you the opportunity to sample one of the neighborhood's eateries, most of which are located just a few blocks down, between East Louisa and East Boston Streets. The offerings include a bakery and several pubs, a longtime Seattle breakfast haven (the 14 Carrot Cafe), a tapas bar, and several Italian restaurants.

the great strike

SEATTLE TODAY SEEMS AS devoted to capitalism as any American metropolis, but during the first four decades of the 20th century the city, and indeed the entire state, was renowned as a bastion of socialism, even moving James Farley, postmaster general under President Franklin D. Roosevelt, to speak of the "47 states and the Soviet of Washington."

The state's leftism became evident as early as 1896, when Washington elected a populist governor. Around that same time the Brotherhood of the Cooperative Commonwealth established a commune on Whidbey Island and worked to secure Washington for socialism. Although they were unsuccessful in that ambitious quest, socialist principles were widely accepted in the state.

The local affinity for socialism was one of the factors leading to the famed Seattle general strike of 1919; the end of World War I was another. Government contracts had brought wartime jobs and prosperity to Seattle, a major shipbuilding center. When the war ended, the government cancelled orders for warships, and the shipbuilding adjustment board cut workers' wages. Shipwrights protested, tension spread to other industries, and eventually workers from 110 Seattle unions joined together and voted to strike.

On the morning of February 6, 1919, about 60,000 workers, representing most of the unions in the city, walked off the job and brought Seattle to a grinding halt. The strike's opponents feared violence and hysteria, but everything remained orderly. As strike leaders had arranged, hospitals and essential services continued to operate, and a kitchen run by strikers provided food to any citizen who might otherwise have been left hungry. Striking workers became "labor guards" and helped the police patrol the streets, which were deathly quiet.

There was talk of anarchy and of a Bolshevik revolution, but in the end nothing changed. Perhaps the strike was too orderly for its own good. News of strike developments never reached the public because newspapers did not print. Strike organizers had no clear idea what they hoped to accomplish by striking, and as the city lay silent, strikers lost their sense of solidarity. The strike ended on February 11, less than a week after it had begun.

The workers won no concessions through their protest, but Seattle mayor Ole Hanson, previously considered a buffoon, found his status considerably enhanced. Quick to assume credit for subduing the strike, Hanson later toured the country lecturing about how he had personally squelched the Bolshevik threat in Seattle.

THE WELL-LOVED LITTLE LAKE:

Distance: 1.6 miles (one way)   **Approximate time:** 2 hours

GREEN LAKE PARK IS THE MOST popular park in Washington, receiving over a million visitors a year according to the Seattle parks department. On a sunny day, the lake can draw as many as 7,200 visitors; the nearly 3-mile walking/cycling trail that circles it is in almost constant use. Although it's one of the city's least spectacular waterfront pathways, it remains the popular favorite—largely because it's centrally located, pleasant, and always hopping. People are at least as interested in looking at other people as at scenery, and the atmosphere at Green Lake Park on a summer day is proof of that.

This one-way walk starts in Ravenna Park, following a relatively secluded forest path. After leaving the park, the route follows a lovely green parkway and emerges amid the gaiety of Green Lake's teeming masses. You may start this walk in isolation and end it in a crowd.

❶ **Start this walk in the parking area of Ravenna Park, off Northeast 58th Street and 20th Avenue Northeast.** This is an entrance to **Ravenna Park**.

Down in Ravenna's ravine

You'll see picnic grounds and a shelter on a lawn surrounded by trees. A small restroom structure is on the left.

starting point

Ravenna Park parking area, off Northeast 58th Street and 20th Avenue Northeast

finish point

Green Lake Park, on East Green Lake Drive North at Ravenna Boulevard Northeast

getting there

parking Parking is available in lots at Ravenna Park and Green Lake Park.

bus connections Enter the University Street bus tunnel station on University Street near Third Avenue, proceed to the northbound side of the tunnel, and catch Route 71 (Wedgwood). Get off on 15th Avenue Northeast near Northeast 58th Street, stroll down 58th for several blocks to 20th Avenue Northeast, and follow the winding, paved road into the parking area. Note: On Sundays, when the bus tunnel is closed, catch Route 71 on Third Avenue near Union Street. (To get information on the bus tunnel or on other bus routes serving this area, see the "Getting Around" section in the introduction to this book.)

To return to your car via bus: Catch Route 48 (Columbia City/Rainier Beach) on Ravenna Boulevard Northeast near East Green Lake Drive North; get off on 15th Avenue Northeast near Northeast 58th Street, and follow 58th to 20th Avenue Northeast.

To return downtown via bus: Catch Route 16 or 26 (Downtown) on Ravenna Boulevard Northeast near East Green Lake Drive North, at one of the two bus stops in front of the supermarket.

Cross the lawn to a wooden sign marking the beginning of the Ravenna Valley Self-Guided Trail. Follow the trail downhill, keeping to the left, until you reach a hillside stairway on the right. Stepping off Ravenna Park's lawn and onto this path through a forested ravine is like stepping into another world. Birds sing, light sifts through the trees, and a creek gurgles happily. The city seems miles away. You cross under a narrow bridge that's high above the trail.

Descend the stairs and cross a wooden footbridge over a stream. The stream is **Ravenna Creek**, at one time the outlet for Green Lake. The creek ran from the west side of Green Lake, along Ravenna Boulevard, and into the University Slough (just south of where the University Village shopping center is today).

Around 1912, when the city lowered Green Lake's water level to increase the strip of parkland surrounding it, this waterway lost its principal source. Today Ravenna Creek is a relative trickle, fed by natural springs and runoff. The creek exits the park through a drainage pipe and ends up in, of all the glorious places, the Metro sewage-treatment plant. A group of citizens known as the Ravenna Creek Alliance is campaigning to again open the creek to daylight east of Ravenna Park.

Stroll along the trail for about a quarter mile. Here the trail has the air of a wooded country lane, bordered by lush ferns on one side and the creek on the other.

Ravenna Park was once a private preserve. In the 1880s William W. Beck and his wife built a music pavilion, a dressing room, and benches amid the old-growth forest in this ravine and charged admission to their natural amusement park, which they named Ravenna after an Italian

green lake

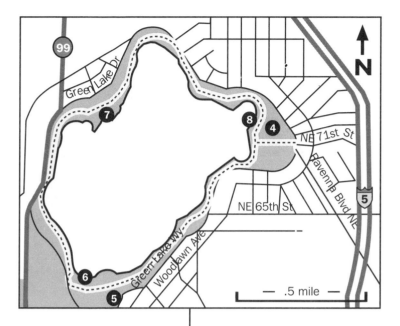

1. Ravenna Park
2. Cowen Park
3. Park Vista apartment building
4. Green Lake Community Center and Evans Pool
5. Pitch 'N Putt Golf
6. Small Craft Center
7. Bathhouse Theatre
8. Boat rentals

ravenna park

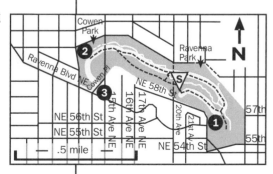

town known for its forests. In 1911, the Seattle parks department acquired the Becks' land and logged it off, but left it undeveloped for many years.

❷ After crossing under a stately bridge that's also a historic landmark, you enter **Cowen Park**, which adjoins Ravenna Park. Here the creek seems to disappear. In 1906 the park's namesake, Charles Cowen, bought 40 acres of what was once swampland north of the University of Washington; a year later he donated these 12 acres to the city, in hopes of spurring development of his lands nearby.

❸ **Leave Cowen Park by following the paved path to the left; turn right onto Cowen Place Northeast and follow it to**

Cottages on Ravenna Boulevard

Ravenna Boulevard Northeast. Directly across from Cowen Park is the elegant brick **Park Vista apartment building** (1924), which was designed to complement the park and Ravenna Boulevard, the tree-lined parkway that will now take you from Cowen Park to Green Lake Park.

Turn right and stroll along Ravenna Boulevard Northeast for about three-quarters of a mile, until it ends at East Green Lake Drive North. Ravenna Creek once flowed along this route. When the creek was cut off from its source by the lowering of Green Lake, this classic boulevard, with its wide green median, rows of trees, and bungalow-style homes, was constructed over the old creekbed. The peaceful parkway gives Ravenna Boulevard an

elegant air. Like many of Seattle's parks and parklike boulevards, it was designed by the Olmsted Brothers, a nationally known landscape architecture firm.

After about half a mile, you pass under Interstate 5. As you near Green Lake Park, on the right is the red-brick **John Marshall School** (1927). Originally a junior high, the impressive Georgian structure now houses an alternative high school and other school-related programs. Its architect, Floyd Naramore, designed more than 20 area schools in a little more than a decade as the architect for the Seattle School District. He and three colleagues later formed a partnership that evolved into the well-known contemporary Seattle architectural firm NBBJ.

A few blocks farther, across Green Lake Drive, the recreational paradise of **Green Lake Park** lies before you. To the right are several eateries, including a sandwich place, an ice cream shop, and the ubiquitous Starbucks.

Cross East Green Lake Drive North to Green Lake Park. In 1910, when the city bought the land that would become Green Lake Park, it was only a narrow strip. The city lowered the lake seven feet, producing the desired wide strip of parkland around the lake but also blocking the lake's drainage and causing it to turn green. (See "Why Is the Lake Green?" on this page.)

If you're energetic, join the parade of pedestrians (and joggers, cyclists, and Rollerbladers) circling

why is the lake green?

GREEN LAKE'S DEPTHS WERE carved out of the surrounding hills by a glacier some 50,000 years ago. Shortly afterward, the lake began silting up and was on its way to becoming a silt-filled meadow when the Seattle parks department stepped into the picture around 1910. The city bought a thin strip of property around Green Lake, and— at the recommendation of the Olmsted Brothers firm, the park's designers—lowered the lake's water level in order to widen its shoreline. This had a dramatic, unexpected effect on the lake: It began to turn green.

When its waterline was lowered, Green Lake lost its outlet, Ravenna Creek. This turned the lake into a stagnant body of water, a hospitable host for billions of algae. It became a murky green soup reeking of algae—no longer very attractive as a recreational facility, to say the least. The government tried dredging the lake and dumping two tons of copper sulfate into it, which was effective for a time. Today the city continues to dredge the lake as necessary, and pumps excess reservoir water through Green Lake to regulate its water quality and occasionally treats it with aluminum sulfate. This hasn't completely solved the problem, but Green Lake is no longer as green as it used to be.

Running around the lake

the lake. If you're not inclined to walk the 2.8-mile loop, you have many other options. At various points around the lake, you'll find courts for tennis and basketball and fields for soccer and baseball. Lounge in the park, take a dip at one of several swimming beaches, or enjoy one of the other Green Lake attractions listed below.

④ Community Center and Evans Pool. Swimming and recreational programs for all ages and interests. The community center operates from a 1929 field house; the pool was added in 1955. Open daily, year-round.

⑤ Pitch 'N Putt Golf. A nine-hole course. Open March through mid-October.

⑥ Small Craft Center. Year-round classes in rowing, canoeing, kayaking, and sailing.

⑦ Bathhouse Theatre. This 1928 bathing pavilion was converted into a theater in 1970. The resident theatrical company specializes in classic European and American plays with a twist.

⑧ Boat rentals. Paddleboats, rowboats, kayaks, canoes, sailboats, and sailboards. Open daily, April through Labor Day.

Green Lake Park marks the end of this walk. After you've explored it to your heart's content, you can return to Ravenna Park (where you parked your car), or travel elsewhere in the city, via the bus routes noted at the beginning of this chapter.

the olmsted legacy

SEATTLE WOULD BE AN ENTIRELY different city without its more than 400 parks and 6,000 acres of parkland. It would have fewer memorable vistas, less neighborly neighborhoods, and an absence of green spaces to walk, bike, and explore. In fact, it wouldn't even be the Emerald City. So it's hard to believe that for its first 60 years, Seattle had hardly any parks at all.

It wasn't until the early 1900s that local leaders, alarmed by the rate at which the city's natural beauty was being destroyed, decided that Seattle needed a park system. To design it, they engaged one of the best landscape architecture firms in the country: the Olmsted Brothers of Brookline, Massachusetts. The firm's principals, John C. and Frederick Jr., were the sons of Frederick Law Olmsted, best known for designing New York's Central Park.

In 1903, when the Olmsted Brothers firm presented its park plan, there were only a few publicly owned open areas in Seattle. Even so, the city's park potential caused John C. Olmsted to wax lyrical: "I do not know of any place where the natural advantages for parks are better than here. They . . . will be, in time, one of the things that will make Seattle known all over the world."

The Olmsted plan featured a chain of parks linked by landscaped parkways, with no house in Seattle more than one and a half miles from a park.

The parkways formed two almost continuous loops from Seward Park to Discovery Park and back, and from Seward Park to Alki and back.

Then as now, not everyone agreed that the city should spend money on parks. A 1908 article in the *Argus*, a local periodical, opposed the notion on the grounds that building parks would be more beneficial to posterity than to Seattle's current residents. It opined: "Seattle is today spending thousands of dollars that will be enjoyed by posterity. But there are some things that posterity should do for itself."

Fortunately for posterity (us), Seattle's voters didn't heed this argument. They approved a city bond for park construction based on the Olmsted plan in 1910, and parks and parkways went up across the city. In addition to Ravenna Boulevard, landscaped parkways designed by the Olmsteds include Interlaken Boulevard, Lake Washington Boulevard, and Magnolia Boulevard. (Parkways planned by the Olmsted firm but never built include one from Seward Park to Beacon Hill, and another from Woodland Park to Discovery Park.) At the time the Olmsted plan was enacted, Seattle had only five public parks (Denny Park, Volunteer Park, Kinnear Park, Rodgers Park, and Woodland Park). Dozens more were constructed as a result of the Olmsted Brothers' work, an invaluable legacy that endures to this day.

THE ORIGINAL CITY:

Distance: 3 miles (one way)   **Approximate time:** 2 hours

STANDING ON ALKI BEACH ON a sunny summer day it is hard to imagine a more lovely setting. This beach has mountain views, a long public shoreline, and a beachfront culture that is reminiscent of a more southerly climate. Alki's flaw may be that it is too popular—it draws thousands of admirers from across the city.

In 1851, this stretch of beach, with its beautiful setting and views, was the first glimpse Seattle's founders had of their new city. When that intrepid party of Dennys, Borens, Lows, Bells, and Terrys disembarked from the schooner *Exact* and landed on this earthly paradise, however, they were not awed. The women in the party took one look around and broke into tears. It was a stormy November, and the view apparently impressed them less than the rain.

Frisbee at Duwamish Head

starting point

Seacrest Park on Harbor Avenue Southwest near California Way Southwest

finish point

Alki Avenue Southwest near 61st Avenue Southwest

parking Free parking is available in the parking lot at Seacrest Park, but not many spaces are available and it's limited to two hours; street parking is available along Harbor Avenue Southwest and Alki Avenue Southwest. Parking can be tight at peak times, but you can usually find a space on Harbor Avenue if you're patient and drive far enough.

bus connections Catch Route 37 (Admiral District) on Second Avenue near Pike Street downtown; get off on Harbor Avenue Southwest past Salty's on Alki, a popular bayfront restaurant that's tough to miss, and walk toward the long pier. Or, in the summer, take Metro's water taxi from Pier 54 or 66, on the downtown waterfront, to Seacrest Park. The water taxi runs approximately every 30 minutes, though there are some gaps in the schedule. Call the Water Taxi Hotline for information, (206) 684-0224. (For more information on bus routes serving this area, see the "Getting Around" section in the introduction to this book.)

To return to your car (or the water-taxi dock) via bus: Catch Route 37 (Downtown) on Alki Avenue Southwest near 61st Avenue Southwest; get off near Seacrest Park, on Harbor Avenue Southwest near California Way Southwest.

To return downtown via bus: Catch Route 37 or 56 (both Downtown) along Alki Avenue Southwest near 61st Avenue Southwest.

The more optimistic souls gave their settlement the name New York-Alki ("Alki" being an Indian trade-jargon word for "by and by"), but after a few months many in the party moved to the inner shores of Elliott Bay, where Pioneer Square is now located.

The heart of this walk is a stroll along the length of Alki Beach Park, which extends along the shoreline for about two miles. You'll start with drop-dead views of Seattle's skyline, enjoy mountain scenery along the way, and conclude with a visit to some historic sites and a diminutive lighthouse.

❶ Start this walk on Harbor Avenue Southwest near California Way Southwest. This is **Seacrest Park**, a waterfront viewpoint that also has a fishing pier and a bait shop. Walk out to the edge of the long pier and enjoy its million-dollar panorama of the Seattle skyline. To the right is a considerably less valuable view of industrial **Harbor Island**, located

at the mouth of the Duwamish River. Harbor Island was constructed of sand and silt dredged from the river when it was straightened in the early 20th century. The island's container port is the fifth largest in the United States and the 20th largest in the world.

Leaving Seacrest Park, turn right onto Harbor Avenue Southwest and follow it to California Way Southwest. The Native Americans of this area used to forage in the rich shellfish bed once located in this place, which they called Skwuh-dkx.

Harbor Avenue is bordered on the left by a tall ridge where houses perch. In winter, this bluff sometimes becomes saturated with rain and gradually shifts. These

alki

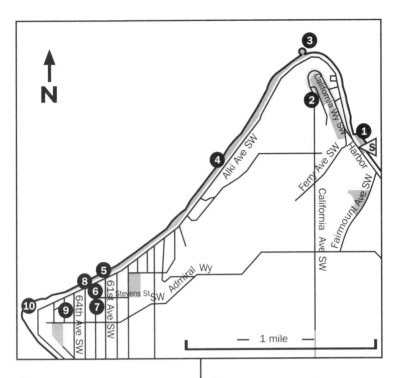

1. Seacrest Park
2. Hamilton Viewpoint
3. Duwamish Head
4. Alki Beach Park
5. Replica of the Statue of Liberty
6. Alki Homestead Restaurant
7. Log House Museum
8. Birthplace of Seattle Monument
9. Seattle's oldest house
10. Alki Point Lighthouse

The unmovable cottage

homes may eventually tumble downhill—but until then, they have wonderful views.

❷ Atop this bluff is a lookout park, called **Hamilton Viewpoint**, which offers the truly energetic a spectacular panoramic view of mountains, water, and skyline. If you're feeling energetic and don't mind lengthening your walk by about a mile, follow California Way up a steep incline to reach the viewpoint, and then retrace your steps to Harbor Avenue.

❸ **Continue on Harbor Avenue Southwest to the tip of the West Seattle peninsula.** The tip of the peninsula is called **Duwamish Head**. While this area is undergoing a condominium boom today, in earlier days Harbor Avenue was lined with tiny cottages. On the left is a remnant of those days: a

small, dilapidated cottage (1023 Harbor Avenue Southwest) whose owner refused to sell her property to developers. Her home is now surrounded on three sides, quite incongruously, by a modern upscale condo building.

Follow Harbor Avenue Southwest as it curves around Duwamish Head and becomes Alki Avenue Southwest. At the tip of the peninsula, on the right, is an inviting bayfront overlook set with benches and what appear to be telescopic viewers, with tablets embedded in the sidewalk nearby in an attractive arching pattern. Have a seat for a moment and enjoy the panoramic view of Seattle, from Magnolia to Harbor Island. If you're lucky, a ferry will glide by and give the scene the crowning touch.

Take a look through one of the viewers, but don't be surprised if you don't recognize what you see. The viewer shows you an image related to the subject of the tablets on the sidewalk. Here it shows the settlement of Alki by Seattle's founders. Watch for other heritage overlooks as you continue along the shoreline.

Just past the overlook, on the right, is **Luna Park**, a small waterfront city park dominated by a large anchor retrieved from Elliott Bay in the 1950s. For a half-dozen years this unassuming spot was the site of a popular amusement park, also called Luna Park, that lit up the night with a thousand electric lights.

Opened in 1907, Luna Park was built over Puget Sound on a 12-acre wooden platform, and at low tide you can still see some of the platform's pilings. Called "the Coney Island of the West," the first Luna Park featured rides such

as the Joy Wheel, the Canals of Venice, the Great Figure Eight Roller Coaster, and the enigmatically named Infant Electrobator. Other attractions included an indoor swimming pool, a movie house, a dance palace, and a cocktail lounge that called itself "the longest bar on the bay."

Passengers could take an eight-minute ferry from downtown Seattle to Luna Park for just a nickel—one of the most convenient and least expensive "getaways" around. In summer, tents were pitched on the waterfront from Duwamish Head all the way to Alki Point, along the same stretch of shoreline covered by this walk.

❹ Enjoy a leisurely stroll along Alki Avenue Southwest for a bit less than two miles, to 61st

A beach cottage at Duwamish Head

Avenue Southwest. Your stroll will take you all the way to Alki Point, which you can see jutting to the right on the horizon. This entire stretch of waterfront is **Alki Beach Park**. From the park you can see Bainbridge Island across Puget Sound and, on a clear day, the Olympic Mountains on the horizon.

The fact that this lovely beach and this view exist today is a credit to the foresight of the Seattle parks department, which bought this land in the early 20th century to preserve it for the public as a park. Had the city not done so, your view would undoubtedly be obscured by homes and condominiums like those lining the opposite side of Alki Avenue.

As it follows the shoreline, Alki Beach Park is alternately a park and a beach. At regular inter-

View from Alki Beach

vals, heritage overlooks with benches, viewers, and tablets in the sidewalk invite you to learn more about such topics as canoes in Native American culture and indigenous flora and fauna.

Near Bonair Drive Southwest, just past the halfway point of your stroll, the beach widens. If it's sunny, you'll likely be surrounded by Seattleites of all ages enjoying the warmth; on a more typical Seattle day (cloudy), you may have the beach all to yourself. If you'd like to experience Alki after dark sometime, note that the park allows campfires in designated spots on the beach; just be sure to observe any burn bans.

This stretch of sidewalk is also punctuated here and there with heritage tablets of a different style than those at the overlooks. In addition to images of local flora and fauna, there's a Native American story about the creation of the

the alki landing: where it all began

MOST MEMBERS OF SEATTLE'S founding party came west in the same wagon train, which included members of the Denny and Boren families who traveled west from Cherry Grove, Illinois, in 1851. They planned to settle together in Oregon's Willamette Valley, but one member of the party, Arthur Denny, picked up other ideas along the way. He heard stories about the Puget Sound area, then largely unsettled because no road yet connected it to the Oregon Trail. He realized that all the Puget Sound area needed was a road and it could contain the West's newest metropolis.

After arriving in Portland, Arthur Denny sent two men ahead to choose a location for his future empire: his younger brother David, a lad of 19, and John Low, who had joined the Denny-Boren party on their way west. They hooked up with another would-be empire builder, Lee Terry, and sailed toward Puget Sound.

The three eventually selected Alki Point as their settlement site, and Denny and Terry set about building a cabin while Low returned to Portland to summon the others. Terry later went off on an extended mission to find a certain tool needed to make shingles for the roof, leaving David Denny alone in a roofless cabin for weeks. In Terry's absence, Denny fell ill, lost most of his provisions to skunks, and injured his foot with an ax, leaving him unable to work or hunt.

Back in Portland, Arthur Denny received John Low's good tidings. A party of 10 adults and 12 children hired passage on the schooner *Exact*, and on November 13, 1851, the group landed and surveyed their promised land. They found a cold, rainy shore; a roofless cabin that was to be the only shelter for two dozen people; and a feverish David Denny, who limped out of the cabin and said to his compatriots, "I wish you hadn't come!"

It was hardly an auspicious beginning, but the adventurers managed to build cabins and survive the winter, naming their settlement New York–Alki (a name bestowed by Terry who was originally from New York). However the site's lack of a deep, protected harbor prompted Arthur Denny to search for a better location. In February 1852 he, Carson Boren, and William Bell settled on Elliott Bay after measuring its depth with a horseshoe and clothesline and discovering its deep harbor. They divided and platted the land from present-day Belltown to Pioneer Square. A good number of Alki's residents joined them, and together they began the rival town that became known as Seattle. Many years later the community at Alki was annexed to the city of Seattle.

Alki's Lady Liberty

butterfly, and even a poem called "Alki Beach," by the late Seattle poet Richard Hugo. These tablets were installed as part of the Mountains to Sound Greenway project. This project is coordinated by a non-profit organization that works to preserve greenspace and construct trails along the I-90 corridor between a location east of Snoqualmie Pass and Puget Sound.

❺ When you reach 61st Avenue Southwest you'll find a small **replica of the Statue of Liberty** opposite the street end on your right. It was donated to the city in 1952 by the Boy Scouts. Its placement may seem odd, until you realize that the community that Seattle's founders established here was called New York-Alki. What would New York be without the Statue of Liberty?

❻ Turn left onto 61st Avenue Southwest and follow it for half a block. On the right is the **Alki Homestead Restaurant**, located in a 1903 log home originally known as Fir Lodge. Built for William and Gladys Bernard, it was constructed of driftwood carried from Alki Beach, and its fireplace is made of scavenged beach rocks. Over the years the house has changed much less than the neighborhood: In 1903 Fir Lodge was a house by the beach, on an almost roadless plateau, in a stand of old-growth forest. The restaurant is open for dinner only, Wednesday through Sunday.

❼ Continue on 61st Avenue Southwest to Southwest Stevens Street. Just past Stevens, on the right, is the **Log House Museum**, located in the former carriage house of the Bernard estate. The displays tell you about this area's place in Duwamish Indian culture and its history as an urban neighborhood. The museum is open limited hours Thursday through Sunday; call for the current schedule, (206) 938-5293. Admission is by donation.

❽ Retrace your steps to Alki Avenue Southwest. Cross Alki Avenue, turn left, and follow it to 63rd Avenue Southwest. Here you will find a park with a lawn, gnarled old trees, picnic tables, and shelters.

On the right is the **Birthplace of Seattle Monument**, an obelisk marking the spot where those who were to found Seattle disembarked from the schooner *Exact* on November 13, 1851. Catycorner, in front of an apartment building across the street, is a plaque marking the spot where David Denny, a scout for the landing party, erected Seattle's first cabin and waited for his compatriots to join him.

Seattle's Birthplace Monument contains a fragment of what is commonly regarded as the nation's birthplace. The small chunk of Plymouth Rock was placed in the base of the obelisk in 1926; a plaque describes its cross-country excursion and how it came to be here.

❾ Continue on Alki Avenue Southwest, then turn left onto 64th Avenue Southwest and follow it for about half a block. This otherwise unremarkable street has one claim to fame. Halfway

down the block on your right is **Seattle's oldest house** (3045 64th Avenue Southwest), a plain brown dwelling with cedar siding and white window frames. Still a private residence, the house was built around 1858 for, and probably by, David "Doc" Maynard. Maynard was one of early Seattle's most colorful characters. He was generous, gregarious, and known more for a love of liquor than for meticulous craftsmanship. That may account for the home's appearance; it's neat and trim, but undistinguished.

Retrace your steps to Alki Avenue Southwest. The next and final site on this walk, the Alki Point Lighthouse, is open only on Saturday and Sunday afternoons, May through September. At other times you're limited to getting a peekaboo view of the lighthouse from its parking lot (there's a sizable house in front of it), but it's a charming sight.

Turn left onto Alki Avenue Southwest and follow it for several blocks as it curves to the left. On the right, a wall of condominiums largely blocks your view of the water. The parks department originally planned to extend Alki Beach Park all the way around Alki Point, but it waited too long: Apartment buildings were constructed here around 1929, making the land too expensive for the city to acquire.

❿ At the tip of Alki Point, on the right, is the **Alki Point Light-**

house, completed in 1913. A residence for the lighthouse keeper
stands nearby; although the lighthouse is fully automated today, it's
still tended. If the lighthouse is
open, take a look at the memorabilia inside and climb the circular
stairs to the top. Admission is free.

**Retrace your steps along Alki
Avenue Southwest and follow it
to 61st Street Southwest.** This
intersection marks the end of the
walk. You can return to Seacrest
Park (where you parked your car
or took the water taxi), or downtown, via the buses noted at the
beginning of this chapter. You can
also choose to savor the view a bit
longer as you enjoy a meal at one
of Alki Avenue's many eateries
opposite the beach.

THE SUBLIME WITHIN THE ORDINARY: montlake

bays, forests, and fairy-tale cottages

THIS CHAPTER PRESENTS three different walks in the Montlake area, which can be taken individually, or linked together loosely to form a longer walk. The first walk meanders uphill and down, past storybook cottages and rhododendron gardens; the second follows a historic path winding through the center of lush, secluded Interlaken Park, and returns via a street lined with cottages; the third explores a marshland trail and strolls along a scenic waterway.

ROUTE 1:

Distance: 1.75 miles
Approximate time: 1 hour
The Montlake neighborhood is blessed with a lovely setting, nestled between Portage Bay and the forested hillside of Interlaken Park. It seems like a typical Seattle neighborhood: congenial and residential, with a melange of architectural styles. It has picturesque English-style cottages, tree-lined streets, and glimpsed water views. There is nothing particularly outstanding about Montlake, but if

ordinary could be so lovely everywhere, this would be a more perfect world.

❶ **Start this walk at Montlake Park, on the corner of East Calhoun Street and 16th Avenue East.** **Montlake Park** features a sports field, tennis courts, and adjacent Tudor Building, now serving as an overly elegant restroom structure. This park was built by the Works Progress Administration in 1933. Before that, a good portion of it was a little bay where houseboats floated. The bay has been filled in, but it often seems to be trying to reclaim its old territory: The park can be a veritable swamp if there has been much rain recently.

❷ **Follow 16th Avenue East for several blocks to East Lynn Street, turn left, and stroll down Lynn to 18th Avenue East.** On the left is a slice of olde England: a neat row of similarly styled **red-brick cottages**, most of which were constructed in 1928. These houses have tidy lawns with flowerbeds and neatly trimmed rhododendron bushes. All along this walk you'll see English-style

getting there

parking Parking is available in a lot at the park, but it's limited to two hours. Street parking is available along East Calhoun Street.

bus connections Catch Route 25 (Laurelhurst) on Third Avenue near Union Street downtown. Get off on Boyer Avenue East near East McGraw Street, follow McGraw to 16th Avenue East, turn left, and follow it to East Calhoun Street. On Sundays, when Route 25 doesn't serve downtown, catch Route 43 (University District) on Pike Street near Third Avenue. Get off on 24th Avenue East near Boyer Avenue East, turn west onto Boyer and stroll past its picturesque cottages for a half mile; then turn right onto 16th Avenue East and follow it for several blocks to Calhoun. (For more information about bus routes serving this area, see the "Getting Around" section in the introduction to this book.)

cottages like these, lending the neighborhood a fanciful air with their steeply pitched roofs, tiny gables, and leaded glass windows.

❸ **Continue on East Lynn Street for about half a block to a parking lot on the right.** You pass more English-style cottages and arrive at the rear gate of **St. Demetrios Greek Ortho-**

Houses near Montlake Park

dox Church, whose unusual modern design features a vaulted concrete roof for the chapel and multicolored panes of glass for the cupola. St. Demetrios sponsors a popular Greek festival, open to the public, on a weekend in late September each year.

Cross the parking lot, passing to the left of the church and joining 19th Avenue East, and continue to Boyer Avenue East. From the front, the church looks far more impressive!

Retrace your steps for a block, turn right onto East Blaine Street, and follow it to 22nd Avenue East. Strolling down this long block of Blaine, lined on both sides with **storybook cottages**, is like walking through a fairy tale. The homes nestled at the base of a hill are predominantly English-style cottages, although they come in many more colors, shapes, and sizes than those you saw earlier on Lynn. Most were built between 1926 and 1928.

montlake

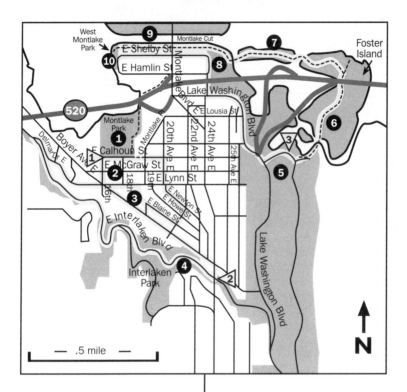

ROUTE 1:
1. Montlake Park
2. Red-brick cottages
3. St. Demetrios Greek Orthodox Church

ROUTE 2:
4. Interlaken bike path

ROUTE 3:
5. Washington Park Arboretum
6. Foster Island
7. Marsh Island
8. Museum of History and Industry
9. Montlake Cut
10. West Montlake Park

Montlake's storybook cottages

Turn left onto 22nd Avenue East, which is at first a stairway, and follow it to East Newton Street. You ascend a forested hill and emerge into another residential area. Here the houses are considerably less English and reflect a more typical Seattle neighborhood mixture: Arts and Crafts, period revivals, and bungalows. To the left, on the corner of 22nd and Newton, is a large, gabled **Shingle-style house** that's worth a second look. With its wide wooden porch, accented with rough "clinker" bricks, it resembles a tranquil mountain cabin. Built in 1912, the rustic home is idyllically located under a spreading maple tree (on its south side).

Turn left onto East Newton Street, following it as it curves to the right and becomes 20th

Avenue East. Continue to East Calhoun Street. About half a block down on the left is a strikingly large three-story **Shingle-style house**, built in 1912, with a white trellised porch. Such a sizable house is a bit out of place on this street graced largely by **bungalows**, modest single-story homes that commonly feature wide porches. As Newton curves, enjoy the peekaboo view of the Montlake Bridge, which spans the Montlake Cut between Union and Portage Bays.

Turn left onto East Calhoun Street, follow it downhill and across 19th Street, and descend the stairway there to Montlake Park, where you started this walk. The stairway becomes a paved path that winds down a hillside covered with ivy and blackberry bushes, leading you back into the park.

starting/
finish point

Interlaken Boulevard East
and 24th Avenue East

parking
Street parking is available along Interlaken
Boulevard East near the start of the walk.

bus connections
Catch Route 43 (University District) on Pike Street near Third Avenue downtown; get off on 24th
Avenue East near Interlaken Boulevard East. (To get information on other bus routes serving
this area, see the "Getting Around" section in the introduction to this book.)

ROUTE 2:

interlaken park

Distance: 2.25 miles
Approximate time: 1.5 hours
On this great urban-forest walk, trees are interspersed with elegant houses and peekaboo views of the University of Washington, Portage Bay, and the rooftops of the Montlake neighborhood below. You follow Interlaken Boulevard through the forested serenity of Interlaken Park, then return via a picturesque avenue lined with charming cottages.

❹ **Start this walk on the corner of 24th Avenue East and Interlaken Boulevard East. Stroll along Interlaken Boulevard East for about half a mile, slightly uphill in places, to 19th Avenue East.** Interlaken Boulevard, designed by the Olmsted Brothers firm in the early 1900s as part of its master plan for Seattle's park system, winds through lush woodland for almost its entire length. Soon after you begin, the boulevard becomes a paved walking/cycling path that's closed to cars. This path was designed by Seattle mayor and bicycling enthusiast George Cotterill in the early days of the sport, and completed around 1897. The bike path later became Interlaken Boulevard.

The park can feel a bit primeval, especially after a rain, when the water drips from moss-covered branches. Lush ferns and ivy carpet the hillside to your left, while to your right is a forested ravine and the rooftops of the Montlake neighborhood. The adventurous may want to follow one of many narrow footpaths leading through the forest.

At 19th Avenue East, the Interlaken bike path again becomes a road. Follow it as it curves to the left, then keep to the right

House on Blaine Street

A slice of old England in Montlake

as it forks, and follow it for a little more than half a mile to Delmar Drive East. Although the bike path has becomes a road, the shady peaceful atmosphere continues. It's a little-used thoroughfare, so few cars disturb your solitude. For a time the trees become more numerous and the views less so, but then a marvelous panorama of the university, the bay, and the rooftops unfolds briefly.

Turn right onto Delmar Drive East and follow it for about a quarter mile to Boyer Avenue East. This lovely street winds along the base of the forested Interlaken Park hillside.

Turn right onto Boyer Avenue East and stroll along it for about half a mile, to 24th Avenue East. Enter a fairy tale once again as you stroll down Boyer, bordered on either side by a seemingly endless row of quaint cottages whose rooftops you peeked at earlier from Interlaken Park. As you near busy 24th and prepare to reenter the real world, the structures along Boyer become somewhat more ordinary.

Turn right onto 24th Avenue East and follow it to Interlaken Boulevard East, where you started this walk.

starting/ finish point

Parking area at the northern end of the Washington Park Arboretum, off East Foster Island Road

parking Parking is available in a lot near the start of the walk.

bus connections Catch Route 43 (University District) on Pike Street near Third Avenue downtown; get off on Montlake Boulevard past East Roanoke Street, just before the bus reaches SR-520. Follow Montlake to Lake Washington Boulevard, turn right and walk about half a mile to Foster Island Road. Turn left and follow East Foster Island Road to its end. (For more information on bus routes serving this area, see the "Getting Around" section in the introduction to this book.)

ROUTE 3:

Distance: 2.5 miles

Approximate time: 2 hours

This walk follows the shoreline of Lake Washington's Union Bay and the Montlake Cut. The cut got its start in the early 1880s as a log canal across a narrow isthmus that once separated Union Bay and Portage Bay. It was moved and widened in 1916 when the ship canal and locks were being constructed.

Today the Montlake Cut is the site of a lovely waterfront trail, and also hosts a festive parade of boats heading out to the locks or into Lake Washington. This picturesque walk begins at the Washington Park Arboretum, follows a marshland trail, strolls along the Montlake Cut, and ends near a tiny park and a yacht club. The marshland trail can be muddy, especially if it's been rainy, so wear appropriate shoes.

The walk begins near the Arboretum's visitor center.

❺ Start this walk from the parking lot at the northern end of the Arboretum, off East Foster Island Road. Follow the footpath that skirts a pond and crosses over a footbridge to Foster Island. About 40,000 trees, shrubs, and vines grace the **Washington Park Arboretum**, whose 200 acres of parkland include the marshland you're about to explore.

❻ Native Americans once used **Foster Island** as a burial site, placing their dead in wooden boxes and hoisting them into the trees. They called this place Stetee'chee, or "Little Island." Today their old burial ground is a popular recreational area, attracting bird watchers, canoeists, and picnickers. The only thing that mars the peace on this scenic walk is the 520 freeway that passes nearby, spewing noise and particulates. However, even that does not destroy the mood.

Continuing on the path, cross under the 520 overpass and walk to the northern end of Foster Island. This vantage point offers a lovely view of Union Bay and Lake Washington. You can see the waterfront homes in Laurelhurst across the bay and the

University of Washington's Husky Stadium to your left. In the fall, football fans moor their boats in Union Bay during games.

When you finish taking in the view, retrace your steps a few hundred feet and look for the signed entrance to the Waterfront Trail on your right.

❼ Follow the Arboretum Waterfront Trail until it ends near the Museum of History and Industry.

Interlaken Park

The **Waterfront Trail** is a walkway built over a wetland, rich with bird life and waterfowl. This trail leads to **Marsh Island** and features a bark path and floating sidewalks between islands. The trail allows pedestrians access to a landscape that would be otherwise inaccessible on foot, cutting a swath through cattails, marsh plants, and wildflowers. Several observation platforms along the way offer views across the bay. In the spring water lilies cluster along the islands' edge and red-winged blackbirds trill from the reeds. You can frequently spot great blue herons fishing from the shore, and there is almost always a healthy population of Canada geese nearby.

❽ Although the Waterfront Trail officially ends near the **Museum of History and Industry (MOHAI),** the path continues through a grassy area toward the Montlake Cut. Before you continue along the trail, consider a visit to MOHAI, which features displays on local products and innovations, and a life-size replica of an early Seattle street, among other attractions. The museum also has rotating exhibits on everything from fish to fashion. It is open daily and there is an admission fee.

❾ Continue along the walkway as it follows the Montlake Cut, goes underneath the Montlake Bridge, and ends at West Montlake Park. The **Montlake Cut** connects Union and Portage Bays. This is the place to be on the first

Sunday in May, when people gather to celebrate the opening day of boating season. That event involves a parade of boats, a rowing competition (the Windermere Cup crew races), a regatta, and a congregation of yachts rafted together in the middle of Union Bay. Pedestrians usually gather along the Montlake Cut to watch the parade. Note the Neo-Gothic control towers on the **Montlake Bridge**, completed in 1925.

10 **West Montlake Park** has the ambiance of a private country club, thanks to two genteel structures bordering it: a lovely white plaster house, with elegant windows, on the park's northeast side, and the striking **Seattle Yacht Club**, a 1919 Colonial Revival structure with a mock lighthouse, at the far end of the park.

Leaving the park, follow East Hamlin Street to Montlake Boulevard East.

To return downtown via bus, catch Route 43 (Downtown) on Montlake Boulevard. To return to your car, read on.

Turn right onto Montlake Boulevard East, turn left onto Lake Washington Boulevard East, and follow it to the East Foster Island Road parking area, where you started this walk. Stay on the right side of Lake Washington Boulevard until you've passed the exit and entrance lanes to SR-520, which are on the opposite side of the boulevard (even though it means walking for a short distance on the side of a grassy slope). Once past the entrance and exit lanes, just before the T where East Foster Island Road enters from the left, *carefully* cross over and follow the road back to the parking lot.

A PROPER LITTLE PARADISE:
madison park

Parks and fine old homes

Distance: 2.25 miles (one way)   **Approximate time:** 2 hours

MADISON PARK IS ALMOST TOO picturesque to be true. Perched on the shores of Lake Washington, the area is graced with charming bungalows, fine old homes, and expansive views across the lake to the Cascade Range and Mount Rainier. It's an older, residential neighborhood with a small business district that offers all the essentials (grocery store, hardware store, pharmacy, and bakery, as well as restaurants and the ubiquitous coffee shops); a self-contained community that feels like a small, lakeside village far away from the city.

This walk begins and ends in parks. In between it goes uphill and down, following a sometimes circuitous path through streets lined with tidy bungalows or magnificent mansions overlooking Lake Washington. It passes through an unofficial memorial to a local rock hero, and offers you a glimpse across the lake to the high-tech home the whole world is curious about.

If you're fortunate enough to take this walk on a sunny day, the neighborhood may seem paradisiacal—almost too nice to be believed. If you arrive on a cold,

The bookstore in Madison Park

gray day, you will be fortunate in a different sense. The climate will have redeemed this shoreline from perfection, and perfection rarely has much personality.

The walk described here is a one-way route from Madison Park to Denny Blaine Park. From

starting point

Madison Park Beach, near the corner of East Madison Street and 43rd Avenue East

finish point

Denny Blaine Park

parking Parking is available near Madison Park Beach and along any of the streets outlined in this walk. It's limited to four hours by Madison Park Beach and one hour along East Madison Street.

bus connections
Catch Route 11 (Madison Park) on Pike Street near Third Avenue downtown; get off near East Madison Street and 42nd Avenue East.

To return to your car via bus: It is possible, though not particularly convenient, to return to Madison Park via bus. Walk half a mile south from Denny Blaine Park on Lake Washington Boulevard to Madrona Drive. There, catch Route 2 (Downtown) and get off at the corner of East Union and East Madison Streets. Transfer to Route 11 (Madison Park) and get off at 42nd and Madison.

To return downtown via bus: Walk half a mile south from Denny Blaine Park on Lake Washington Boulevard to Madrona Drive and catch Route 2 (Downtown).

Denny Blaine, you can return to Madison Park via the loop indicated on the map, which will take you along McGilvra Boulevard East, a broad, lovely street with striking homes and peekaboo glimpses of the lake. This adds an additional mile and a quarter to the walk, but it's well worth the effort. Alternatively, you can walk south from Denny Blaine Park for half a mile along Lake Washington Boulevard, to the bus stop at the base of Madrona Drive. From there, you can return to Madison Park (by taking two buses) or travel elsewhere in the city.

Note: All the houses on this walk are private; none are open to the public. Please admire them from a respectful distance.

❶ **Start this walk on the corner of East Madison Street and 43rd Avenue East.** Just east of here is **Madison Park Beach**, once a popular amusement center. Madison Park was created in the 1890s to encourage ridership of the streetcar line that ran from here to downtown. People came here to waltz at the dance pavilion, attend baseball games, and rent canoes to row their sweethearts

out on the lake. An old scow converted into a floating stage hosted productions of Gilbert and Sullivan operas for an audience sitting along the beach.

Today's Madison Park is no longer an amusement park; its streets are lined with bungalows rather than vacation cabins. Before you begin the walk, you may want to have a bite to eat at one of the neighborhood cafes in the small business district along Madison Street. If the sun is out, sit at a sidewalk table, or order your food to go and enjoy a picnic on the beach.

❷ **With the lake on your left, walk south on 43rd Avenue East to East Garfield Street.** A short distance past the park, where East Blaine Street intersects 43rd, is **Pioneer Hall**, a brick building constructed for the Pioneer Association of the State of Washington in 1910. Pioneer Association members must be able to trace their Washington ancestry back to at least 1889. A genealogical

madison park

1. Madison Park Beach
2. Pioneer Hall
3. Gated community
4. Alexander Pantages house
5. Walker-Ames house
6. Bush School
7. Lakeview Park
8. Viretta Park
9. Denny Blaine Park

Alexander Pantages house

library and a small historical museum are housed here, open only on the second Sunday of each month, 1–4 P.M. Admission is free.

Beyond Pioneer Hall are a couple of high-rise condominiums, occupying land that was a popular summer campground in the late 19th century.

❸ At East Garfield Street, turn right, go one block, and then turn left onto 42nd Avenue East. Follow it to the T, which is East Lee Street. A curious **gated community**—small, overgrown, mysterious—occupies the lakefront between East Garfield and East Lee. Through the fence you can catch glimpses of the tennis courts, winding lanes, and coordinating white wooden houses of this little enclave, which dates from the mid-1930s.

During the 1860s this plot of land was the estate of Madison Park's principal developer, Judge John McGilvra, a Chicago lawyer appointed by President Lincoln as U.S. attorney for the Washington Territory. McGilvra loved this country retreat, which he called Laurel Shade.

At the T, turn right onto East Lee Street and walk a few blocks uphill to 39th Avenue East. Turn left and follow 39th Avenue East for a couple blocks to East Prospect Street. At the bottom of the hill, many of the homes are tiny cottages, reminders of the time when Madison Park was a summertime, beachfront community. Toward the top of the hill, the houses are larger and more grand—long-established residences with cloistered gardens and unobstructed views across the lake.

Turn right on East Prospect and go steeply uphill to 36th Avenue East. Thirty-sixth Avenue, a stately street lined with towering elm trees, is the address of some of Seattle's finest old homes. Most were built by the city's movers and shakers in the early part of the 20th century. The variety of architectural styles one sees here is typical of Seattle—an eclecticism that does not detract from the street's elegance. Thirty-sixth follows the hill's crest, providing many of the homes with spectacular vistas from their upper stories (although the houses and trees obscure the views from passersby).

❹ Turn right onto 36th Avenue East and walk half a block downhill. This short detour takes you to the **Alexander Pantages house** (on your left at 1117 36th Avenue East). This unusual mansion, with its creamy-white plaster walls, intricate window designs, and red tile roof, was built in 1909 for the quite substantial sum of $50,000, which made possible such luxuries as a ballroom on the third floor.

Pantages was a self-made man who built a well-known circuit of theaters throughout the West Coast during the early part of the 20th century, basing his operation in Seattle. He first got a taste of theatrical success in Nome, Alaska, during the Klondike gold rush, when he struck it rich by taking over a failing theater, where he charged $12.50 for tickets. When he brought his entrepreneurial spirit to Seattle several years later

he charged only 10 cents. Crowds flocked to his affordable entertainment. He opened two more theaters in Seattle before starting to accumulate a circuit of theaters along the Pacific coast, ultimately coming to own 30 playhouses and have control over 42 others.

When it came time to sell his theater circuit, Pantages had excellent timing. He sold the circuit for $24 million in 1929, just before the stock market crash plunged the country into the Great Depression. Several theaters bearing his name still exist, including one in Tacoma and one in Hollywood.

❺ Turn around and retrace your steps back up 36th Avenue East to East Valley Street. On your left, set back from the street by a broad lawn and circular drive, is

Walker-Ames house

Bush School

the impressive **Walker-Ames house** (808 36th Avenue), an imposing brick mansion with classical detailing, built in 1906–07. The owners willed their house to the University of Washington for use as the university president's home, and it still serves that purpose today.

The corner of 36th Avenue and Valley Street affords a fine view of Capitol Hill. The large dome visible atop the hill belongs to the **Holy Names Academy**, a parochial girls' school. The steeple of the nearby **St. Joseph Catholic Church** is also visible in the background.

❻ Continue along 36th Avenue East for a couple blocks down the hill to Lake Washington Boulevard. At the bottom of the hill, glance to your left. A drive-

way leads up a short rise to the **Bush School** (405 36th Avenue East), a private school for about 500 students in grades K–12. The school's most striking building is a converted brick Tudor Revival house, built in 1915–17. Other buildings belonging to the Bush School are located on the opposite side of Lake Washington Boulevard. Founded in the 1920s by Helen Taylor Bush after her husband's health forced him to retire prematurely, the school has a progressive philosophy that includes community service and "learning by doing."

❼ Turn left onto Lake Washington Boulevard, then right (at the street island) onto 37th Avenue East. Walk along 37th Avenue East as it winds around and becomes Dorffel Drive East. On your left, just as you turn onto 37th Avenue, is **Lakeview Park.**

Sprawling down a gentle slope and across a grassy knoll, the park resembles a clearing in a forest, its lake view framed by giant Douglas fir, cedar, and maple trees.

Just past Lakeview Park, also on the left, are the **Storey houses** (260–270 Dorffel Drive East), built in 1903–05. With their dark, cedar-shake siding and elaborate white window framings, these house have an elegant rusticity, aptly demonstrating their architect's Swiss chalet and Arts and Crafts influences. Ellsworth Storey was probably Seattle's first academically trained architect, and his designs are still well regarded. He built the first of the two homes you see here for his parents, just after he moved to Seattle after graduating from college. He added

Former Cobain home from Viretta Park

the second for himself later. Most of Storey's designs used materials readily available in the Northwest. They have a certain dark beauty that harmonizes well with gray skies and old-growth forests.

Continue on Dorffel Drive East to East John Street, and turn left.
On the corner of John Street and Maiden Lane, behind a wrought-iron gate, is the **former home of Theodore Roethke**, the Pulitzer Prize–winning poet and University of Washington professor from 1947 to 1963. Northwest imagery infuses much of Roethke's poetry, such as in these lines from "And Time Slows Down," which could describe the view across the lake from his garden: "The vine-like dead branches of the madrona arch over the water, / Creaking slightly with each light wind-shift; / The

wave shimmers play back the parched leaves."

⑧ Follow East John Street to its end and cross 39th Avenue East to Viretta Park. A tiny green space on two levels, **Viretta Park** has developed an unusual double life as park and informal memorial. The upper level—a broad, flat lawn with a bench and carefully tended shrubs and trees—appears at first glance to be the front yard of the large home next to it. Down a steep flight of steps, the lower level offers broad views of the lake, with the Evergreen Point floating bridge prominent in the foreground, and (on clear days at least) Mount Baker rising above the distant horizon. The lower level also abuts the fenced-in yard of the **former home of Kurt**

Dorffel Drive from Lakeview Park

Cobain, lead singer of the grunge-rock band Nirvana, who committed suicide in the home's greenhouse in April 1994. Even years later, fans still leave flowers under a large cedar tree near the house or decorate the park benches with memorial graffiti (which then gets cleaned off or painted over by the parks department). The house itself is a beautiful two-story stone and cedar-shake structure built in 1900–01 for E. F. Blaine, an early Seattle lawyer and real estate speculator for whom Denny Blaine Park was named.

⑨ Leaving Viretta Park, turn left onto Lake Washington Boulevard and follow it for one block. To your right is **Denny Blaine Park**, which sits between two large houses. On the left is a brick Georgian Revival home with terraced grounds. It was built in 1914 by Jules Redelsheimer, a clothing store owner known for his ingenious marketing ploys. The sidewalk in front of his store featured a mosaic made of silver dollars, he held pie-eating contests and mule races, and he occasionally tossed bundles of merchandise from the roof of the store.

As a man who thought big, Redelsheimer wanted a big house. He commissioned a home with 26 rooms, 141 feet of lakeshore, a boathouse, a cabana, and tennis courts—and it was almost ready for occupancy when he suffered a stroke and died. The house survives as a monument to his marketing ability.

There's a small beach at Denny

Gate leading to the Redelsheimer estate

Blaine Park. If you stand at the waterfront and look over the lake, you'll see Mount Rainier to your right (if the mountain is out). Across the lake the highrise buildings of the city of Bellevue peak over the hill, and almost straight across the lake, toward the floating bridge, is Microsoft cofounder **Bill Gates' complex.** Built into the hillside along the lake shore, the Gates' complex covers 45,000 square feet, the size of a small shopping mall, and took more than seven years to complete. Originally it was to cost a "modest" $10 million, but expenses escalated; the final cost was an estimated $50 million. The home's many unusual, high-tech features include video walls for displaying digital artwork throughout the home and an electronic system that keeps track of all the house's occupants using pre-programmed pins attached to their clothes. The system turns the lights on and off for people, plays their favorite music, and rings only the phone closest to them when they get a call.

Denny Blaine Park marks the end of this walk. Follow the loop route outlined on the accompanying map to return to Madison Park, where you started this walk. The route takes you a short distance up Lake Washington Boulevard and then right along McGilvra Boulevard. It's about one and a quarter miles back to Madison Park, but a pleasant stroll past more lovely homes and yards, along mostly flat terrain. Or walk down Lake Washington Boulevard for half a mile to Madrona Drive. There you can return to Madison Park or travel elsewhere in the city, via the bus routes noted at the beginning of this chapter.

bill gates: the wonder boy grows up

IN JUNIOR HIGH SCHOOL, BILL Gates once boasted to a classmate that he would be a millionaire by the time he was 30. That would sound like an idle boast coming from most young men, but from Bill Gates it now seems almost modest. In Gates' 30th year, Microsoft, the internationally known software company he cofounded, brought in revenues of $140 million. At the age of 37, Gates became the second-richest man in the United States; a few years later, he became the richest man in the world.

Bill Gates grew up in Seattle's Laurelhurst neighborhood in a family of privilege. The private school he attended, Lakeside, was one of the first schools in the country to offer its students access to computers. Gates became hooked immediately, spending every spare minute, and many nights, in the computer room—sometimes in the company of an upperclassman named Paul Allen.

In Gates' sophomore year at Harvard, Allen showed up at his door bearing an article about a newly developed computer, the Altair, which did not yet have a programming language. In a marathon eight-week session in Harvard's computer lab, they wrote the first BASIC interpreter—a version of the BASIC programming language—for what would be the world's first microcomputer. While still at Harvard they cofounded the company that would come to be known as Microsoft, but by 1977 Gates had dropped out to devote himself to the business full-time.

In the ensuing years, of course, Microsoft has come to dominate the personal computer industry. It has also had a marked effect on the Seattle economy and culture, attracting thousands of high-tech employees, many of whom have become "Microsoft Millionaires" from vested stock options. (Paul Allen left the company some years ago to pursue varied interests, although he's still a major stockholder.) Gates is a smart and shrewd—some would say devious—businessman, although with his "geek" persona he may not look the part of a typical CEO. His manner may seem unpolished and his hair often uncombed, but he more than makes up for that with his apparently unbounded ambition. As a child, Gates was known to pursue every competition to its logical limit. He clearly still has that determination.

THE URBAN FOREST:
leschi to mount baker

A ramble through the pastoral city

Distance: 3.25 miles (one way)   **Approximate time:** 2.5 hours

SEATTLE COMBINES BOTANICAL and architectural splendor as well as any city in the world, and the scenery along this route is a good example this. The walk traverses some of Seattle's greenest parkways, following Lake Washington Boulevard past lakeshore parks and winding through forested hillsides. Traveling this forested boulevard makes the cares of city life seem remote, even though the forest is

Mount Baker Park beach

actually in the middle of a city.

Along these green boulevards you will also encounter elegant mansions and cozy cottages. The walk is quite long and much of it goes uphill, but the scenery makes the trek worthwhile. It can also be easily divided into two 2-mile loops, one through the Leschi area and the other through the Mount Baker neighborhood. The two loop routes are briefly described in the text and indicated on the accompanying map.

starting point

Madrona Park Beach, on Lake Washington Boulevard South just south of Madrona Drive

finish point

Mount Baker Park, on Lake Washington Boulevard South at Mount Baker Boulevard South (one direction only) or Madrona Park Beach (loop)

getting there

parking Parking is available near Madrona Park, Leschi Park, and all the other parks along Lake Washington. It's limited to two hours at Leschi Park, but there's no limit at Madrona Park.

bus connections Catch Route 2 (Madrona Park) on Third Avenue near Union Street downtown; get off near Madrona Park. (For more information on bus routes serving this area, see the "Getting Around" section in the introduction to this book.)

To return to your car via bus: From Mount Baker Park, walk back down the hill to Colman Park. At 36th Avenue South and South Atlantic, catch Route 27 (Downtown). Get off at Leschi, before the bus turns up the hill on East Alder, and walk the short distance back to Madrona Park Beach where you started.

To return downtown via bus: Catch Route 14 (Downtown) at South McClellan Street near Mount Baker Boulevard South.

❶ Start this walk on Lake Washington Boulevard just south of Madrona Drive. This is the entrance to Madrona Park. On a warm day, **Madrona Park Beach** is one of the city's best people-watching spots, where the human spectacle is set against an extraordinarily scenic backdrop. You may hear conversations in three or four different languages and watch children of every race frolicking in the water.

The community of Madrona adjoins the Central District, which has been the location of Seattle's predominantly African American neighborhood since the late 1800s. A number of African Americans moved to Seattle at that time, in part because they found the city more tolerant than many others. The city government even passed a civil rights bill in 1890 establishing penalties for racial discrimination. Unfortunately, Seattle's tolerance was probably not due to its innate decency, but to the relatively small size of Seattle's African American population. The city's tolerance waned slightly in 1895, when an amendment to the civil

rights bill removed penalties for violation and rendered the law toothless.

❷ Find the path along the lakeshore that parallels Lake Washington Boulevard. With the water to your left, follow the path for about three-quarters of a mile, until it ends. This is the **business district of Leschi**, a neighborhood named for a prominent Nisqually Indian who, in the 1850s, fought the territorial government's attempts to move all Indian tribes to reservations. At the time, white settlement was becoming more widespread in Washington and the native population was being pushed from their lands. These territorial tensions brought about the attack. (See "The Tragedy of Chief Leschi" on page 196.)

The Leschi area has a small grocery/deli and a number of eateries. If you return to Leschi by bus after the walk, or take only the Leschi loop, you could end your day with a picnic in Leschi Park, or a meal at one of the cafes.

leschi to mount baker

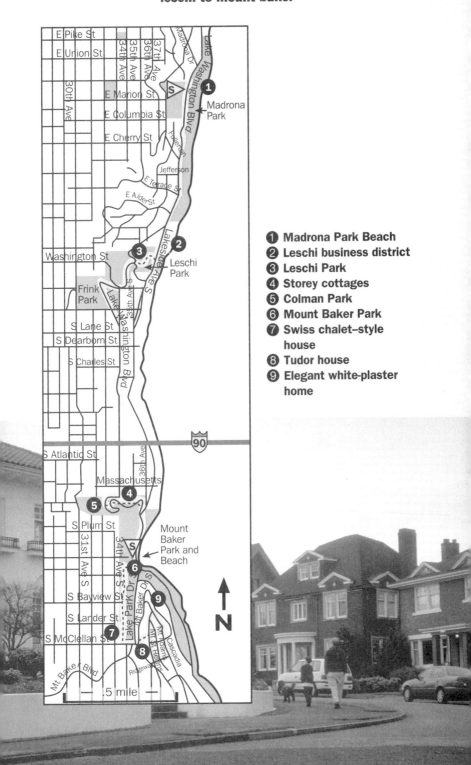

1. Madrona Park Beach
2. Leschi business district
3. Leschi Park
4. Storey cottages
5. Colman Park
6. Mount Baker Park
7. Swiss chalet–style house
8. Tudor house
9. Elegant white-plaster home

Gift from Kobe, Japan

❸ Walk through the business district, and then cross Lake Washington Boulevard to Leschi Park. Leschi Park was once a recreation center with a bandstand, a fish pond, and a small zoo. A cable-car line once connected the park with Pioneer Square, and a cable-car trestle, constructed in the late 1880s, spanned the ridge in today's **Frink Park**. The concrete bridge that was the end of the

wooden trestle is still standing. Two hundred twenty feet high in places, the trestle was known to creak and wobble in the wind. The cable cars featured stained-glass roofs, were open to the weather on the sides, and were lit by gaslight.

Walk uphill through Leschi Park, turn left onto Lake Washington Boulevard South. Walk along the boulevard as it winds up the hill. Lake Washington Boulevard here is a quiet, sheltered road that winds up the hill through a lush, dense forest, crisscrossed by tiny streams. The boulevard is part of the vast system of parks and parkways designed for the city by the celebrated landscape architects John C. and Frederick Law Olmsted in the early 1900s, and the winding street is one of their trademarks. You may find it hard to believe you are in a city neighborhood as you pass beneath the towering trees. When the boulevard emerges from the forest, it levels out, becoming a residential street, lined with relatively new homes, that cuts across the crest of the hill above the lake.

If you want to shorten this walk by dividing it into two loops, you can start closing **the first loop**, through Leschi, here. Go down the stairs that are on the left side of the boulevard, just past the sign indicating Frink Park. At the bottom of the stairs, go a block to an unmarked blacktop lane, right after 35th Avenue South. Turn left and follow the lane back to Leschi Park, then back through the business district and along the lake to your car, completing the Leschi loop.

For **the second loop**, which goes through the Mount Baker neighborhood farther down the lake, drive or take the bus (Route 27) down Lakeside Avenue to Colman Park. There is ample parking in the lot next to the lake. From there, pick up the Mount Baker loop, starting at the swimming beach and going up through Mount Baker Park, site ❻.

If you want to continue the one-way walk, read on.

Follow Lake Washington Boulevard South across the top of the hill for about half a mile to the East Portal Viewpoint over I-90. The most interesting aspect of this stretch of the boulevard is the view. Lake Washington stretches out beneath you, and on clear days the foothills and peaks of the Cascade Range line the eastern horizon, Mount Rainier looming in the south, Mount Baker in the north. Two highways cross Lake Washington via floating bridges, connecting Seattle and the cities of the Eastside. The SR-520 bridge (commonly referred to as the Evergreen Point bridge) is to the south. The **East Portal Viewpoint** looks out over the multiple lanes of the I-90 bridge, which extends across the lake to Mercer Island and then to the lake's eastern shore. Beneath you is the I-90 tunnel. The highway cuts through the hill to Rainier Valley and then on to I-5. There is even a separate tunnel exclusively for bicycles, and a bike lane along the left side of the I-90 bridge.

❹ **Continue along Lake Washington Boulevard for less than a quarter of a mile.** Not far after the bridge overlook, the boulevard changes back to a sheltered road

Historic home at 2704 34th Avenue S

the tragedy of chief leschi

THE NISQUALLY INDIANS HAD long been living in the Puget Sound area when white settlers began to arrive in the 1800s. The tribe welcomed the whites, offering them land and protection. But after Washington became a U.S. territory in 1853, its first governor, Isaac Stevens, made it his top priority to move all Indians onto reservations.

Stevens set about securing treaties and selecting "chiefs" (including Leschi, a prominent Nisqually) to speak for the tribes. The first of the dozen treaties he made was the Medicine Creek Treaty, which he presented on December 26, 1854, to 62 chiefs representing various tribes in western Washington.

By signing the treaty, the assembled chiefs ceded about 2.5 million acres of land to the U.S. government, in return for hunting and fishing rights, a $32,500 cash payment over 20 years, and several thousand acres of reservation land. The treaty would have moved the Nisquallys to gravelly and forested land on a high bluff, far from the rivers and pastures they needed for their horses.

Accounts of the signing vary; while Leschi's "X" (the tribes did not have a written language) appears on the treaty along with those of the other 61 chiefs, Indians say he refused to sign.

Afterward he repeatedly met with those close to Stevens to argue for better terms, but had no success. In the spring of 1855 he traveled to eastern Washington to speak with family members and tribal leaders there about the unfairness of the treaty and the inferiority of the lands to which they were being relegated. Gold had been discovered not too long before in the eastern part of the state, and there had already been scattered attacks on prospectors by Indians, who saw the goldseekers as invaders.

The series of attacks and skirmishes collectively known as the Puget Sound Indian Wars, which would last through the spring of 1856, soon began. The territorial government ordered militia members to take Leschi into protective custody, but he evaded them. In a particularly alarming attack in the fall of 1855, Indians raided settlers' cabins on the White River, near present-day Kent and Auburn, burning homes and murdering some of their white inhabitants. In early January 1856, Leschi requested another meeting to discuss a treaty, but Stevens refused; on January 26, Indians attacked the city of Seattle, which at that time consisted of only 50 settlers (along with 140 soldiers on the warship *Decatur*, which had been stationed in Elliott Bay in response to the fears about Indian attacks). The Indians were outclassed by the *Decatur*'s gun power, and only two settlers died in the attack.

Eventually, tired of being a fugitive and wishing to return home, Leschi tried to surrender, even offering to cut off his right hand to prove his peaceful intentions. But friendly whites advised him to remain in hiding because Stevens was determined to execute him. Leschi was eventually betrayed by a relative and captured in November 1856; he was tried for murder, convicted, and sentenced to be hung. While being led to the gallows, Leschi told his executioner that he "bore a grudge against none save one man, and on him he evoked the vengeance of heaven."

In one small way, Leschi's troops were victorious: In August 1856, perhaps because of pressure from Washington, D.C., Stevens met with the Puyallup and Nisqually tribes and granted them the good land they'd sought. The Nisquallys regard Leschi as a hero and a martyr: "He fought for our country and died to save our reservation lands for us," said George Leschi, his nephew, at the 1895 reburial of Leschi's remains on the Nisqually reservation.

winding through trees. Just before it begins to curve downhill, look on the left for the **Storey cottages** (1706–1710 Lake Washington Boulevard South). Ellsworth Storey, perhaps the first academically trained architect in Seattle, designed these cottages as rentals, and they were built in 1910–15. During the Depression, when architectural commissions were few and far between, Storey survived primarily on rent from these cottages. With their simple and rustic design, the cottages look perfectly at home nestled beneath the trees.

To the right of the Storey cottages is a **small house designed by Victor Steinbrueck** (1714 Lake Washington Boulevard South), a University of Washington architecture professor best known for spearheading the successful campaign to save Pike Place Market from redevelopment. The cottage was his last completed building project; it was finished in 1980, and he passed away in 1985. ❺ Lake Washington Boulevard South winds down the hill into **Colman Park,** a forested parkway. On the right, just past a **picturesque bridge,** a community garden climbs the slope. This is one of Seattle's P-Patch gardens. City residents can rent a garden plot here for a small fee.

After crossing the bridge, turn onto the footpath to the right and follow it through Colman Park to the bottom of the hill. Another cluster of Storey cottages (1800–1816 Lake Washington

Boulevard South) extends along the left side of Lake Washington Boulevard as it makes its second sweeping turn down the hill. To see the cottages, you need to leave the path about two-thirds of the way down the hill and cross the street. The cottages were built 1912–1916; six face the boulevard, two more front 36th Avenue South at the base of the hill.

If you have divided this walk into two loops, you can pick up the **Mount Baker loop** here, at the base of Colman Park.

At the bottom of the hill, turn right onto Lake Washington Boulevard South and follow it along the lakeshore for a quarter mile. A **swimming beach** is to the left. From here you can see **Mercer Island**, about a half mile away. It's currently an upscale suburb, but according to Duwamish

View from Colman Park

Indian legend, the island is the heart of the lake. The Duwamish believed that Lake Washington was a monster that ate its heart (Mercer Island) every evening and regurgitated it every morning.

❻ Just past the beach a road heads uphill through a grove of trees. Take the pedestrian path to the right of the road, and follow it partway through Mount Baker Park. At the entrance to **Mount Baker Park** is a pagoda-shaped stone lantern, a gift from Seattle's Japanese sister city, Kobe, in 1911. A stream runs through the center of the park, and houses perch on the hill to the right. One in particular is worth climbing the hill to see.

❼ About two-thirds of the way through the park, just past a white clapboard house, take the path that climbs the hill. The **Swiss chalet–style house** to the

left of the path (2704 34th Avenue South) looks like a 200-year-old European country house, though it was built relatively recently. The cedar-shake structure was designed by Ellsworth Storey, the architect of the Storey cottages you saw earlier on this walk. The house is sided in cedar shake and plaster. Its aged wood and deep eaves give it a particularly massive character.

Retrace your steps to the pedestrian path and continue through Mount Baker Park. At the playground, turn left onto South McClellan Street and follow it to Mount Baker Drive South. If you like, stop for a snack at **Bakers Beach Cafe**, on the corner of South McClellan Street and South Mount Baker Boulevard. It's an especially popular spot for weekend brunch.

Turn left onto Mount Baker Drive South. Look for a small pedestrian walkway on the right side of the boulevard, winding up the hill. The entrance to the walkway is framed with tree branches and looks as if it leads through someone's yard.

❽ Follow the walkway up to Mount St. Helens Place, turn right, and follow it to South Ridgeway Place. This part of the Mount Baker neighborhood was designed by the Olmsteds and has their trademark winding streets. Perched atop the ridge, this small enclave has expansive views across the lake, and many of the streets are named for peaks in the Cascade Range. Fine, imposing homes, graced with carefully manicured yards, line the streets. Just one example is the grand **Tudor house** (2812 Mount St. Helens Place South). Constructed in 1911, it has 17 rooms.

❾ Turn left onto South Ridgeway Place; then turn left onto Cascadia Avenue South and follow it to Mount St. Helens Place South. Cascadia Avenue has great views and meticulously maintained mansions. At the far end of the avenue is a viewpoint from which you can survey Lake Washington, Mercer Island, and the suburbs on the lake's eastern shore. On the corner, facing out toward the lake, is an **elegant, white-plaster home** (2601 Cascadia Avenue South), with red tile roof, tall windows, and a sunroom. Built in 1920, the mansion seems almost too grand for even this marvelous setting. It calls to mind a country estate, with acres of landscaped gardens, where women in starched dresses and men in white linen jackets sip tea or play lawn tennis.

Turn left onto Mount St. Helens Place South, follow it back to the walkway, and descend to Mount Baker Drive South. Mount Baker Park marks the end of this walk. You can return to Madrona Park Beach (where you started) by going back down the hill to Colman Park and catching the Route 27 bus. Or you can return downtown, via other bus routes noted at the beginning of this chapter.

THE VIEW FROM THE BLUFF: magnolia bluff

Spectacular scenery and a crumbling cliff

Distance: 1.5 miles   **Approximate time:** 1.5 hours

THIS WALK INTRODUCES YOU
to Magnolia Bluff, one of the
Magnolia neighborhood's most
scenic attractions and one of Seattle's best vantage points. Magnolia
Boulevard runs along the bluff,
offering grand vistas of the city,
Puget Sound, and the Olympic
Mountains, framed by madrone
trees. Large houses border the
boulevard, but only on the side of
the street that's farthest from the
water, so they can enjoy the spectacular view without blocking it
from pedestrians.

After following Magnolia
Boulevard for a time, this walk
loops back on Perkins Lane, a
charming but precariously situated
country road where houses perch
on the side of Magnolia Bluff.
Parts of the bluff, as well as some
of the homes, have been known to
slide down toward the water after
heavy rains.

1 **Start this walk on Magnolia
Boulevard West and 34th Court
West. With the water to your
left, stroll along the boulevard
for about a quarter mile, to just
past 36th Avenue West.** As you
begin your stroll, the boulevard
curves to the right and offers an

Madrone trees on Magnolia Bluff

outstanding view of Puget
Sound, Bainbridge Island, and the
Olympic Mountains beyond,
framed by picturesque **madrone
trees**.

Although the Pacific madrone
is a native of the Northwest, it
looks exotic in this gray climate.

starting/ finish point

Magnolia Boulevard West and 34th Court West

getting there

parking Street parking is available on Magnolia Boulevard West.

bus connections Catch Route 24 (Magnolia) on Fourth Avenue near Pike Street downtown; get off just after you cross the Magnolia Bridge, near West Galer Street and Thorndyke Avenue West. (To get information on other bus routes serving this area, see the "Getting Around" section in the introduction to this book.)

Note: The starting point of the walk is a little more than half a mile from where you get off the bus, but it's a scenic stroll on its own. Turn right onto West Galer Street and follow it as it winds along a bluff overlooking the Sound and passes a portion of Magnolia Park on the left. Turn left on to the West Howe Street bridge, which crosses a charming tree-lined lane; then turn left onto Magnolia Boulevard West and follow it to 34th Court West.

The madrone's peeling bark is a beautiful red color that turns gold when caught by the setting sun, and its stiff, leathery leaves are an almost tropical shade of green. Navy geographer George Davidson was captivated by the madrones, which he mistook for magnolias, and misnamed this area after them in 1897. (A different Seattle neighborhood, Madrona, is also named after these trees.)

❷ Just past 36th Avenue West is a

The slippery slope of Perkins Lane

chain-link fence on the left; look beyond the fence to see the **remains of several houses**. Formerly nestled along Magnolia Bluff, they slid off their foundations in the winter of 1996–97, when the bluff became saturated after unusually heavy rains and began to crumble.

❸ A bit farther, also on the left,

magnolia bluff

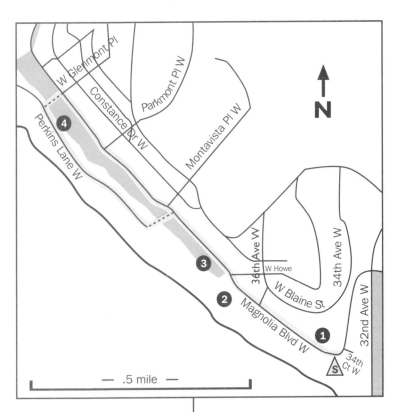

1 Madrone trees
2 Remains of houses

3 Magnolia Boulevard viewpoints
4 Perkins Lane

A view of boats from the bluff

Magnolia Boulevard viewpoint

are the **Magnolia Boulevard viewpoints**, an official city park with a sign and a small parking area of its own. Look back over your shoulder for a **stunning view of the Seattle skyline**. Appearing regularly along the left side of Magnolia Boulevard are smaller, more unofficial-looking parklike spots and viewpoints to enjoy, some with inviting benches.

Continue on Magnolia Boulevard West for about a half mile to Glenmont Lane West. Descend the stairway leading down the bluff to the street below. *Be careful—the stairs are steep!* Bordered by lush trees and vines on either side, the many steps take you a long way down the steep hillside. It's so quiet here that you can hear the water lapping at the shore below.

❹ Turn left onto the unmarked street, which is Perkins Lane West. Follow it for about a half mile, past the "Street Closed" sign, until it ends. **Perkins Lane** has a completely different personality from Magnolia Boulevard. It looks like a country lane in an exclusive rural seaside community—except for the steep hillside to your left, abounding with vine-covered trees and lush ferns. The waterfront homes here are charmingly varied in their sizes and styles, but during an unusually wet winter, some may be in danger of being crushed or carried away by the slowly eroding bluff.

Perkins Lane didn't always end where it does now. It used to continue a few hundred feet farther, but that part of the road was closed when all the houses fronting it slid down the hill after heavy rains a few years ago. The half-demolished dwellings you viewed earlier from the top of the bluff are those unlucky homes.

Ascend the steep stairway nearby to Magnolia Boulevard West. You emerge at the Magnolia Boulevard viewpoints, which you passed earlier. The spectacular view of the Seattle skyline from here is worth a second look.

Turn right onto Magnolia Boulevard and follow it to 34th Court West, where you started this walk.

PITTSBURGH LOST: kirkland

Art and history in the suburbs

Distance: 1.75 miles   **Approximate time:** 1.5 hours

ON THE EASTERN SHORE OF
Lake Washington sits Kirkland,
a small community filled with
condos, boutiques, and art
galleries. It boasts fashionable
coffeehouses, a large collection of
public art, and a pleasant lakefront
boulevard dotted with parks and
viewpoints. A small historic district
is filled with stately brick buildings
dating from the 1890s, remnants
of early Kirkland's unrealized
ambitions.

This charming suburban community was once determined to
become a large city with a steel
industry to rival Pittsburgh's.
Kirkland's namesake, Peter Kirk,
gathered a group of investors
to finance a steel mill to make
this dream a reality. The mill
was complete and ready to open
when the panic of 1893 prompted
investors to withhold stock sub-
scriptions. Kirkland's steel industry
came crashing down before it had
produced a single ingot.

The town of Kirkland managed
to outlive its first industry, becoming something quite different than
what Peter Kirk had envisioned.
Rather than a large industrial city
blackening the skies above north-
eastern Lake Washington, modern

Joshua M. Sears Building

Kirkland is a quiet, upscale suburban community.

starting/ finish point

The corner of Seventh Avenue W and Market Street

① Start at the corner of Seventh Avenue West and Market Street. The buildings at this intersection were the first commercial structures in a town that Peter Kirk and his associates hoped would one day be a metropolis. Kirk had originally wanted to locate the town's center along the waterfront, south of Central Way, where Kirkland's main business district is today. When he could not convince landowners further south to sell, Kirk established a town center here.

Three of the five buildings that were constructed on this corner in the 1890s survive today. On the northwest side of this intersection is the **Joshua M. Sears Building** (1891), a triangular building with terra-cotta accents, designed to conform to this triangular corner. The Sears Building was constructed as a bank, and developers hoped it would eventually handle payrolls for the Kirkland steel mill and other industries that would develop around it. Bank vaults were installed in the basement, but no bank ever opened here. In the 1900s children would peer through the Sears Building's basement windows and speculate on the possibility that large sums of money remained in the vaults.

getting there

parking Free street parking is available along Market Street where this route starts.

bus connections Catch Route 251 (Woodinville) or Route 254 (Redmond) on Fourth Avenue near Pike Street downtown. Get off at Lake Street South and Kirkland Avenue Northeast and follow Lake Street to Central Way Northeast. Turn left on Central Way, walk two blocks, then turn right on Market Street and head uphill to Seventh Avenue Northeast. Neither of these bus routes run very frequently, so call ahead to check the schedule. (For more information about bus routes serving this area, see the "Getting Around" section in the introduction to this book.)

Everyone knew that a million dollars had been lost in the steel mill fiasco. Children figured that the "lost" money might well be here.

Opposite the Sears building, on the northeast corner of this intersection, is the **Campbell Building** (1890), which originally held a grocery. Today it houses an upholstery shop and a Masonic hall.

The final historic building at this intersection is the turreted **Peter Kirk Building**, originally the headquarters for the Kirkland Land and Improvement Co., which platted and developed Kirkland. Today this building is home to the Kirkland Arts Center, which provides classes and studio space for local artists. There is a gallery inside the main entrance that sells locally produced art (mainly pottery and ceramics).

② Leave the Arts Center and turn left on Market Street. Walk two blocks downhill to Waverly Way. Turn right and walk two blocks. On the west side of Waverly Way is a large playfield with an architectural remnant of an old junior high school and a historical marker at its far end.

kirkland

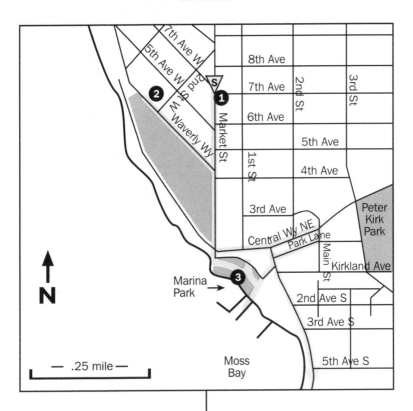

8th Ave
7th Ave W
5th Ave W
2nd
Waverly Wy
S
8th Ave
7th Ave
6th Ave
5th Ave
4th Ave
3rd Ave
Market St
2nd St
3rd St
1st St
Central Wy NE
Park Lane
Main St
Kirkland Ave
Peter Kirk Park
Marina Park
Moss Bay
2nd Ave S
3rd Ave S
5th Ave S

N

— .25 mile —

1 **Joshua M. Sears Building**
2 **Peter Kirk's estate**
3 **Marina Park**

Kirkland's downtown waterfront

First Romance, *by*
Prince Monyo Mihailescu-Nasturel

This property was once part of **Peter Kirk's estate.** Kirk had a mansion in the 200 block of Waverly Way, a gabled and turreted Victorian structure that he called Fir Grove. After Kirk's steel mill closed (or rather, never opened), he continued to live here for some time, even though locals blamed him for the town's fate. Kirk finally left in the early 1900s, and moved to San Juan Island. His estate was eventually sold, and in 1916 developers tore down Fir Grove and used its lumber to build a string of smaller houses along Waverly Way. The home at 202 Waverly Way, constructed in 1917, may well be one of them. Though Kirk's estate is long gone, you can still stand on Waverly Way and admire what was once his view over Lake Washington.

❸ Retrace your steps to Market Street. Turn right and continue for a block, passing the busy intersection with Central Way Northeast. The road ends at **Marina Park.** Directly ahead is a boat launch/fishing pier and a large pavilion skirted by a waterfront path. On a grassy knoll east of the pavilion you'll encounter the first of Kirkland's many art installations, a bronze sculpture called ***Puddle Jumpers,*** by Glenna Goodacre. It depicts a row of children clasping hands and preparing to leap down the side of the hill. Further east along the waterfront is the abstract sculpture ***Centennial Fountain,*** by James FitzGerald.

Opposite the park is a parking lot facing a row of shops and restaurants. At the center of this lot is the ***Plaza of Champions,*** Kirkland's hall of fame. If you have ever wondered whether any Kirkland residents have a claim to fame, the bronze plaques in this plaza will satisfy your curiosity. Honorees include numerous sports heroes, a former Miss USA, and a recipient of the Congressional Medal of Honor.

Cross the street again to Marina Park's swimming beach and a dock where visiting boats moor. This dock was once a landing for ferries that brought passengers across Lake Washington. When the I-90 bridge, formerly called the Lake Washington floating bridge, opened in 1940, Kirkland's ferry service was slowly strangled. Before the floating bridge, Kirkland was a relatively remote community. The only way its residents could reach Seattle easily was by boat. After the bridge was built, Kirkland became a suburb.

Actually, Kirkland still has a ferry of sorts. A 1924 car ferry that was converted to a sightseeing boat offers tours of Lake Washington from this dock. Known as the **MV Kirkland**, this boat originally ferried passengers and vehicles across the mouth of the Columbia River from Astoria, Oregon. During World War II it was commandeered by the military to lay mines in the river's mouth, but has since returned to the tourist trade here in Kirkland.

From opposite the dock, follow Kirkland Avenue for one block inland. On the northwest corner of Kirkland Avenue and Lake Street is an information board with a directory of downtown Kirkland's businesses. You can pick up a downtown map and shop directory here.

Cross Lake Street South, turn left and walk one block to Park Lane. Turn right. Park Lane is lined with trees, antique shops, art galleries, and restaurants. Here you will find a store that sells products made from hemp, a Scandinavian gift shop, as well as public art works (two works in bronze by Sherry Salari Sander).

One of the galleries on Park Lane, the Howard/Mandville Gallery, is featured in Kirkland's Art Walk, held the second Thursday evening of each month. Many of Kirkland's art dealers coordinate show openings and artist receptions for this event. Stop at the

Scene along Lake Washington Drive

peter kirk's land

WHEN PETER KIRK FIRST ARRIVED in Seattle in 1886, the place that would eventually become Kirkland was a tiny, nameless community of about 100 settlers. At that time, neither Kirk nor the community realized the impact they would have on one another.

Kirk came as the representative of the Moss Bay Hematite Iron and Steel Company of Workingman, England, to meet with founders of the Lakeshore and Eastern Railroad. His Seattle connections had told him of iron deposits in the Cascade Mountains, and Kirk was considering opening a steel mill here. His business in England was sagging, and the United States' westward expansion made it a strong market for steel railroad ties.

Kirk soon decided to open a mill and started looking for a site. But while he searched, a law was passed that prohibited all foreigners from owning land in the United States. To circumvent the new law, Kirk formed a partnership with Leigh S. J. Hunt, publisher of the *Seattle Post-Intelligencer*. Together, Kirk and Hunt attracted eastern capital for their enterprise, which would be called the Great Western Iron and Steel Works. They also purchased and developed a wide plat of land surrounding their steel mill. Kirk named this new town after himself and called the nearby cove on Lake Washington Moss Bay, after a bay in the Irish Sea near Kirk's English home.

Construction of the smelter started in 1890, and the steel mill's other facilities soon followed. Excitement grew in what promised to become "the Pittsburgh of the West." The population of Kirkland increased by nearly 5,000 souls in just three years. By September of 1892, the steel mill was complete, and Kirkland's citizens were busy speculating on the town's imminent prosperity.

The plant closed that same month, supposedly for the winter. When the financial panic of 1893 hit, the Great Western Iron and Steel Works crumbled along with the nation's economy. In the unstable financial market, stock subscribers withheld subscription payments. Though the plant had been completed, there was no money to meet operating expenses; it never reopened.

About one million dollars was lost in Kirkland's steel mill fiasco. Many of the town's residents lost their savings speculating on Kirk's venture, but Kirk appeared relatively unscathed. He retained his Kirkland estate and continued to live there for several years in spite of his neighbors' resentments. Kirk maintained his belief that Kirkland was destined to become a major manufacturing center, even after he finally abandoned the town to move to San Juan Island.

Howard/Mandville Gallery to pick up a map of participating galleries.

Turn left on Main Street and walk one block to Central Way Northeast. Cross Central Way and turn left. Central Way features a toy train shop, a chocolate shop and a store that sells Christmas decorations throughout the year, but art galleries and furniture shops predominate. You'll also encounter two more art installations: *Swan Lake*, a bronze of a ballerina enclosed in a swan's wings, by husband and wife team Jacques and Mary Regat, and *Cow and Coyote*, by Brad Rude. The latter is a realistic depiction of an unusual situation: a coyote hitching a ride on a cow. This piece once stood in Seattle's Pioneer Square neighborhood.

At the intersection of Central Way and Lake Street, you can choose to walk back to Market and complete the loop or turn left and take the long lake stroll along Lake Washington Boulevard. (See "Lake Washington Boulevard" on page 214. The route described can be walked, but it is perhaps more enjoyable as a drive.) To complete the loop read on.

Cross Central Way to its south side and view one more bronze sculpture on this street. *Close Quarters*, by Dan Ostermiller, a depiction of two monumental bronze rabbits nuzzling, overlooks the sidewalk tables of a nearby coffeehouse. Ostermiller works in bronze, but cites taxidermists as his greatest influence. Working in his father's taxidermy shop as a young man gave Ostermiller an intimate familiarity with the animal form.

Follow Central Way Northeast to Market Street, turn right, and walk three blocks north to complete this route.

Pavillion at Marina Park

lake washington boulevard

SOUTH OF KIRKLAND IS A SCENIC, lake-view drive that passes several parks. It can be done as a walk rather than a drive, but traffic tends to zoom by. If you go on foot, it will add 1.75 miles to the overall route. If you drive, stopping at the parks along the way, you can take in the points of interest without having to endure the long trek or loud traffic.

To start this drive, head south on Lake Street South in downtown Kirkland. After a few blocks, Lake Street becomes Lake Washington Boulevard. In recent years Kirkland has become a hot condominium market, and new condos continually squeeze themselves in along Lake Washington Boulevard. They wall off much of the view, but several parks along the way open it back up. The first is **David E. Brink Park**, which has a tiny beach, graceful willow trees, and a fishing pier. However, Brink Park's most noticeable feature (other than its lake view) is the bronze sculpture **Water Bearer,** by Glenna Goodacre, which depicts three life-size Native American women gathering water at a landscaped stream. This work won a silver medal in the Solon Borglum Memorial Exhibition in 1975.

The park was named for the Kirkland park director who worked aggressively to improve old parks and establish new ones in the 1960s. At that time Kirkland's waterfront contained a haphazard mixture of industrial and commercial buildings, as well as single- and multi-family dwellings. Today it is much more scenic and orderly.

Across the street from Brink Park is a condominium complex with a landscaped public walk that passes by a small waterfall. A historical marker here tells about the Shumway mansion, which stood on this spot until it was moved to make way for the condominiums.

Back on the other side of Lake Washington Boulevard, a short distance south of Brink Park, is the start of a **waterfront walkway** that passes in front of a couple of developments (though it may be partially closed due to construction). The walkway eventually merges into Lake Washington Boulevard.

Heading south, the next point of interest is **Marsh Park,** named for Louis Marsh, who donated a large waterfront parcel to the city of Kirkland. The park holds another tiny beach, a fishing pier, and, on the south side of the park, an art installation of royal lineage. Sculpted by a prince, *Leap Frog* depicts two bronze boys at play, observed by a bronze girl. The sculptor, Prince Monyo Mihailescu-Nasturel, was a young man in Romania in 1948 when Communists took over his country and threw him in prison. There his body nearly withered away (his weight dropped to only eighty-two pounds), but his imagination took flight. His mind was filled with vivid images and mental pictures. When he was finally released from prison years later, he brought these imagined forms to life, establishing a career as both a sculptor and a painter.

Opposite Marsh Park is a newly built condominium complex that looks authentically historic. Its units are elegant, half-timbered Tudor buildings that would have made Kirkland's namesake, Englishman Peter Kirk, feel at home.

Continue south on Lake Washington Boulevard to **Houghton Beach Park**. This park has a swimming beach and a fishing pier, as well as a playground and more art installations. The art here includes another bronze by Prince Monyo Mihailescu-Nasturel called *First Romance,* and a granite abstract by Peter Skinner called *Winter.*

A large shipyard built shortly after the turn of the century was located just south of here until the close of World War II. It was originally a small operation run by John Anderson in his spare time. Anderson bought old boats, fixed them up, and sold them at a profit. Over the years, the Anderson Shipyard gained momentum and started to build its own boats. It eventually became the Lake Washington Shipyard, which employed thousands and was one of the largest naval construction shipyards during World War II, producing over 500 ships.

Today the site of the old shipyard is home to a large office/retail/hotel/condominium complex called Carillon Point. A landscaped **waterfront walkway** passes in front of this complex, starting a short distance south of Houghton Beach Park. This path leads you past several art installations and historical markers, then crosses a bridge over a small stream that was planted with coho salmon fry in 1993. During spring, you may be able to see the fry if you look closely.

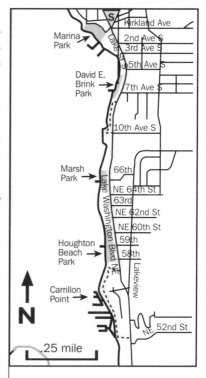

The path eventually comes to a marina. Opposite the marina is a flight of stairs that leads to a plaza lined with shops and restaurants. Beyond this plaza the pathway passes an office building, then follows a dock for a short distance before it returns to Lake Washington Boulevard. If your car is parked at Houghton Beach Park, turn around and return the way you came. If you walked all the way from Kirkland, follow the path to Lake Washington Boulevard. There, at the intersection of Northwest 52nd Street and Lake Washington Boulevard, you can catch Routes 251, 254, or 230 back to Kirkland.

215

BY LAND AND BY SEA: bainbridge

A ferry ride to a laid-back island

Distance: 2 miles   **Approximate time:** 3 hours (including ferry ride)

ACROSS PUGET SOUND FROM
Seattle is the small community of
Winslow, which sits beside a snug
harbor on Bainbridge Island.
Winslow is a popular excursion in
part because getting there is half
the fun. You visit Bainbridge via
the Washington State Ferry system, which, as every Seattleite
knows, is really a low-budget
cruise line. For the price of a tuna
sandwich you can sit on the ferry's
upper deck, sip a latte (the ferry
food-service version of cham-
pagne), and watch the world glide
by. The mountains, islands, and
water are a scenic backdrop, and
Seattle's skyline looks better from a
ferry than from anywhere else.

The trip to Bainbridge Island
would be spectacular even if there
were nothing noteworthy to see
on the other side. The fact that the
ferry lands at a charming waterfront community is icing on the
cake.

This chapter presents a walking
tour of downtown Winslow as
well as a description of some additional Bainbridge attractions that
are accessible by car or bicycle,
should you choose to bring either
(or both) on the ferry with you. If
you're taking a car, be aware that

The ferry to Bainbridge

long backups can occur during the
evening rush hour and on holiday
weekends; if you walk on the
ferry, on the other hand, you
never have to wait.

**Start this walk in downtown
Seattle at Marion Street and**

starting/ finish point

Washington State Ferry terminal in downtown Seattle, at Marion Street and Alaskan Way

ferry facts Ferries leave the Alaskan Way terminal, at Marion Street and Alaskan Way in downtown Seattle, about every hour. The crossing takes about 35 minutes. It is recommended that you walk or bicycle onto the ferry, instead of driving on. You won't need a car for the walking tour on Bainbridge. Taking a car on the ferry is not only expensive, it also means arriving at the terminal an hour or more ahead of departure time during peak hours. (For information on ferries, see the "Getting Around" section in the introduction to this book.)

parking Near the ferry terminal, parking is hard to find and limited to two hours; it's easiest to park in a commercial lot.

bus connections Most Seattle buses pass through downtown Seattle and can leave you within a few blocks of the ferry terminal; get off near Marion Street, walk downhill to First Avenue, and follow the pedestrian overpass right into the terminal.

by car If you take your car on the ferry, then at the Winslow terminal drive up the short hill to the first light and turn left into town, on Winslow Way. After a block, turn left on Bjune Drive Southwest and follow it to find parking in Eagle Harbor Waterfront Park. Street parking is also available in downtown Winslow. It's limited to two hours on Winslow Way and four hours at other locations, including Waterfront Park.

bike rentals You can rent a bike from Bainbridge Island Cycles (162 Bjune Drive); reserve one in advance on summer weekends, (206) 842-6413.

Alaskan Way. This is the **Washington State Ferry terminal**. The ticket booths for walk-on passengers are on the second floor.

After boarding the ferry and enjoying a scenic cruise across Puget Sound, you arrive at the port of **Winslow**. From the ferry it may look like nothing more than a big parking lot, but don't despair. Downtown Winslow is over the rise a few blocks; this is just the loading lot for cars waiting to drive onto the ferry. At the tourist information booth just outside the ferry terminal, you can pick up maps and brochures about local attractions.

Exiting the ferry, walk up Highway 305 for about half a block. Turn left to cross at the crosswalk opposite an auto repair shop. Follow the unmarked road for a short distance. The road is a private drive for Eagle Harbor Condos, but it's also the beginning of a public walkway.

❶ **When a paved path joins the road from the right, follow the**

path. The path skirts a parking lot but eventually crosses a picturesque footbridge and brings you to **Eagle Harbor Waterfront Park**. ❷ This park has a forest and a lawn, picnic tables, a trail along the waterfront, and a small boat-shaped stage where free concerts are held in the summer. Toward the far end of the park is the **Winslow town dock**, where **Bainbridge Boat Rentals** operates. You can rent a kayak, canoe, rowboat, or swan boat, and paddle around Eagle Harbor.

Leave the park, passing the restrooms. Walk past the community center on the left and cross the supermarket parking

winslow

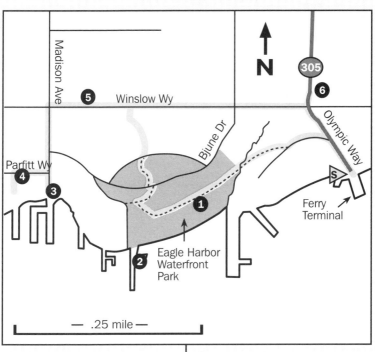

.25 mile

1 **Eagle Harbor Waterfront Park**
2 **Winslow town dock**
3 **Viewpoint over Eagle Harbor**

4 **Captain's House Bed and Breakfast**
5 **Bainbridge Island Farmer's Market**
6 **Bainbridge Island Winery**

Church on Winslow Way

Boat in Eagle Harbor

lot. Turn left onto Winslow Way and follow it to Madison Avenue. Downtown Winslow's main street is **Winslow Way**. Like other towns that thrive on the tourist trade, Winslow has an abundance of antique stores, art galleries, and restaurants. There are also quite a few bookstores, which is appropriate since the island is said to count more than 100 authors among its 19,500 residents. Among the writers making Bainbridge their home are Jack Olsen, who has been called the master of true crime, and Rebecca Wells, author of *Divine Secrets of the Ya-Ya Sisterhood* and other works set in the South.

Many Bainbridge residents live here because they want to be in the country yet remain within commuting distance of the city. Forty percent of the island's popu-

lation commutes to Seattle. In fact, Bainbridge locals may have more in common with Seattleites than with their rural neighbors. Almost 50 percent of Bainbridge adults are college graduates, compared with 20 percent of other Kitsap County residents.

❸ Turn left onto Madison Avenue and follow it to the end. Here you'll find several restaurants, a boat moorage, and a **viewpoint over Eagle Harbor**. This very popular anchorage is usually full of boats. A number of sailors anchor here permanently, living rent-free on the water, to the dismay of many land-based residents.

This harbor was once a landing spot for the Mosquito Fleet, the collective name for the many small steamers and private ferries that plied the waters of Puget Sound between the 1860s and the 1940s.

Supposedly given its nickname because the boats were so numerous, the Mosquito Fleet saw its business begin to decline in the 1920s, after Washington State Ferry service was established.

④ Return to Madison Avenue, turn left onto Parfitt Way Southwest, and follow it for half a block. The **Captain's House Bed and Breakfast**, with its rose-covered picket fence and river-rock porch, was once the home of Eban Franks, cofounder of the Eagle Harbor Transportation Company, a steamer service that was part of the Mosquito Fleet. The Franks lived in the house from about 1913 until 1956.

Across the street from the Captain's House, in a converted historic home, is a pub called **Harbour Public House.** The pub's waterfront deck, with its view of the harbor and Seattle's skyline, is a nice place to enjoy a drink. One of the house's original occupants was Amanda Grow, a member of the local temperance union; she must love the way her home is being used today!

⑤ Retrace your steps, turning right onto Winslow Way and following it toward the ferry for several blocks. If you're here on a Saturday morning between April and October, stop by the **Bainbridge Island Farmers Market** for locally grown produce and flowers. Look for it in the parking lot behind Harold's Square (210 Winslow Way), an office/retail complex.

⑥ Turn left onto Highway 305 and follow it for a short distance. You'll see the entrance to **Bainbridge Island Winery** on the right. Open Wednesday through Sunday afternoons, this small winery has a tasting room and a small wine museum as well as a picnic garden. Its wine is produced on the island, from locally harvested grapes, and is sold only at the winery by the producing family.

Leaving Bainbridge Island Winery, turn left on Highway 305 and follow it down to the ferry terminal. Board the ferry and return to downtown Seattle, where you started.

Waterfront Park

garden spots and nature trails

THESE BAINBRIDGE ISLAND gardens and trails can be visited by car or bicycle.

Ⓐ Bloedel Reserve. Located seven miles from the ferry terminal (7571 Northeast Dolphin Drive, (206) 842-7631), this 150-acre garden can be the highlight of a trip to Bainbridge Island. Stroll through a variety of different environments—a Japanese garden, an eerily prehistoric moss garden, a Zen sand garden, a rhododendron glen—amid a forest reserve that was formerly the Bloedel family estate. Swans glide across the pond in front of an elegant mansion (now a visitors center) overlooking the water, adding to the sense of peace. It's advisable to make a reservation a week in advance during the spring and summer; only 200 visitors are allowed per day, in order to preserve an atmosphere conducive to contemplation (no picnicking or pets, either). Bloedel Reserve is open Wednesday through Sunday, and there's an admission fee.

You can reach the Bloedel Reserve by bus on weekdays by taking Route 94 (Agate Pass) from the ferry terminal to Dolphin Drive. The bus runs about once an hour; schedules are available at the tourist information booth near the ferry terminal.

Ⓑ West Port Madison Nature Trail. A five- to ten-minute walk on this trail leads to a picnic spot overlooking Puget Sound. There's also a beach, but to reach it you must descend a bluff on a rope ladder. The entrance to the trailhead is off a dirt parking area just past the turn, just west of where West Port Madison Road becomes County Park Road.

Ⓒ Bainbridge Gardens. Located about four miles from the ferry terminal (9415 Miller Road Northeast), this nursery specializes in exotic plants and even has a cafe where you can take a break amid the greenery. Bainbridge Gardens has a long history, one that is reminiscent of Bainbridge author David Guterson's best-selling *Snow Falling on Cedars*. Zenhichi Harui opened the nursery in 1912, originally featuring elaborately landscaped gardens, reflecting pools, and stone lions. Tragically, the Harui family was forced to relocate to a Japanese internment camp during World War II. When Harui was finally able to return, his gardens were in ruins, and they remained untended for many years. In 1989, Harui's son Junkoh reestablished his father's business on its original site, and is working to recreate gardens like those that were abandoned during World War II.

D Nathan Bucklin Trail.
This trail goes through a 61-acre wetland preserve and passes the historic Nathan Bucklin Farmhouse, which now serves as a middle school. Take Bucklin Hill Road to the fire station, park behind it, and cross the street. The trailhead is a bit hard to find; it's located at the back of the playground on the southwest side, amid the trees, marked by a small gate. You must walk across school property to reach it, so don't use it during school hours.

E Stanley T. Berg Memorial Nature Trail. This 1.3-mile trail passes a marsh and some marked tree species. Park by the basketball courts next to the school on Blakely Avenue. The trailhead can be found at the back of the school playground, between two sets of playground equipment. Once again, don't use it during school hours.

F Fort Ward State Park Trail. This one-mile loop offers views of the mountains and Sound, blackberry bushes, and the ruins of several military facilities. Enter the park off Pleasant Beach Drive and park by the boat ramp. The trailhead is just east of the boat launch and is clearly marked.

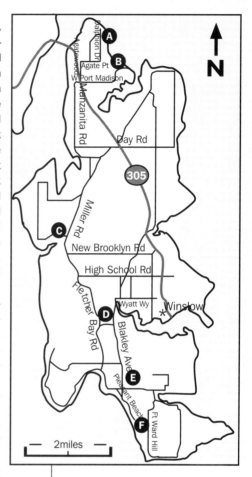

EXPLORING THE CITY PRIMEVAL:
parks and nature walks

Flora and fauna in the city

THE SEATTLE AREA HAS AN abundance of beautiful natural areas, waterfront walkways, and promontory vistas. This chapter provides an overview of natural attractions located throughout the city. Bus routes that reach each of the parks are listed.

❶ burke-gilman trail

bus connections for the Ballard trailhead: Route 28 from Broadview or downtown

This popular cycling/jogging trail, which follows the grade of an old railroad, is often clogged with people on sunny weekends. It's probably better suited for cyclists than walkers, since it's quite long (about 14 miles) and not always scenic; vegetation or houses surround much of it on either side, and there are often long stretches between vistas. The trail begins at 8th Avenue NW and NW Leary Way in Ballard and ends at Tracy Owen Station, a park in Kenmore.

❷ carkeek park

bus connections Route 28 from Broadview or downtown

This park, which covers almost 200 acres and includes 23 acres of beaches, is a great place to come whether you're looking for a secluded forest walk or a festive day at the beach. The park encompasses Piper's Canyon as well as Piper's Creek, a spawning place for chum salmon. The salmon, whose numbers are growing thanks to the efforts of dedicated volunteers, return every October or November to spawn, and can be seen from several places in the park. This is a good reason to get out of the house if November's drizzle has kept you hostage for too long. Just be careful not to approach the creek or allow unleashed dogs in the area.

❸ discovery park

bus connections Routes 19, 24, or 33 from downtown

Set on a bluff overlooking Puget Sound, this expansive park offers sweeping views, grassy hills, a historic military barracks, a Native American cultural center, a picturesque lighthouse, and miles of forest trails and beach walks. A trail to the beach goes past a sewage treatment plant, but not even that diminishes the park's popularity.

The park has 534 acres and two miles of beaches. A pair of bald eagles nest in the trees, and orca whales can sometimes be seen from the beach. Ask at the visitors center (3801 West Government Drive) about the spotting scope that may be set up to allow viewing of the eagles' nest from March through August. (See map on page 228.)

④ golden gardens

bus connections Route
17 from downtown

At this park you can walk along the beach at sunset, then roll out a blanket and build a campfire (in designated fire pits). There's a boat launch, a fishing pier, basketball courts, almost a mile of beach, and several forest trails (east of the railroad tracks), some of which are quite steep. A stairway/trail leads from the streets above the park down to the beach.

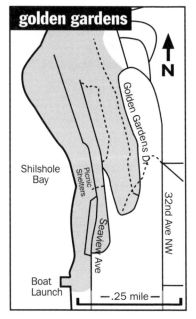

parks and nature walks

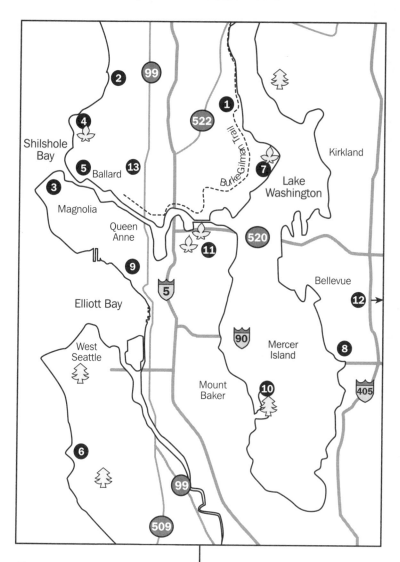

1 Burke-Gilman Trail
2 Carkeek Park
3 Discovery Park
4 Golden Gardens
5 Hiram M. Chittenden Locks
6 Lincoln Park
7 Magnuson Park

8 Mercer Slough/Bellefields Nature Park
9 Myrtle Edwards Park and Elliott Bay Park
10 Seward Park
11 Washington Park Arboretum
12 Wilburton Hill Park and Bellevue Botanical Gardens
13 Woodland Park Zoo

⑤ hiram m. chittenden locks

bus connections Routes 44 from the University of Washington or Wallingford

Known by most Seattleites simply as the Ballard Locks, this intriguing contrivance is one of Seattle's most popular tourist attractions. The Locks were constructed in 1917 as a sort of water elevator for boats traveling between Lake Union and Puget Sound. Today people come here to see yachtsmen taking their boats out to sea, to stroll through a botanical garden, and to watch salmon making their way up the fish ladder.

Just north of the Locks are the Carl S. English Jr. Botanical Gardens, which feature 500 species and 1,500 varieties of trees and plants. The garden's namesake, a landscape designer for the U.S. Army Corps of Engineers, spent over 40 years designing and tending this garden. Maps are available in the visitors center (3015 Northwest 54th Street).

The fish ladder south of the Locks is another popular attraction. You can usually see at least a few migrating salmon through the huge viewing windows; during July or August, when the largest runs of chinook and sockeye come through, it's like an underwater salmon freeway.

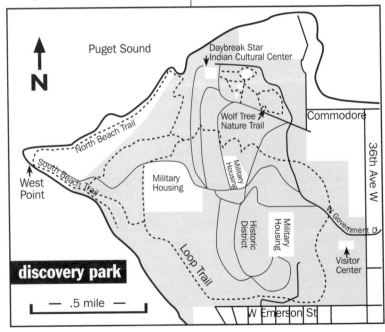

⑥ lincoln park

bus connections Route
54 from downtown or White Center

This is one of the city's best water-front parks. You can walk north for about a mile along the beach, then climb the bluff overlooking Puget Sound and walk through trees on the way back. This beach is much less crowded than the one at Alki to the north, but it's no less scenic. The ferry to Vashon Island docks just south of the 130-acre park. The park's attractions include a heated outdoor swimming pool (open in the summer only), 11 acres of ballfields, two tennis courts, horseshoe pits, play-grounds, and forested pathways.

⑦ magnuson park

bus connections Routes
74 from the University District and 75 from Ballard or the University District

Seemingly a world away from the rest of the city, this park sits on the northwest side of Lake Washing-ton alongside a recently decom-missioned naval base. Amenities include a boat launch, a swimming beach, a knoll popular with kite flyers, and acres of blackberry bushes, but the park's most out-standing feature is its arid land-scape; you may feel you've left the wet, temperate Northwest alto-gether. The park's windblown grasses, small gnarled trees, beach, and mountain view are reminis-cent of a Mediterranean resort.

Just north of Magnuson Park are the offices of the National Oceanic and Atmospheric Admin-istration (NOAA). The NOAA campus features a waterfront walk-way that leads you past several art installations. (A gate between Magnuson Park and NOAA is often left open after hours so the public can view the art.) Just north of the gate is the most notable, if not the most beautiful, art installa-tion: Douglas Hollis' *Soundgarden* (yes, this is where the Seattle-based alternative-rock band got its name). The artwork looks like a collection of wind-velocity indica-tors but is actually a group of musical instruments played by the wind. The music you hear changes as you walk between the flutelike pipes.

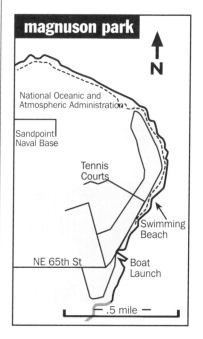

magnuson park

N

National Oceanic and
Atmospheric Administration

Sandpoint
Naval Base

Tennis
Courts

Swimming
Beach

NE 65th St

Boat
Launch

.5 mile

⑧ mercer slough/ bellefields nature park

bus connections Routes
222 from Bellevue transit center or Over-
lake, 226 from Bellevue transit center or
downtown Seattle, 240 from Clyde Hill or
Renton, and 340 from Shoreline or Burien

Extending along the eastern shore of Lake Washington, this park includes the largest remaining wetlands on the lake, and offers opportunities for various types of exploration. You can canoe through 1.5 miles of waterways (ask about canoe tours at the visitors center), cycle on 3 miles of paved trail around the park's periphery, or hike along boardwalk and wood-chip trails. This is a great spot to bird-watch, stroll among many varieties of trees and shrubs, and perhaps encounter some of the park's four-legged inhabitants, such as coyotes, foxes, beavers, deer, otters, and tree frogs. A house built in 1929 currently serves as the visitors center, where environmental education programs are offered.

⑨ myrtle edwards park and elliott bay park

bus connections Routes
2 from Queen Anne or Madrona, 18 from
North Beach/Ballard or downtown, 33
from Discovery Park or downtown, and the
Waterfront Streetcar from the International District

These parks follow Elliott Bay's shoreline from near the end of Denny Way to Pier 90 at Smith Cove, making them a wonderful place to walk or jog. A 1.25-mile paved path affords an excellent view of the Seattle skyline. There are separate walking and cycling trails, a rose garden, and even a physical fitness course. Metered parking spaces are located at Myrtle Edwards Park's entrance off Alaskan Way, but on sunny weekends finding a space there, or on the streets nearby, can be a challenge.

⑩ seward park

bus connections Route 39

What is today Seward Park was once a private estate on an island. The estate became a park after it was purchased by the city in 1911; the island became a peninsula when Lake Washington was lowered during the construction of the ship canal in 1917, and a narrow neck of land emerged. Today this is one of the most scenic parks in Seattle's extraordinary collection. Seward Park has a paved walking and cycling trail around its periphery that provides breathtaking views of Mount Rainier, Mercer Island, and Lake Washington. It also skirts Andrews Bay, the only place in Lake Washington where boats can legally anchor. The bay is usually crowded with boats on warm sunny days. The park also features a ceramics studio, tennis courts, picnic shelters, and an amphitheater.

Seward Park's interior still holds a stand of old-growth timber. Stepping into this forest is like entering a green cathedral made

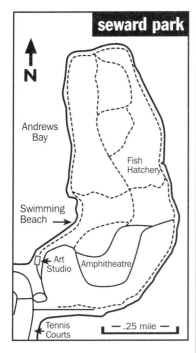

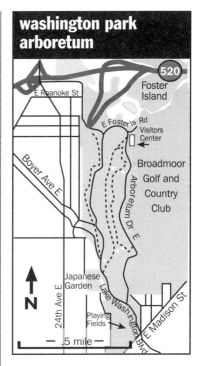

of towering Douglas fir, hemlock, and Western red cedar. To walk the paths through the old-growth forest, drive up the hill and park at the first lot at the top.

⑪ washington park arboretum

bus connections Routes
11 from downtown, and 48 from Loyal Heights, Capitol Hill, or Rainier Beach.

The best time to visit the Arboretum is in the spring, when the cherry trees are in bloom, or in the fall, when the leaves change color, but there really is no bad time to visit: It's beautiful all year. The Arboretum has 40,000 trees, shrubs, and vines growing in 200 acres of parkland. Pick up a trail guide or get more information on

plant species at the visitors center, located at the northern end of the Arboretum. Don't miss the Japanese Tea Garden at the southern end, across Lake Washington Boulevard East from the main park. The tranquil setting is marred only slightly by the traffic zooming by on the boulevard. There's a small admission fee for the Japanese garden, but the Arboretum is free.

⑫ wilburton hill park and bellevue botanical gardens

bus connections Routes 271 from Issaquah or the University District, 920 from Totem Lake, and 921 from Factoria.

This free park includes an exquisitely landscaped section that was named one of the country's top 50 public gardens in 1996 by Garden Design Magazine. Winding footpaths pass various themed gardens: a rhododendron glen, an alpine rock garden, a groundcover garden, and a Japanese garden, to name a few. Much of this park was once the private estate of Calhoun and Harriet Shorts, who donated their home and property to the city of Bellevue in 1989. The city added several more acres and opened this park in 1992. The Shorts house currently serves as a gift shop and visitors center for this free public garden. There are also two historic cabins built by early settlers within the park.

Outside the botanical garden, Wilburton Hill Park consists of second-growth forest. The Lake to Lake Trail that travels between Lake Sammamish and Lake Washington crosses through this park.

⑬ woodland park zoo

bus connections Routes 5 and 6 from downtown or Shoreline, and 359 from downtown or Bitter Lake

When the zoo opened in 1904 it featured a collection of cold concrete and iron enclosures and a listless menagerie, but in the 1970s it underwent a remarkable transformation, and is today reputed to have some of the best-simulated native habitat of any zoo in the country. The flora is almost as fascinating as the fauna; if the zoo had no animals, it could be a botanical garden. The Tropical Rain Forest exhibit alone includes over 20,000 plant species. Just east of the zoo is Woodland Park, which offers both sports fields and forested trails. The lovely Woodland Park Rose Garden is just outside the zoo's south gate. There's an admission fee for the zoo, but the park and the rose garden are free.

FORAGING IN THE THICKETS:
blackberries

These wild fruits are ubiquitous in late July and August, their bushes forming an impenetrable tangle in most of the city's vacant lots and untended backyards. If you leave any plot of land alone for more than a month, it will probably be sprouting blackberries when you return. However, the landscaper's bane is the forager's delight, and it's possible to range widely through the city and graze on blackberries almost everywhere you go. The following parks offer exceptionally good picking. (See the overview map at the beginning of this chapter for locations.)

Magnuson Park: In terms of sheer volume, this is the best place to pick blackberries in the city. Just be sure to wear heavy clothes, since filling your bucket may require some bushwhacking.

Golden Gardens: Blackberries on the beach—what more could you ask? (OK, so the berries are along a railroad track and across a parking lot from the beach, but still. . . .) There are also bushes in the forested section of Golden Gardens, east of the railroad tracks.

McCurdy Park: Located northwest of the Arboretum near the Montlake Cut, this excellent blackberry park has the wide-open spaces that blackberries love, plus lots of little trails between bushes to make bushwhacking unnecessary.

Interlaken Park: Blackberry bushes can be found along the many paths through this park. Because most of the area is shaded, the berries are not quite as sweet as those found in sunnier locations.

Blackberry-Picking Tips
• Don't wear white. Blackberry juice spreads easily, and it stains.
• Wear long pants, a long-sleeved shirt, and closed-toe shoes to prevent thorny injuries.
• The sweetest (and most prolific) berries grow in sunny locations.
• Blackberries turn black before they are completely ripe. Ripe berries are less shiny than unripe ones, and they fall into your hand with only a slight nudge. If you have to pull berries from the vine, they are probably not ripe yet.

THE CITY'S
ancient forests

You don't have to drive to the Olympic Peninsula to see ancient forest; Seattle is fortunate to have four parks with pockets of timber that have never been cut. (See the overview map at the beginning of this chapter for locations.)

Seward Park: This park has the largest stand of old-growth forest in the city.

Schmitz Park: Ferdinand and Emma Schmitz donated a large part of this park, located directly east of Alki Point in West Seattle, to the city in 1908. They gave the land on the condition that its forest never be cut.

Fauntleroy Park: Located in West Seattle, southeast of Lincoln Park, this is the smallest of Seattle's old-growth forest stands. It features a well-used, though sometimes soggy, trail through the woods. It's situated on the south side of Barton Street, four blocks east of California Avenue SW.

O. O. Denny Park: Located north of Kirkland, on the northeast side of Lake Washington, this park was donated by the Dennys, one of Seattle's founding families. The park's old-growth forest is in a ravine just across Holmes Point Road from the landscaped lakefront section of the park.

other parks worth seeing

Several notable parks and nature walks are not included in this chapter because they are included in other chapters. These are summarized below.

Alki Beach Park: A popular beach with spectacular views. Chapter 12 (Alki).

Foster Island Park/Montlake Cut: A scenic waterfront path. Chapter 13 (Montlake).

Freeway Park: Waterfalls and intriguing spaces. Chapter 3 (Downtown and Seattle Center).

Green Lake Park: A walk around the lake on Seattle's most popular pathway. Chapter 11 (Green Lake).

Magnolia Boulevard Viewpoints: Overlook Puget Sound from Magnolia Bluff. Chapter 16 (Magnolia).

Parks on Lake Washington: Madison Park, Madrona Park, Leschi Park, and Mount Baker Park. Nestled on the lake these parks have swimming beaches and waterfront paths. Chapter 14 (Madison Park) and 15 (Leschi to Mount Baker).

Ravenna Park: A serene forested ravine. Chapter 11 (Green Lake).

Volunteer Park: A lively city park. Chapter 7 (Capitol Hill).

selected bibliography

Binns, Archie. *Northwest Gateway.* Portland, Ore.: Binfords & Mort, 1941.

Cornish, Nellie C. *Miss Aunt Nellie: The Autobiography of Nellie C. Cornish.* Seattle: University of Washington Press, 1964.

Crowley, Walt. *National Trust Guide Seattle: A Guide for Architecture and History Travelers.* New York: John Wiley and Sons, 1998.

De Barros, Paul. *Jackson Street After Hours: The Roots of Jazz in Seattle.* Seattle: Sasquatch Books, 1993.

Dorpat, Paul. *Seattle Now and Then, vols. I, II, and III.* Seattle: Tartu Publications. 1984–89.

Droker, Howard. *Seattle's Unsinkable Houseboats: An Illustrated History.* Seattle: Watermark Press, 1977.

Ely, Arline. *Our Foundering Fathers: The Story of Kirkland.* Kirkland, Wash.: Kirkland Public Library, 1975.

Ferguson, Robert L. *The Pioneers of Lake View: A Guide to Seattle's Early Settlers and Their Cemetery.* Bellevue, Wash.: Thistle Press, 1995.

Johnson, Norman J. *The Fountain and the Mountain: The University of Washington Campus 1895–1995.* Woodinville, Wash.: Documentary Book Publishers, 1995.

Kreisman, Lawrence. *Apartments by Anhalt.* Seattle: Office of Urban Conservation and Department of Community Development, 1978.

Morgan, Murray C. *Skid Road: An Informal Portrait of Seattle.* New York: Viking Press, 1951.

Ochsner, Jeffery Karl, ed. *Shaping Seattle Architecture: A Historical Guide to the Architects.* Seattle: University of Washington Press, 1994.

Paulson, Don, with Roger Simpson. *An Evening at the Garden of Allah: A Gay Cabaret in Seattle.* New York: Columbia University Press, 1996.

Reinartz, Francis Key. *Queen Anne: Community on the Hill.* Seattle: Queen Anne Historical Society, 1993.

Ruby, Robert H., and John A. Brown. *A Guide to the Indian Tribes of the Pacific Northwest.* Norman, Okla.: University of Oklahoma Press, 1986.

Sale, Roger. *Seattle Past to Present.* Seattle: University of Washington Press, 1978.

———. *Seeing Seattle.* Seattle: University of Washington Press, 1994.

Strong, Tracy B., and Helen Keyssar. *Right in Her Soul: The Life of Anna Louise Strong.* New York: Random House, 1983.

Takami, David. *Executive Order 9066, Fifty Years Before and Fifty Years After: A History of Japanese Americans in Seattle.* Seattle: Wing Luke Asian Museum, 1992.

Wallace, James, and Jim Erickson. *Hard Drive: The Making of the Microsoft Empire.* New York: John Wiley and Sons, 1992.

Woodbridge, Sally B., and Roger Montgomery. *Guide to Architecture in Washington State.* Seattle: University of Washington Press, 1980.

index

Boldface entries and page numbers indicate greater detail.

237

243